THE SENTENCING COMMISSION AND ITS GUIDELINES

The Sentencing Commission and Its Guidelines

Andrew von Hirsch
Kay A. Knapp
Michael Tonry

Northeastern University Press
Boston

Northeastern University Press

Library of Congress Cataloging in Publication Data

von Hirsch, Andrew.
   The sentencing commission and its guidelines.

   Bibliography: p.
   Includes index.
   1. Sentences (Criminal procedure)—United States.
I. Tonry, Michael. II. Knapp, Kay A. III. Title.
KF9685.V66   1987   364.6′0973   86-33116
ISBN 1-55553-009-5 (alk. paper)

Designed by Sandra Calef.

Composed in Sabon by Seham Associates, Metuchen, New Jersey.

Printed and bound by Halliday Lithograph, Hanover,
Massachusetts. The paper is Warren's #66 Antique, an acid-free
sheet.

MANUFACTURED IN THE UNITED STATES OF AMERICA
92 91 90 89 88 87   5 4 3 2 1

Contents

Acknowledgments　　　　　　　　　　vii
Preface　　　　　　　　　　　　　　　ix

PART 1

Why Have a Sentencing Commission?

1

The Sentencing Commission's Functions
Andrew von Hirsch　　　　　　　　　　3

2

Sentencing Guidelines and Their Effects
Michael Tonry　　　　　　　　　　　16

PART 2

Writing Sentencing Guidelines

3

Numerical Grids or Guiding Principles?
Andrew von Hirsch　　　　　　　　　47

4

The Enabling Legislation
Andrew von Hirsch　　　　　　　　　62

5

**Structure and Rationale:
Minnesota's Critical Choices**
Andrew von Hirsch   84

6

**The Sentencing Commission's Empirical
Research**
Kay A. Knapp   107

7

Organization and Staffing
Kay A. Knapp   117

P A R T   3

The Implementation of Guidelines

8

**Implementation of the Minnesota
Guidelines: Can the Innovative Spirit
Be Preserved?**
Kay A. Knapp   127

9

**Enforcing Sentencing Guidelines:
Plea Bargaining and Review Mechanisms**
Michael Tonry and John C. Coffee, Jr.   142

Appendix

**A Summary of the Minnesota,
Washington, and Pennsylvania
Guidelines**   177

Notes   189
Bibliography   207
Index   217

Acknowledgments

The idea for this book came to us during a conference we attended in the fall of 1984, on the proposed New York State sentencing guidelines. The discussion convinced us of the need for a book that would address the sentencing commission and the functions of its guidelines.

We are grateful to Nella Lee and to Michael Markowitz for their assistance in reviewing and revising the manuscript and preparing the notes and bibliography. We would also like to thank Joan Schroeder, who typed the manuscript, for her skill and patience.

We are indebted to our colleagues who devoted their valuable time to reviewing our original sketch of the book and individual draft chapters: Bill Bowers, Judith Greene, Milton Heumann, James Jacobs, Sheldon Messinger, Roxanne Park, Nicole Hahn Rafter, and Joan Vermeulen.

The book could never have been written without the encouragement and enthusiasm of Deborah Kops of Northeastern University Press.

In a number of chapters, we have used (with considerable alterations or additions) portions of articles that have been published elsewhere. We are grateful to those who have permitted us to make use of those articles:

Manchester University Press, Manchester, England, for the essays by Michael Tonry and Andrew von Hirsch, chapters 2 and 3, respectively, which originally appeared in *Sentencing Reform: Guidance or Guidelines?*, edited by Ken Pease and Martin Wasik, 1987.

Acknowledgments

Hamline Law Review for part of chapter 5, which originally appeared in 1982 as "Constructing Guidelines for Sentencing: The Critical Choices for the Minnesota Sentencing Guidelines Commission," by Andrew von Hirsch, in vol. 5, pp. 591–634 of that journal.

University of Chicago Press, for chapter 9, which originally appeared in a somewhat different version as "Hard Choices: Critical Trade-offs in the Implementation of Sentencing Reform through Guidelines," by John C. Coffee, Jr., and Michael H. Tonry, in *Reform and Punishment,* edited by Michael H. Tonry and Franklin E. Zimring, pp. 155–203, 1983.

We also wish to thank John C. Coffee, Jr., Professor of Law at Columbia University, for his kind permission to include our revised version of this last-cited essay.

Preface

The sentencing commission was first proposed in 1972 by an influential federal judge, Marvin E. Frankel. The commission was to be an independent, expert rule-making agency that wrote guidelines for criminal sentences. Frankel's proposal attracted widespread attention. Three states—Minnesota, Washington, and Pennsylvania—have created sentencing commissions whose guidelines are already in effect. The United States Sentencing Commission, established by law in 1984, has been writing its standards. Other states may follow suit.

There has been, however, no single work that examines this reform in systematic fashion. Why have a sentencing commission, and precisely what should its functions be? Should the guidelines be in numerical form, or provide more general guidance? What has been the experience with sentencing commissions to date? How should the legislation creating the commission be drafted? How, and toward what penal ends, should the guidelines be written? What might the effect of the guidelines be on other stages of the criminal process, such as plea bargaining? While some of these issues have been addressed in the scholarly and professional journals, others have not. The purpose of this book is to give a more comprehensive view of the sentencing commission.

This volume goes to press before the guidelines of the U.S. Sentencing Commission are issued in their final form. However, it supplies principles for judging those (and other jurisdictions') guidelines. What needs chiefly to be looked at, we suggest, is (1) the quality of the commission's deliberative process, (2) whether the guidelines reflect a coherent and fair penal rationale, (3) whether the guidelines' impact on correctional resources has systematically been taken into account, (4) whether the standards provide sufficient guidance to assist in the resolution of actual sentencing cases, and (5) how much the guidelines actually change sentencing patterns toward the directions intended. While we fervently hope the federal guidelines fare well when judged by these standards, it is premature to say whether they will.

The utility of the sentencing commission should not, however, be judged by the federal commission's efforts alone. The sentencing commission and its guidelines were pioneered at the state level, and most common crimes are governed by state law. It is thus state guidelines that chiefly will determine the future of this reform, and it is these our book in large part addresses.

The book is organized as follows. Part 1 describes the mission of a sentencing commission: deciding a rationale, setting prison-population targets, and developing a tariff. It also supplies a survey of sentencing guidelines to date, and their known effects.

Part 2 considers the writing of the guidelines. We begin by examining whether guidance can best be achieved through detailed, numerical standards—or through broader narrative norms. Next we examine the legislation creating a sentencing commission, to see how the commission's guideline-writing functions should be defined by law. Then comes a discussion of how the commission should decide the crucial questions of the guidelines' rationale and structure. We also address what research the commission needs to undertake, and how organizational and staffing issues may be handled.

Finally, in Part 3, we examine guidelines' effects on sentencing practice. We analyze the impact of Minnesota's guidelines, and consider how plea bargaining and appellate review can affect the implementation of guidelines.

Few true innovations have been attempted in criminal justice in recent decades. The sentencing commission is one. However historians ultimately judge it, this reform surely warrants our attention.

January 1987

PART 1

Why Have a Sentencing Commission?

CHAPTER 1

The Sentencing Commission's Functions

Andrew von Hirsch

Sweeping discretion in the determination of sentence prevailed during the first six decades of this century. In Europe, penal codes gave sentencing judges wide leeway, but in the United States that leeway was wider still. Typically, American statutes set only the maximum penalties for different crimes, and the judge had the choice of *any* sentence within that limit: a fine, probation, a jail sentence, or a shorter or longer term in state prison. When the offender was sentenced to prison, the parole board could release him at any time after a specified fraction (in most states, one-third) of his sentence had elapsed. Within these wide limits, no standards governed the decisions of sentencing judges or parole boards, and those decisions ordinarily could not be appealed.

This wide discretion was ostensibly justified for rehabilitative ends: to enable judges and parole officials familiar with the case to choose a disposition tailored to the offender's need for treatment. Actually, the discretion may not have helped the cause of penal rehabilitationism much, because it was a blank check which judges and parole officials could use as they wished. Rather then ensuring sentences designed for treatment, it permitted individual decision makers to pursue *whatever* aims or policies they personally preferred (or no coherent aims at all) when deciding sentence. Such difficulties, however, were long overlooked: there was little challenge to the idea that there should be wide sentencing discretion, in order to facilitate the rehabilitation of offenders.

Beginning in the 1970s, disenchantment with discretionary sentencing began to develop. It stemmed, in part, from growing skepticism about the therapeutic model of punishment. The story of the decline of penal rehabilitationism has been told too often to warrant my retelling it in detail here.[1] Penal treatments did not seem to be working well: once tested carefully, few such programs

3

had a measurable influence on recidivism.[2] Aside from such program failures came a broader loss of faith in human malleability. Not only in sentencing but in other state interventions into the lives of persons whose conduct was deemed deviant, the difficulties of compelling or inducing changed behavior were becoming apparent.[3] Finally, the fairness of the rehabilitative sentence came into question: was it really fair to make the severity of the offender's penalty depend, not on the degree of reprehensibleness of his own criminal choices, but on someone else's estimate of his supposed "needs" for treatment?[4]

As rehabilitationism lost its dominance, other penal philosophies came to the fore. One influential school of thought emphasizes the offender's deserts and would make the sentence comport with the gravity of his criminal conduct.[5] Another school emphasizes incapacitation: imprisoning offenders whose early criminal records and social histories suggest they are likely to return to crime.[6] There have been sharp disagreements between these schools of thought, which I shall mention in later chapters and have elaborated upon in a recent book.[7] But both philosophies are suited to embodiment in explicit standards for sentencing. If penalties are to be based on the seriousness of offenders' criminal conduct, then guidelines can help judges gauge the conduct's gravity and the appropriate, deserved penalty. If penalties are to be based, instead, on the statistical probability of offending again, such probabilities, and the appropriate incapacitative measures, can also be set forth in explicit standards.[8]

As these shifts in penal philosophy were occurring, broad sentencing discretion itself came under fire. Unguided authority to sentence, it began to be recognized, allows discrepant decisions. When judges and parole boards are free to determine the quantum of punishment without standards or guidelines, they are apt to decide similar cases differently. While some courts seem to have developed "going rates" of sentence for various typical situations, these are little more than statistical norms—from which individual judges are free to deviate whenever and for whatever reason they choose.[9]

More fundamentally, critics asserted, discretionary sentencing meant sentencing uncontrolled by considered policy.[10] Dispositional patterns in a particular state emerged largely by happenstance, the product of the attitudes and practices of those occupying the bench at the moment. There was no coherent pattern of sentences sought, and hence no opportunity to consider the wisdom or practicability of seeking such outcomes. The time seemed ripe for bringing purpose and order to sentencing.

The Unsuitability of Legislative Standards

As interest in regulating sentencing grew, the method of regulation initially most used was legislative: the state legislature would prescribe a detailed schedule of prescribed or recommended sanctions for various crimes. California started the trend in 1976, with its Uniform Determinate Sentencing Law. This law prescribed the terms that were to be served for different felonies when judges committed offenders to state prison. The parole board's releasing power was abolished for most cases, and the offender was to serve the sentence in full, less a one-third "good-time" deduction if he or she behaved peaceably in prison. Indiana adopted its determinate sentencing law in the same year. The law prescribed a normally recommended prison term for each of the four statutory felony classes; allowed wide variation from that sentence for aggravating and mitigating circumstances; eliminated parole release; and required the offender to serve his full sentence minus 50 percent off for good behavior. Illinois, Colorado, Alaska, New Mexico, and North Carolina followed suit with analogous legislation.[11]

Of these legislative efforts, the most complex was California's. The California sentencing code, when first enacted in 1976, had an explicit guiding principle: terms of imprisonment should be proportionate to the seriousness of the criminal conduct. An effort was made by the drafters of the code to grade penalties to reflect the gravity of offenses. The prescribed durations of confinement were based on previous averages for time served, and the legislature resisted proposals for wholesale escalation of penalties when drafting the original statute.[12]

Since its original writing in 1976, however, California's legislation has deteriorated. A number of bills have been enacted to lengthen the prescribed terms for various crimes and to restore discretion by widening the range between the presumptive term and the aggravated term. These piecemeal changes were made with little apparent concern for preserving proportionality or consistency among penalties.

In the other states where the legislature attempted to fix definite penalties, the situation was worse than in California from the outset. An example is Indiana. That state's sentencing code bears marks of haste in drafting; it prescribes draconian penalties for many felonies; and, despite its alleged discretion-limiting aim, it reserves vast powers for judges to choose aggravated or mitigated terms and for correctional administrators to confer or withdraw the very large (50 percent) good-time allowance.[13]

Perhaps these jurisdictions' choice of rule maker—the legislature—contributed to the disappointments. When called upon to write specific punishments for crimes, a legislative body has two vulnerabilities. First, it has little time available: given the press of other legislative business, it cannot devote much effort and thought to developing a coherent rationale; comparing proposed penalties with one another; projecting the standards' impact on sentencing practice and on the limited resources of the correctional system; and, once the penalties have gone into effect, reviewing the manner in which they have actually been administered. Second, legislatures face particularly troublesome pressures in the sentencing field. Many voters fear crime and criminals, and few convicted offenders do (or even may) vote. Once a legislative body begins debating specific penalties, legislators have considerable incentives to adopt posturing stances of "toughness" and few incentives for giving thought to the *justice* of proposed penalties—for considering seriously whether the proposed sanctions would treat convicted criminals (that unpopular minority) fairly and deservedly.[14] With such difficulties apparent, observers began to ask whether the legislature might better delegate the task of setting sentencing standards to a specialized body—one more insulated from political pressures and with more time and expertise to devote.

One such alternative rule maker might, surprisingly enough, be the parole board. Traditionally, parole boards were hostile to writing explicit rules for their decisions regarding release. In part because of that hostility, parole authorities in several jurisdictions have lost their authority to decide when to release prisoners.[15] But where authority to grant parole release has been retained, the parole board could become the vehicle of more definite penalties. By writing explicit standards for its release decisions, the board could begin to regulate duration of confinement.[16] The board's standards could reduce prisoners' sense of uncertainty about the lengths of their confinement by requiring that they be informed, soon after entry into prison, of their expected dates of release.[17] The United States Parole Commission has developed guidelines of this nature.[18]

Parole guidelines, however, cannot be the ideal solution. Those guidelines cannot regulate judges' critical "in-out" decisions of whether to imprison offenders or not. Parole guidelines, in many states, also only partially control the duration of imprisonment: judges may appreciably influence the length of stay in prison through the decisions they make affecting the date of first parole eligibility and the maximum sentence. Explicit standards for *judges'* sentencing decisions therefore are a necessity. To write such standards, a standard-setting body is needed: not the legislature, but a specialized rule maker.[19]

The Sentencing Commission

The idea for such a rule-making body can be credited to a former law professor and federal judge, Marvin E. Frankel. In a 1972 book, he proposed creation of a sentencing commission.[20] The commission would be authorized by statute to write detailed guidelines for sentencing. Its members would be appointed by the jurisdiction's chief executive, with senatorial advice and consent; they would consist of judges, prosecutors, defense attorneys, scholars, and citizens, backed by a full-time professional staff. Judges would be required to follow the guidelines in their sentencing decisions, except where they could give satisfactory reasons for deviation. Under the enabling statute, the guidelines would become law either automatically after the commission approved them (in the absence of a legislative resolution of disapproval), or else upon submission to and approval by the legislature.[21] In either case, the commission would be responsible for writing the guidelines, and was supposed to have enough leisure, expertise, and insulation from outside pressures to draft them with care. After the guidelines went into effect, the commission would collect information on their implementation and amend and refine them accordingly.

The sentencing commission's mission was to be prescriptive: to decide the future direction of sentencing policy. The study of past sentencing practice would be a useful first step, indicating what factors had been given primary emphasis in judges' everyday sentencing decisions. The next and critical step, however, would be a *normative* evaluation of that past practice. Is it rational? Is it fair? Ought the practice continue to be followed? If not, how should it be changed? The sentencing commission, in Frankel's proposal, was supposed to address those issues of policy explicitly. The commission would have its rule-making powers granted by law, in order to give it clear authority to formulate policy.

The commission's guidelines were supposed to structure the judge's discretion, not eliminate it. Judges still would interpret and apply the guidelines and could deviate from them in special circumstances. They would be called upon to do what their legal background has trained them to do: to apply generalized norms to particular cases, with whatever complexities of interpretation that involves, and to decide when there are sufficient grounds for departing from those norms in unusual situations. They would no longer be called upon to act in a legal void—to make decisions about people's liberty without explicit standards to guide their actions.

Frankel's proposal generated a great deal of interest, and by the end of the 1970s, several states began taking action. Three jurisdictions—Minnesota, Washington, and Pennsylvania—have created sentencing commissions whose guidelines are now in effect. (Those guidelines are summarized in the appendix to the present volume.) Two other states—New York and South Carolina—also established sentencing commissions, but the resulting guidelines did not survive legislative scrutiny. For federal crimes, the U.S. Sentencing Commission has been established and is in the process of writing its guidelines as this book goes to press. Of these various efforts, the first—and in many respects the most sophisticated to date—has been Minnesota's guidelines. We therefore will concentrate on Minnesota's experience to elucidate the principal issues.[22]

The Format of the Guidelines

Let me begin a sketch of sentencing commission guidelines with a description of their usual format. The guidelines are numerical and definite. Usually, their principal feature is a sentencing grid: a two-dimensional table of prescribed sanctions. The vertical axis of the grid, or offense score, grades the seriousness of various species of criminal conduct. The horizontal axis, or offender score, rates characteristics of the offender—such as the extent of his prior criminal record. Across the grid is drawn a so-called dispositional (or in-out) line. Above the line are prescribed prison sanctions of varying duration, and below it are lesser sanctions. In each grid cell above the line, a numerical range of imprisonment is prescribed: the grid cell applicable to convicted armed robbers having two prior felony convictions might contain a range of, say, thirty-eight to forty-four months in prison.

The grid is, however, only one of a variety of possible formats for numerical guidelines. It is the one used in the guidelines that have been adopted to date and thus is the one we shall focus upon here. Another possible format, however, would be a step-by-step formula: first, crimes are rated by their seriousness; then, adjustments are made for other relevant factors (such as prior criminal history); the result is a "sanction score" that can be converted into periods of imprisonment and appropriate lesser sanctions. Different formats may reflect differences in style more than substance. It may take only elementary mathematics to convert a sentencing grid into a step-by-step formula or vice versa.

In a grid, the range in any particular cell prescribes only the *normally* appropriate sentences. A sentencing court is authorized to deviate from the cell range on account of aggravating and mitigating circumstances. Such deviations are to be invoked, however, only in unusual situations—and the guidelines themselves may contain a suggested list of factors that qualify as mitigating or aggravating.[23]

Once established, the guidelines system is policed through appellate review. The higher courts are authorized to hear sentence appeals and to determine compliance with the guidelines. In so doing, those courts are supposed to develop a supplementary jurisprudence—on, for example, how to interpret the commission's list of aggravating and mitigating factors.

The sentencing commission remains in existence to study patterns of implementation of the guidelines and to note areas of difficulty. Frequent departures from the cell ranges for a particular type of case, for example, may suggest that the ranges themselves need amendment. Through such "feedback," the commission can alter and try to improve the guidelines over time.

The Guidelines and "Disparity"

One of the major charges against discretionary sentencing was, as I noted, its apparent tendency to produce disparate outcomes. It has thus been tempting to define the sentencing commission's mission purely as that of promoting consistency or reducing disparity. Such a formulation of the guidelines' aim, however, is insufficient.

Disparity cannot be determined in a vacuum. It consists of differences in sentence that cannot be accounted for on the basis of the purpose or purposes sought to be achieved. Does it constitute disparity when unemployed offenders receive more severe sentences than employed ones? That depends upon the rationale. If the aim is to punish offenders as they deserve, it *is* disparity—because an offender's employment status ordinarily is not germane to the reprehensibleness of his criminal conduct. If, on the other hand, the aim is to sentence offenders according to their risk of recidivism, it is not necessarily disparity, because available studies suggest a link between joblessness and recidivism.[24] In order to combat or even to identify disparity, the first step needed is the specification of a rationale. Yet that is precisely what is missing in a discretionary sentencing system.

Consistency is, also, no guarantee of the rationality or fairness of a system. Sentencing offenders invariably according to their height or weight would be consistent but nevertheless irrational. What is needed is a *considered* judgment of what the basis of the sentence should be. Only then has a standard been created against which "disparity" can be measured and judged.

What, then, is the mission of a sentencing commission? It is threefold: selecting a rationale, considering prison population constraints, and developing a tariff. Let me examine each of these functions.

Choosing the Rationale

The sentencing commission, in fashioning its guidelines, must choose a rationale. Should the system emphasize punishing offenders proportionately to the gravity of their crimes? Or should it rely, instead, more heavily on the degree of risk offenders pose? Or should there be some other purpose? The choice of rationale is critical because it will determine what features of the offense or of the offender should be relied upon in determining the punishment. On a rationale emphasizing proportionality and desert, the factor primarily to be relied upon is the seriousness of the current crime.[25] On a predictive rationale, however, the primacy would shift to factors that are indicative of risk—chiefly, as we will see, the offender's previous criminal record and his social and employment history. The commission does not have to choose one rationale to the exclusion of all others, but, where a hybrid rationale is used, it is still necessary to decide which aim should have preeminence.[26]

10

A sentencing commission is well suited to this task: it can consider the rationale for the system as a whole and make its choice in an *informed* fashion. When considering treatment or deterrence, the commission can inform itself of the extent and limits of present knowledge of treatment and deterrent effects. When considering incapacitation, it can examine prediction research to see how well we can forecast recidivism, and where the empirical and ethical problems lie. When considering desert, it can—by examining the literature on that subject—acquaint itself with the criteria for proportionality.[27]

With the rationale formulated, the commission is in a position to identify the factors chiefly to be relied upon and the comparative weight they should be given. Choosing between desert and incapacitation, for example, enables the commission to decide the weight to be given the current offense relative to the prior record and other information about the offender.[28]

A striking illustration of this policy-making process has been provided by Minnesota's sentencing commission. The Minnesota commission studied judges' decisions about whether or not to impose a prison sentence. It found that, under previous judicial practice, the main determinant of an offender's going to prison was the length of his criminal record. An offender with a string of lesser felonies would be imprisoned; a first offender with a considerably more serious conviction would not. In other words, the dispositional line on the grid—the line separating prison from nonprison dispositions—would be steep (emphasizing the criminal record) were past practice made the basis of the guidelines. The commission then proceeded to consider whether this practice was desirable and should be continued.

To make that decision the commission developed models comparing the slope of the dispositional line on two rationales: a desert rationale, and an incapacitative one relying on prediction of risk. After consulting the literature on desert and prediction, the commission determined that a desert rationale would have a relatively flat line, giving primary weight to the seriousness of the current offense—whereas a predictive rationale would (because of the link between previous record and recidivism) have a much steeper line, emphasizing the prior record, as the state's previous practice did. With this in mind the commission was able to debate the rationale, and eventually it decided that a more desert-oriented rationale was preferable.[29] The commission thereupon chose as its dispositional line one which, it asserted, reflected a "modified" desert conception;

11

the line was flat for most cases, albeit steep for offenders with lengthy criminal histories. The result of this decision was a substantial change from prior policy. The seriousness of the offense is given considerably more importance in the guidelines than it had under the state's past practice, and the extent of the criminal history is given much less.[30]

Since I do so later in chapter 5, I shall not discuss here the merits of Minnesota's particular solution for the slope of the dispositional line. What is of interest is the commission's technique: of selecting the primary rationale for the sentencing system and using it to determine the structure of the guidelines.

Controlling the Growth of Prison Populations

Many jurisdictions, both in the United States and elsewhere, have been experiencing sharp rises in prison populations. The result has been prison overcrowding, with its attendant evils of deteriorating living conditions. If crowding is endemic and serious, the conventional palliatives offer little hope. Emergency release, accelerated parole, and similar stopgap measures are only short-term solutions—and soon generate opposition, as involving the "premature" release of undeserving or dangerous felons. New prison construction is costly, time-consuming, and (if prison commitments continue unabated) creates space that itself soon will be filled. Crowding can be effectively prevented only by controlling the inflow into the prisons and the length of stay there.

Inflow and length of stay can be influenced through sentencing guidelines. Minnesota, again, provides the model. The Minnesota sentencing commission devised its guidelines so that, given anticipated conviction rates, the aggregate prison population would not exceed the capacity of the state's prisons. The commission accomplished this by projecting the impact of its tentatively proposed guidelines on prison populations, comparing those projections with the rated capacity of the state's prison system, and then making the appropriate adjustments to yield the final guidelines.[31]

Minnesota's approach involves "freezing" prison populations at existing levels. A variant of the technique might involve setting a population target that is either somewhat higher or lower than existing institutional capacity. Then—as long as any increased commitments were not to take effect until necessary space had been built—the guidelines still would perform the function of restraining prison populations within available space.

The effectiveness of the Minnesota projection technique depends upon grid ranges that are fairly narrow and departure rules that are fairly stringent. With wide ranges, it would be difficult or impossible to project actual sentence levels and hence the impact. Eventually, the Minnesota commission's projections proved reasonably accurate—prison commitments have remained within capacity, after a transition period in which some adjustments had to be made (see chapters 2 and 8). The state is no longer experiencing a problem of uncontrolled prison-population increases.

Why should a sentencing commission adopt such population targets? The plainest reason is ethical. Overcrowding makes the daily discomforts of prison life much worse, and it exacerbates frictions that can lead to violence. A civilized society should not commit offenders to institutions that lack room for them.

A population constraint has another use: it forces those who write sentencing guidelines to treat them as a choice of priorities. When a population constraint is imposed and population projections are systematically used in writing the guidelines, the commissioners are made aware that they are dealing with a system of scarce resources—which cannot possibly imprison all those whom various constituencies might prefer to see confined. With explicit population targets it becomes clear that a choice must be made of whom it is *most important* to imprison: those whose crimes are serious or those who have substantial criminal records can be chosen, but not all of both groups. The need to make such a choice can promote consensus within the commission and can also help the commission explain its work by pointing out the tradeoffs: how getting tougher with one group of offenders would necessitate more leniency with another group. In Minnesota, such a strategy of argument proved helpful for obtaining agreement within the commission and for generating outside support for the guidelines.[32]

It is sometimes said to be unjust or inappropriate to let prison space influence punishment levels. This claim seems plausible on a retributive theory of punishment: why should offenders' deserts depend on how much room there is in penal institutions? On closer analysis, however, the claim does not stand. Granted, it would not be appropriate to use space constraints to impose unequal punishments on offenders convicted of equally reprehensible conduct. But if parity among equally blameworthy offenders is maintained, and if punishments are graded according to the gravity of the criminal conduct, then—for reasons suggested in chapter 5 and elaborated by me elsewhere—desert principles allow some leeway in determining the anchoring points and overall severity levels of the penalty scale. To the extent such leeway exists, resource availability may be a legitimate factor in deciding overall severity levels.[33]

On a utilitarian sentencing philosophy, the objection to considering space availability lacks even plausibility. Sentences, in such a view, are to be determined by weighing the crime-preventive benefits of a given sentencing policy against its costs, human and financial.[34] A major cost is that of building and maintaining prisons.

Beyond such philosophical arguments stands another, simpler reason for considering prison space: namely, to ensure that the guidelines are implemented as written. To the extent that their full application would overtax available penal resources, the guidelines will have to be disregarded in everyday sentencing decisions. If dissatisfied with existing punishment levels, the commission might decide that increased or reduced aggregate use of imprisonment is appropriate. If it wishes an increase, then it would have to take into account whether the legislature is willing to fund such an increase and how long it would take before the added space becomes available. But to write a sentencing "policy" for which the necessary resources are lacking is posturing, not policy making.

Developing the Tariff

The third task for the commission is to develop a tariff: to provide specific guidance on the amount of punishment ordinarily called for by various types of cases. Such a baseline for everyday sentencing decisions is what has been lacking from discretionary systems.

If the guidelines use a grid format, the commission develops the tariff by filling in the cells in the grid. By supplying ranges in the grid's cells, the commission indicates when imprisonment is called for, and what periods of imprisonment ordinarily are appropriate. The judges' role then becomes that of applying and interpreting the tariff in their everyday sentencing decisions and deciding when to deviate from the tariff in suitable special circumstances.

This tariff-construction work is the commission's most laborious task. Different species of criminal conduct must be graded in seriousness—which involves assessing the harm and culpability of a wide variety of criminal acts. Offenders' criminal histories, and any other appropriate offender factors, need also to be graded (see chapter 5). Finally, the ranges of normally prescribed punishments need to be decided upon—work involving complex comparative judgments, in which the commission needs to bear in mind its chosen rationale and its prison-population targets. The guidelines are only as good as the tariff. Little is accomplished if the chosen rationale is ignored when the numbers are written in the grid cells, or if the prescribed punishment ranges are too broad to provide significant guidance to judges.

Once the tariff is thus developed, the question of departures needs also to be addressed. What burden of persuasion must be met before departures from the grid's ranges are permitted? What are the permitted grounds for departure? If departures are too readily permitted, the guidelines become merely precatory; if they are stringently restricted, then the guidelines become too rigid.

With this brief description of guidelines' format and purpose in mind, we should survey the salient features of the guidelines that have become law already, and summarize their known effects. That is the topic of the next chapter.

CHAPTER 2

Sentencing Guidelines and Their Effects

Michael Tonry

To many observers the story of sentencing reform in America is the Minnesota story. Minnesota combined two new ideas—the sentencing commission and presumptive sentencing guidelines—with an old idea, appellate sentence review. The Minnesota guidelines were principled; they expressed ideals of racial, social, and sexual neutrality; they constituted a serious attack on sentencing disparities; and they were intended to alter Minnesota sentencing practices substantially. To the surprise of skeptics, they "worked." Trial judges adhered to the guidelines. Minnesota sentencing patterns shifted in the intended ways. Sentencing disparities were reduced. And, for the first time in the United States, a meaningful system of appellate sentence review developed.

Half a dozen other states have had sentencing commissions. Sentencing commissions in Pennsylvania and Washington have promulgated guidelines. Commissions in Connecticut, New York, Maine, and South Carolina tried but failed; others are at work. In late 1984 the U.S. Congress enacted the Sentencing Reform Act of 1984, establishing a federal sentencing commission which must present its proposed guidelines to the Congress early in 1987.

Entities known as "sentencing commissions" have been established in as many as fifteen states. Many of these, however, have been study groups or advisory boards instituted to study sentencing and formulate recommendations to a governor or a legislature or a chief justice. Others have been committees of judges impaneled to develop voluntary guidelines. In this chapter, I use the term "sentencing commission" to refer to a body which is created by legislation and which is supposed to write sentencing guidelines having some binding force.

The Idea

The "sentencing commission model" incorporates three main elements—the sentencing commission, presumptive sentencing guidelines, and appellate sentence review. Each is an inseparable part of the Minnesota story. The *sentencing commission* was indispensable because it possessed the institutional capacity to develop sentencing standards of greater subtlety and specificity than a legislature could. *Presumptive sentencing guidelines* provided a mechanism for expressing sentencing standards in a form that has more legal authority than voluntary guidelines, is less rigid than mandatory sentencing laws, and is much more specific than the maximum and minimum sentences specified by criminal-law statutes. *Appellate sentence review* provided a mechanism for assuring that trial judges either imposed sentences that were consistent with the applicable guidelines or had adequate and acceptable reasons for imposing sentences that were different.

The attraction of the sentencing commission model is its merger of the three elements. Appellate sentence review has been available in various jurisdictions from time to time throughout this century, and probably earlier. It seldom amounted to much, however, because there was no substantive sentencing law. Most criminal statutes simply authorized maximum lawful sentences. If the maximum for robbery was fifteen years, there were no standards to guide a judge in deciding whether probation, five years, ten years, or fifteen years was the appropriate sentence to impose. By contrast, in most legal matters, when an appeal is taken from a trial judge's decision, the appellate court can look to the applicable statutes and case law for guidance in deciding whether the trial judge's decision was correct.

In most jurisdictions that allow sentence appeals, the scrutiny given to appealed sentences has been slight, and doctrines of extreme deference to the trial judge have developed. It is hard to see what else could have happened. The long maximum sentences in indeterminate sentencing systems were intended to permit judges to individualize sentences. For an appellate judge to have reversed a sentence, in the absence of established standards for evaluating the appropriateness of sentences, would have seemed, and been, ad hoc and arbitrary.

Presumptive sentencing guidelines changed that. The judge is supposed to impose a sentence consistent with the guidelines unless there is a good reason to do otherwise. This system contrasts with "voluntary" guidelines, from which there is no legal appeal. It is also what makes appellate sentence review feasible. There is no significant difference, in principle, between considering whether a trial judge rightly decided a question of contract law and whether a trial judge rightly decided to impose a sentence that deviates from the applicable guidelines. In both instances, the appellate judges must consider the standard rule and any cases that apply or interpret it and then decide whether the reasons given for the disputed decision are persuasive.

When the sentencing commission model was first proposed by Marvin Frankel in 1972, his basic argument was that sentencing was "lawless": no substantive criteria existed to guide either the trial judge's sentence or the appellate judge's review of that sentence. Judge Frankel observed that legislatures are unlikely to be very good at developing detailed sentencing standards. Instead he urged creation of a special-purpose administrative agency that had the institutional capacity, and might develop an institutional competence, to establish substantive sentencing rules.

Shortly thereafter, a workshop at Yale Law School met over an extended period under the auspices of the Guggenheim Foundation, and attempted to work out the details of Judge Frankel's proposal. The workshop generated a book proposing the creation of a federal sentencing commission.[1] Slightly revised, the proposal was introduced in the ninety-fourth Congress by Senator Edward Kennedy as Senate Bill 2699. The sentencing commission legislation was reintroduced in subsequent congresses, initially as a separate sentencing commission bill, later as a part of the successive federal criminal code bills, and finally was enacted in October 1984 as part of the Sentencing Reform Act of 1984.

Still, ten years passed between the introduction of the first federal sentencing commission bill and the passage of the 1984 law. That first bill was the legislative prototype, but the operational prototype was created in Minnesota.

The Experience

Minnesota (which had been one of the first jurisdictions to adopt parole guidelines) became the first jurisdiction to establish a sentencing commission. Minnesota's nine-member commission was created in 1978 and was directed to submit guidelines to the legislature on January 1, 1980. The commission met regularly, conducted frequent public meetings, took its task seriously, and invested substantial energies and resources in training practitioners in use of the guidelines. After implementation, an elaborate and intensive monitoring system was established.

The Minnesota commission made a number of bold policy decisions. First, it decided to be "prescriptive" and to establish its own explicit sentencing priorities; every previous scheme of sentencing guidelines had purported to be "descriptive," to attempt to replicate existing sentencing patterns. Second, the commission decided to de-emphasize imprisonment as a punishment for property offenders and to emphasize imprisonment for violent offenders; this was a major sentencing policy decision, because research on past Minnesota sentencing patterns showed that repeat property offenders tended to go to prison and that first-time violent offenders tended not to. Third, in order to attack sentencing disparities, the commission established narrow sentencing ranges (for example, thirty to thirty-four months, or fifty to fifty-eight months) and to authorize departures from guideline ranges only when "substantial and compelling" reasons were present. Fourth, the commission elected to adopt "just deserts" as the governing premise of its policies concerning who receives prison sentences. Fifth, the commission chose to interpret an ambiguous statutory injunction that it take correctional resources into "substantial consideration" as a mandate that its guidelines not increase prison populations beyond existing capacity constraints. This meant that the commission had to make deliberate trade-offs in imprisonment policies. If the commission decided to increase the lengths of prison terms for one group of offenders, it had also either to decrease prison terms for another group or to shift the in-out line and divert some group of prisoners from prison altogether. Sixth, the commission forbade consideration at sentencing of many personal factors—such as education, employment, marital status, living arrangements—that many judges had believed to be legitimate. This decision resulted from a policy that sentencing decisions not be based on factors that might directly or indirectly discriminate against minorities, women, or low-income groups. Two recent studies by Kay Knapp provide a full account of the commission's work.[2]

The Minnesota commission had a number of advantages. It was blessed with an unusually talented staff. Its first chairman was actively involved in the commission's work and, because she was politically knowledgeable and effective, was able to anticipate and avoid political problems that later overwhelmed commissions in other states. Key members were able both to represent the interests of their "constituencies," notably the judiciary and the prosecutors and, later, to persuade their constituencies not to oppose the commission and its product. The commission early decided that its work would be an "open political process" in which the views, opinions, and concerns of the affected constituencies and interest groups would be solicited. When the commission elected to take principled positions or to undertake bold policy initiatives, it was able to test those decisions on the affected constituencies, to modify those decisions when opposition appeared intractable, and once those constituencies were won over, to be relatively confident that they would not be seriously opposed before the legislature.

Minnesota's guidelines initially proved more successful than even the commission anticipated. Rates of compliance with the guidelines were high. More violent offenders and fewer property offenders went to prison. Disparities in prison sentences diminished. Prison populations remained under control.

Later there was backsliding; as time passed, sentencing patterns came to resemble those that existed before the guidelines were implemented (see chapter 8). Few would deny, however, that the Minnesota guideline system has been an impressive effort with important long-term consequences. Before discussing the guidelines' impact in detail, however, the sentencing commission experience in other states should be summarized. Aside from Minnesota, six states—Maine, Connecticut, New York, Pennsylvania, South Carolina, and Washington—illustrate the range of experience to date.

Maine

In June 1983 the Maine Legislature created the Maine Sentencing Guidelines Commission and charged it with making "recommendations of sentencing guidelines" to the legislature. The commission's primary recommendation, in a five-page report in November 1984, was "that a new commission be created to continue the responsibilities of this commission."[3] The commission did not give a detailed explanation of why it had failed to develop guidelines.

The Maine Sentencing Guidelines Commission suffered from a number of limitations. A sizable number of its members apparently decided early on that Maine did not need sentencing guidelines; as a consequence, institutional momentum seems never to have developed. Most of the Maine commission's nine part-time members had little prior knowledge of sentencing reform developments elsewhere. No full-time professional staff was appointed. State funding was insubstantial and outside funding was neither sought nor obtained.

Maine's judges constitute a major obstacle to creation of a presumptive guidelines system. At present, they arguably have more control over sentencing than judges in any other American state. Parole release was abolished in 1976. Unlike the other states that abolished parole release, however, Maine did not simultaneously establish either a statutory determinate sentencing system or a sentencing guideline system. As a result, judges do not share their sentencing discretion with a parole board or a sentencing commission. By contrast, judges in indeterminate sentencing states have discretion over who goes to prison but little control over the lengths of prison terms; parole boards control the latter decision. Judges in determinate sentencing states are bound either by statutory standards or criteria or by sentencing guidelines. Maine's judges appear to enjoy their unusual power and appear loathe to give it up.

In January 1986, Maine's governor signed legislation to reestablish the Maine commission. Whether its prospects of success will be any greater the second time around will be known only as events unfold.

Connecticut

The Connecticut legislature created a sentencing commission in 1979. The commission undertook research on past sentencing practices and developed a "descriptive" sentencing grid based on that research. Rules were developed for departures and for the role of aggravating and mitigating circumstances. Still, "[a]fter developing this sentencing guidelines system, the Sentencing Commission went on record stating that it was strongly opposed to the adoption of the sentencing guidelines system, but rather recommended the replacement of the indeterminate sentencing system in Connecticut with a determinate sentencing scheme."[4] The legislature heeded that advice and, effective July 1, 1981, abolished parole and established a statutory determinate sentencing system.

New York

Appointed in 1983, the New York State Committee on Sentencing Guidelines had a larger budget and a larger staff than those of any other sentencing commission. The members of the committee were sophisticated and many of them were well aware of developments in other jurisdictions. One member, Robert Morgenthau, had chaired a gubernatorial advisory committee that had in 1979 recommended that New York adopt the sentencing commission model. The staff director had worked on a major statewide sentencing guideline project in an urban industrial state, and the staff counsel was a veteran of political wars in New York. The New York committee met regularly, and occasionally lengthily, and generated a substantial volume of proposals, staff papers, working drafts, and impact projections. A report setting out recommendations was presented to the New York Legislature in April 1985; the report met with considerable hostility and was not approved.

The committee's work had suffered throughout from political posturing and interest-group politics. No consensus was reached about the goals or premises of the committee's recommendations, and the resulting ad hoc compromises pleased virtually no one. Robert Morgenthau, the Manhattan district attorney, dissented from the committee's report, thereby undermining its credibility and shattering any illusions that the committee had reached consensus positions.

The guidelines that were proposed had few vigorous proponents. The committee apparently never achieved a sense of collective mission and, perhaps as a consequence, never adopted a rationale or set of rationales for their work. If the committee had adopted a retributive, incapacitative, or other rationale, or some coherently integrated set of rationales, the resulting guideline proposals might have possessed an apparent logic.

The committee ducked most of the difficult policy choices. Rather than proposing sentencing ranges based on explicit policy choices of its own, it proposed ranges based on statistical averages of time served by inmates released in 1982 and 1983. Rather than recommend sentencing ranges that would significantly constrain discretion, the guideline ranges were extremely wide—sometimes with the top of the range exceeding the bottom by 100 percent. A person with no prior convictions who was convicted of armed robbery, for example, was subject to a guideline range of forty-five to ninety months' imprisonment after taking account of time off for good behavior. The committee also decided not to treat available prison capacity as a constraint on its policy recommendations.

A *Newsday* feature on the New York experience captured the result: The committee's "final report, in April, also drew contradictory complaints. It reduces mandatory minimums. It is too tough.

It is too soft. It will lead to an explosion in prison populations. It won't do enough to reduce sentencing disparity."[5]

The New York Committee on Sentencing Guidelines continued to exist for a time, and a few members still attended meetings. The staff director had resigned much earlier, as did the general counsel, who had succeeded him as director.

Pennsylvania

The Pennsylvania Commission on Sentencing was established in 1978 and began its work in April 1979. The commission proposed guidelines to the legislature in January 1981 under a statutory provision by which the guidelines would take effect automatically six months later unless rejected by the legislature in their entirety. They were rejected in March 1981, and the commission was directed to revise and resubmit the guidelines, to make the sentencing standards more severe (in a variety of specified ways), and to increase judicial discretion under the guidelines. In numerous ways the commission complied, and the resulting guidelines were submitted to the legislature in January 1982 and took effect on July 22, 1982.[6]

For every offense, including misdemeanors, the guidelines specify three "ranges"—a normal range, an aggravated range, and a mitigated range. The judge may impose a sentence from within any of the three ranges and may do so for any reason, as long as he or she states a reason. The guidelines set no general criteria for imposition of aggravated or mitigated sentences, or for "departures" from the guidelines, and no special findings of fact need be made. There are in addition no rules governing circumstances under which consecutive sentences may be ordered.

Pennsylvania publishes annual statistical analyses of the guidelines' impact. Overall compliance rates are very high, but it is unclear what this means; the guidelines are so broad (for example, nine to thirty-six months) that substantial disparities can occur even within the guidelines, because judges can use the aggravated and mitigated ranges at will, and because no efforts have been made to account for the role of plea bargaining.

Pennsylvania only vaguely represents the sentencing commission model. The guidelines concern only minimum sentences—that is, the time when the defendant becomes eligible to be considered for parole release. They do not regulate the parole board's release decisions. Actual duration of confinement is determined in large part by the board's discretionary release decisions. Moreover, because the guidelines are broad and furnish no rules governing when judges may depart from the normally recommended ranges, it is difficult for the Pennsylvania appellate courts to have any basis for evaluating sentence appeals. This is precisely the reason hypothesized above for the failure of meaningful appellate sentence review to develop in the United States. An interesting unpublished paper by a member of the commission's research staff analyzes the sentence appeal case law and concludes that, to date, the courts have dealt primarily with procedural issues and have not dealt with the substantive bases of sentences.[7]

In fairness, the Pennsylvania commission's initial, ultimately rejected guidelines were considerably more ambitious than those that took effect. The original proposed guidelines had much narrower guideline ranges, provided rules on consecutive sentencing, and set forth specific criteria for aggravation or mitigation.[8] These features disappeared from the final guidelines.

There appear to be a number of reasons for the Pennsylvania commission's failure to establish meaningful guidelines. From one perspective the legislature can be blamed, for it passed a law calling for presumptive sentencing guidelines to operate in conjunction with parole, and yet rejected the commission's initial, more meaningful guidelines. The commission had its own difficulties as well. During the period when the guidelines were being developed, it seems not to have developed a sense of collective mission. Several commission members took little interest in the commission's work and seldom appeared at meetings. Finally, little effort was apparently made to obtain the participation of affected interests and constituencies in the guidelines development process. As a result, when the guidelines reached the legislature, the commission had few allies or supporters and, in a law-and-order climate, did well to survive at all.[9]

South Carolina

The South Carolina Sentencing Guidelines Commission was appointed by the governor of that state in 1982, and, somewhat later, separate enabling legislation was passed. The commission was chaired by a supreme court justice, and its members included judges, legislators, and prosecutors. Its guidelines were proposed to the legislature for adoption in 1985 but were rejected. To a considerable extent, the rejection apparently resulted from the commission's inability to gain support from the judiciary. Politically, judicial support is more important in South Carolina than it would have been in most states. The South Carolina legislature selects the South Carolina judges, many of whom—perhaps not surprisingly—are former legislators.

Washington

The one apparent success story, besides that in Minnesota, occurred in Washington State. The commission had most of the same ingredients as had been present in Minnesota: a capable staff, an effective chairman, an adequate budget, a sense of mission among the commission's members, a comprehensive and principled approach to policy problems, and an understanding of the need for compromise during development of the guidelines. When the proposed guidelines were submitted to the Washington legislature, they passed amid relatively little controversy and have been in effect since July 1, 1984.[10]

The Washington guidelines (summarized in the appendix) resemble Minnesota's. Sentencing ranges are much narrower than those in Pennsylvania but are somewhat broader than those in Minnesota. The guidelines set out illustrative aggravating and mitigating circumstances and, as in Minnesota, permit departures only in "substantial and compelling" circumstances. Also as in Minnesota, the commission decided to shift sentencing policy toward more incarceration of violent offenders and less incarceration of property offenders. Washington has eliminated not only discretionary parole release, but parole supervision as well.

The Washington legislature had learned a number of lessons from the Minnesota experience and built them into the enabling legislation. Unlike the Minnesota guidelines, which provide detailed standards only for felony prison sentences, the Washington guidelines apply to all felonies and to both jail and prison sentences. The commission was directed to be sensitive to prison population capacity constraints and to promulgate statewide prosecutorial charging and bargaining guidelines. This last feature is a Washington original and resulted in part from the frequent observation that determinate sentencing in general, and narrow ranges of guidelines in particular, increase the power of prosecutors. The Washington solution was to try to structure the discretion of the prosecutor.

The preliminary evaluation of Washington's first year under guidelines suggests considerable successes. The shift toward imprisonment of violent offenders and away from imprisonment of property offenders is happening, and compliance with the guidelines has been high. Trial rates have not increased significantly.

The Minnesota and Washington experiences suggest that the combination of sentencing commissions and presumptive guidelines can be a viable approach for achieving consistent and coherent jurisdiction-wide sentencing policies. The experiences in Maine, New York, Pennsylvania, and South Carolina, however, counsel that the sentencing commission approach will not necessarily succeed. Six jurisdictions are too few to support any but the most tentative generalizations about success and failure. Still, it is clear that local legal and political cultures shape the environments in which the commissions work. Minnesota and Washington, for example, are both relatively homogeneous states with reform traditions. In neither state were criminal justice issues highly politicized. New York and Pennsylvania, by contrast, are heterogeneous states in which criminal justice issues are highly politicized and law-and-order sentiment is powerful. In states where trial judges are politically influential, they may be able to resist efforts to limit their own discretion. Perhaps the only generalization that can be offered concerning political and legal culture is that the potential and the effectiveness of a sentencing commission will depend on how it addresses and accommodates constraints imposed by the local culture (see chapter 4).

The Impact of Commission Guidelines

The staff of the Minnesota commission prepared a series of exhaustive impact evaluations; the most recent was published in 1984 and covered the experience of the first three years. One independent statistical analysis of Minnesota impact data has been published. The Pennsylvania commission has published a series of sketchier statistical reports on sentencing in Pennsylvania, and one article by members of its staff has been published. In addition, several unpublished papers have been presented at academic meetings. Finally, Washington has undertaken an in-house evaluation from which a preliminary report became available in November 1985; a more comprehensive report was released in January 1986.[11]

A number of questions can be asked about the effect of sentencing guidelines on sentencing patterns. Did judges comply with guidelines and to what extent? Were sentencing patterns under guidelines different from the patterns that existed before guidelines? Did sentences become more severe? Did disparities increase or decrease? What was the interaction between the guidelines and plea bargaining?

Finally, were there important adverse effects of guidelines on the operation of the courts? For example, did trial rates or case processing times increase? Did the appellate courts become inundated by sentence appeals? The following sections discuss these questions in sequence. To anticipate the conclusions:

- All three guideline systems achieved high compliance rates
- All three guideline systems apparently had some success in changing sentencing patterns (the evidence for such success is weakest in Pennsylvania)
- The lengths of sentences received by imprisoned offenders increased in Minnesota and Pennsylvania (information is not yet available from Washington)
- Sentencing disparities apparently decreased in Minnesota and Pennsylvania during the first years of guideline experience; in Minnesota there was slippage in the second and third years
- Prosecutors in Minnesota have changed charging and bargaining practices in an effort to circumvent the guidelines, with some success; and there are indications that this may be happening in Pennsylvania and Washington
- In Minnesota and Washington there were no significant increases in trial rates or case processing times under guidelines; sentence appeals were filed in only 1 percent of cases.

The findings of the evaluations are relatively clear. What is less clear is what the findings mean. For example, high rates of compliance with guidelines may mean that sentencing guidelines are successfully inducing judges and lawyers to defer to sentencing policies set by the sentencing commissions, or they may mean that judges and lawyers are identifying the sentences they wish to have imposed and are then ensuring through bargains and charge dismissals that the defendant is convicted of an offense bearing the appropriate sentence. Similarly, an increase in sentence severity may result from promulgation of the guidelines, or it may be the product of other causes. As findings are reviewed below, an effort is made to identify alternative explanations for evaluation findings.

Compliance Rates
All three sentencing commissions have achieved relatively high compliance rates. In the following discussion, "dispositional de-

parture" is a sentence to state prison when the guidelines prescribe an "out" (nonprison) sentence, or an "out" sentence when the guidelines prescribe state prison. A "durational departure" is a prison sentence for a term outside the applicable guideline range.

Minnesota Compared with sentencing patterns in 1978, Minnesota sentencing patterns changed significantly after guidelines took effect and became more consistent. Minnesota's rate of dispositional departures increased slightly during the first three years, and departures were about evenly divided between departures upward (imprisonment when the grid provided nonprison) and downward (the reverse). Durational departure rates were stable; downward departures exceeded upward departures by two to one. Table 2–1 shows both kinds of departure rates for 1978 and for the first three years after the guidelines were implemented.

In 1981, 6.2 percent of Minnesota sentences were dispositional departures (3.1 percent upward; 3.1 percent downward). In 1982, 7.0 percent of sentences were dispositional departures (3.4 percent upward; 3.6 percent downward). In 1983, the dispositional departure rate had climbed to 8.9 percent (4.5 percent upward; 4.4 percent downward). Projected dispositional departures under the guidelines, if they had been superimposed over 1978 sentences, would have been 19.4 percent, suggesting that the guidelines had significantly increased the consistency of sentencing. Or, viewed

Table 2–1

Dispositional and durational departure rates in Minnesota, 1978 and 1981–1983

Year	Dispositional Departures				Durational Departures			
	Total (%)	Up (%)	Down (%)	No. of Cases	Total (%)	Up (%)	Down (%)	No. of Cases
1978	19.4	12.0	7.4	4,369	—	—	—	—
1981	6.2	3.1	3.1	5,500	23.6	7.9	15.7	827
1982	7.0	3.4	3.6	6,066	20.4	6.6	13.8	1,127
1983	8.9	4.5	4.4	5,562	22.9	6.0	16.9	1,124

Note: Dashes indicate that data are unavailable.
Sources: Minnesota Sentencing Guidelines Commission, *The Impact of the Minnesota Sentencing Guidelines*, tables 2, 6, 8, 9, 13, 15, and *Preliminary Report on the Development and Impact of the Minnesota Sentencing Guidelines*, fig. 3, p. 22.

from the opposite angle, in the first three years of Minnesota's experience with guidelines, the dispositional compliance rates were 93.8 percent, 93 percent, and 91.1 percent.

To some extent, the increased dispositional departure rates in 1982 and 1983 resulted from the anomaly that 75 defendants in 1982 and 111 defendants in 1983 requested to go to prison rather than receive nonprison sentences. The Minnesota Supreme Court has ruled that such a request generally should be honored. These cases are counted as departures, and therefore inflate the departure rate.

The compliance figures are less impressive than first appears. Minnesota has very low imprisonment rates for persons convicted of felonies. In 1978, before guidelines took effect, 20.4 percent of convicted felons received prison sentences. In 1981, imprisonment was the presumptive disposition, and also the actual disposition, in 15.0 percent of cases. In 1982, imprisonment was the presumptive disposition in 18.7 percent of cases and the actual disposition in 18.6 percent of cases. Thus nonimprisonment is the presumptive sentence in 80 to 85 percent of felony cases each year, and it would take a very large shift toward greater severity in sentencing of persons convicted of less serious offenses significantly to alter dispositional compliance rates. Conversely, as many as a quarter of offenders whom the grid would imprison could receive nonprison sentences and alter the overall dispositional departure rate by only a few percentage points.

Durational departure rates, also shown in Table 2-1, do not appear to follow any clear pattern. Comparisons with durational patterns before guidelines were implemented are not shown because the parole release decisions in 1978 could not easily be compared with sentencing decisions made after guidelines were put into effect.

Pennsylvania   Dispositional and durational compliance with the guidelines in Pennsylvania has been much lower than in Minnesota. Table 2–2 shows published Pennsylvania dispositional data for 1983 and 1984. Even with the very wide guideline ranges that result when Pennsylvania's three ranges are combined, Pennsylvania's dispositional departure rates of 13 percent in 1983 and 14 percent in 1984 are much higher than Minnesota's range of 6.2 to 8.9 percent in the first three years.

Table 2–3 shows Pennsylvania's durational departure rates of 7 percent in 1983 and 1984. The rates appear lower than Min-

Table 2–2

Dispositional departure rates in Pennsylvania, 1983 and 1984

Year	Departure Down (%)	Mitigated Range (%)	Standard (%)	Aggravated Range (%)	Departure Up
1983	12.0	5.0	80.5	1.0	1.0
1984	12.0	5.6	78.5	1.7	2.0

Note: Percentages do not total 100 because of rounding.
Sources: Pennsylvania Commission on Sentencing, *1983 Report*, fig. 1, table 1, and *1984 Report*, fig. G, table 6.

nesota's rates, but probably nothing can be concluded from this. The effect of Pennsylvania's three wide ranges allows enormous scope for variation without departures. For example, the combined guideline range in Pennsylvania for a person convicted of an aggravated robbery who had previously been convicted of a robbery would be nine to thirty-six months. Under the Minnesota guidelines, the guideline range would be thirty to thirty-four months.

Even Pennsylvania's modest rates of compliance with the grid ranges must be considered with skepticism. These data are heavily influenced by high compliance rates for minor offenses. For example, of 25,694 sentences imposed in the one-year period covered by the Pennsylvania commission's 1984 report, 6,987 of those cases (more than a quarter) fell in the category "crimes code misdemeanors"—of which 97 percent resulted in sentences in the normal guideline range (the normal guideline range is zero to six months); that single offense category therefore constitutes more than 25 percent of the statewide compliance with Pennsylvania's guidelines. Other misdemeanors, totaling 3,143 sentences in 1984,

Table 2–3

Durational departure rates in Pennsylvania, 1983 and 1984

Year	Departure Upward (%)	Departure Down (%)
1983	1.0	6.0
1984	2.0	5.0

Sources: Pennsylvania Commission on Sentencing, *1983 Report*, table 3, and *1984 Report*, table 8.

experienced dispositional compliance rates ranging from 94 to 99 percent.

Further evidence of low levels of compliance in Pennsylvania is shown in a recent article by executive and associate directors of the Pennsylvania commission.[12] Table 2–4, taken from that article, shows compliance rates in 1983 for selected offenses. "Compliance" means imposition of any sentence from within the aggregate mitigated, standard, and aggravated ranges. The offenses set out in that table (excepting drug misdemeanors) are generally felonies and therefore are comparable with the offenses (only felonies) that are affected by Minnesota's guidelines. Pennsylvania's level of compliance for felony sentences appears lower than Minnesota's even when the different widths of "compliant" guideline ranges are ignored. Compliance rates for aggravated assault, arson, burglary, drug felonies, rape, and robbery range from 64 percent to 83 percent.

Unfortunately, because of plea bargaining, even the weak evidence summarized above for compliance with Pennsylvania's guidelines may be overstated. Table 2–5, taken from the Pennsyl-

Table 2–4

Compliance with guideline sentences imposed in Pennsylvania in 1983 for selected offenses

Offense	N	Comply (%)	Above (%)	Below (%)
Aggravated assault	574	70	0	30
Arson	95	64	1	35
Burglary	2538	77	3	20
Criminal trespass	451	93	0	7
Drug felonies	872	80	2	18
Drug misdemeanors	646	100	0	0
Escape	99	40	0	60
Forgery	450	85	0	15
Involuntary deviate sexual intercourse	69	68	0	32
Rape	75	76	4	20
Retail theft	611	84	1	15
Robbery	1020	83	5	12
Terroristic threats	130	92	0	8
Theft-felony	906	89	1	10
Weapons	454	81	1	18

Source: Kramer and Lubitz p. 490.

vania commission's 1983 report, shows guideline conformity rates for selected offenses. The offenses shown are sets of related offenses of variable severity and they exhibit certain common features. Mitigated departure rates are very high for persons convicted of the *most serious* offense of a class (aggravated assault, 46 percent; arson, 77 percent; burglary, 29 percent; retail theft, 25 percent; robbery, 25 percent). Persons convicted of the *least serious* version of the offense, however, tend to be sentenced from within the standard range (aggravated assault, 70 percent; arson, 62 percent; burglary, 78 percent; retail theft, 91 percent; robbery, 85 percent). These patterns support a number of hypotheses about variations in plea bargaining practices. In courts in which sentence bargaining is the norm, the parties may agree to conviction on the offense charged but with an understanding that the sentence will be reduced substantially. This would explain the high downward departure rates for the most serious form of an offense. In charge bargaining courts, the parties may agree to conviction on a reduced charge and imposition of a sentence from within the standard range. This would explain high rates of sentences within the normal guideline ranges for the least serious form of an offense. If these hypotheses are valid, one cannot conclude anything about compliance from the aggregate data. Whether these hypotheses are valid can be tested by participant observation research on plea bargaining in Pennsylvania. The data suggest, however, how high compliance rates might be compatible with extensive plea bargaining.[13] (Critics of sentencing guidelines have suggested that greater predictability allows the prosecutor increased power. Or, in jurisdictions in which plea bargaining is the norm, the specificity that accompanies determinate sentencing may allow bargaining to work backward from the sentence to the offense. That is, counsel can agree on an appropriate sentence, locate it on the sentencing grid, and then reach agreement concerning the offence to which the defendant will plead guilty. The validity of these criticisms will be examined more fully in chapter 9.)

Table 2–6 shows, for 1983, "sentence conformity" for the offenses "violations/firearms-loaded" and "violations/firearms-unloaded." It, likewise, illustrates conformity patterns that may be artifacts of plea bargaining. The loaded-firearms offense is more serious than the unloaded-firearms offense. Of persons convicted of the more serious offense, only 30 percent received sentences from the standard range and 52 percent received sentences below both

Table 2–5
Statewide conformity with guidelines in Pennsylvania, 1983

Offense	Standard (%)	Aggravated (%)	Mitigated (%)	Departure Up (%)	Departure Down (%)
Aggravated assault					
F2	36	4	12	2	46
F3	100	0	0	0	0
M1	70	1	10	0	19
Arson					
F1	13	0	10	0	77
F2	62	0	11	5	22
Burglary					
ogs 7	39	3	25	3	29
ogs 6	49	3	14	4	31
ogs 5	78	2	5	2	12
Retail theft					
F3	62	2	9	1	25
M1	91	0	4	0	5
Robbery					
F1	48	6	10	15	25
F2	67	4	6	6	20
F3	85	1	4	2	17

Note: In the first column, "F" and "M" refer to felony and misdemeanor, and the number after those letters (e.g., "F3") refers to the statutory offense category. "Ogs" refers to the commission's offense gravity scale, and the number thereafter (e.g. "ogs 5") refers to the grid's offense-gravity ranking.
Source: Pennsylvania Commission on Sentencing, *1983 Report*, table 2.

the standard range and the mitigated range. The high rate of downward departures suggests that in courts where sentence bargaining is the prevalent pattern of plea negotiation, counsel negotiated a below-guideline sentence in a majority of cases.

Of persons convicted of unloaded-firearms offenses, however, 94 percent were sentenced from within the standard range. That suggests that in many jurisdictions charge bargaining was the norm and defendants charged with loaded-firearms violations pled guilty to the unloaded-firearms offense and received the expected standard sentence.

Table 2–6
Dispositions in firearms cases in Pennsylvania, 1983

Cases	Number Sentenced	Standard Range (%)	Aggravated Range (%)	Mitigated Range (%)	Departures Above (%)	Departures Below (%)
Violations/firearms-loaded	155	30	1	15	1	52
Violations/firearms-unloaded	252	94	1	1	2	2

Source: Pennsylvania Commission on Sentencing, *1983 Report*, table 1.

Table 2–7
Sentencing severity in Pennsylvania, 1983 and 1984

Year	Percentage of Defendants Incarcerated	Minimum Average Incarceration (Months)	Maximum Average Incarceration (Months)	Average Minimum Jail Sentence (Months)	Average Maximum Jail Sentence (Months)	Average Minimum Prison Sentence (Months)	Average Maximum Prison Sentence (Months)	Percentage of Minimum Sentences in Excess of Five Years
1983	55	12.1	33.4	6.4	20.5	24.4	61.5	3.3
1984	57	—	—	6.8	22.2	28.7	70.0	6

Note: Dashes indicate that data are not available.
Source: Pennsylvania Commission on Sentencing, *1983 Report*, p. 17, and *1984 Report*, p. 22.

Washington Washington has relatively narrow guidelines, only one guideline range for each offense and offender, and a demanding standard for departures. Only 3.4 percent of sentences in the first six months of 1985 were "exceptional" sentences that satisfied the "substantial and compelling" test and therefore were "departures."[14] Washington has, however, a special "first offender" provision (for persons convicted of a nonviolent, nonsexual offense who have no prior felony conviction); this option permits the judge to order a treatment-oriented sentence and jail time not to exceed ninety days in place of whatever sentence the guidelines might prescribe. The first-offender provision applied to 23.2 percent of offenders, of whom about half benefited from the special provision; it is unclear how to factor these cases into compliance rates. The special first-offender provision is unlikely significantly to affect the size of the departure rate. Almost by definition, first offenders convicted of nonviolent, nonsexual offenses are unlikely in any jurisdiction to fall within a part of a guidelines grid that specifies an incarcerative sentence. If even 10 percent of those offenders received incarcerative sentences, the overall departure rate would increase to only 5.4 percent. The Washington compliance rates are possibly even more impressive than Minnesota's since the guidelines cover both felonies and misdemeanors.

Changes in Sentencing Patterns

Both the Minnesota and the Washington commissions decided, as a matter of policy, to attempt to change patterns of prison use by emphasizing the use of prison for persons convicted of violent offenses, including first offenders, and by de-emphasizing the use of imprisonment in nonviolent cases, including those involving offenders with extensive criminal records. In Minnesota, in the first year of experience with guidelines, 78 percent of offenders convicted of serious violent offenses and having a minor criminal record, or none at all, were imprisoned; that constituted a 73 percent increase over preguideline practices. Conversely, of those convicted of minor property offenses and having moderate to extensive criminal records, only 15 percent were imprisoned under the sentencing guidelines during the first year; that constituted a 72 percent reduction. During the second and third years, sentencing began to shift back toward traditional patterns. Imprisonment rates for violent offenders remained higher than preguideline levels but were lower than in 1981 and 1982.[15] By 1983 the imprisonment rate for low-severity property offenders was at almost the preguideline level (see chapter 8). This fact, however, may camouflage the guidelines' actual impact. Many offenders, as mentioned already, were imprisoned because they *requested* incarceration. Some offenders did so because they were being imprisoned for another, more serious, offense, and wanted the sentences to run concurrently. Others, however, who constituted 4 percent of prison admissions in 1981 and 10 percent in 1983, apparently preferred incarceration because it seemed less onerous than an "out" sentence. Under anomalies in the Minnesota guidelines, some "out" sentences are potentially harsher than "in" sentences. A person receiving a one-year prison term would, assuming good-time was credited, be released in eight months. An "out" sentence might include twelve months in jail plus a lengthy term of probation with conditions, and if probation were revoked, a state prison sentence of twelve to thirty months might be imposed. If the anomalies were eliminated so that this category of offenders did not request imprisonment, the imprisonment rate for low-severity property offenders in 1983 would probably be not much higher than the 1981 rate.

Washington also seems to have succeeded in altering sentencing patterns. In 1982, before implementation of guidelines, 46 percent of persons convicted of violent offenses received prison sentences; during the first six months of 1985, under the guidelines, 63.5 percent of persons convicted of such offenses were imprisoned. Conversely, in 1982, 84 percent of persons convicted of nonviolent offenses received nonprison sentences; during the first half of 1985, that percentage had increased to 90.8. The Washington data are cruder than those for Minnesota, for they do not distinguish among either violent or nonviolent offenses in terms of their relative gravity, but the pattern is clear. In both jurisdictions during the first year under guidelines, substantial shifts toward the direction contemplated by the creators of the guidelines took place in the patterns of sentences imposed.

Sentencing Severity

Only Minnesota and Pennsylvania data are relevant. The early Washington reports do not discuss changes in sentencing severity. The Pennsylvania evaluations showed increases in sentencing severity in each of the first two years of experience with guidelines. A 1983 commission report concluded that "incarceration rates and incarceration lengths increased substantially over previous levels, especially for violent crimes." The commission's conclusion in 1984 was that "sentencing severity for serious crimes increased over previous levels," for the second year. By every measure shown in Table 2–7, sentencing in Pennsylvania appears to have been more severe in 1984 than in 1983.[16]

In Minnesota, sentencing severity also appears to have increased but to a more modest extent. During the first year under the guidelines, 1981, judges imposed an average sentence of 38.3 months, and the projected actual incarceration (taking good time into account) was 25.5 months. Those figures increased in 1982 to 41 months and 27.3 months. They would likely have increased again in the third year but for a series of changes made by both the Minnesota Legislature and the commission aimed at reducing sentence lengths (and prison overcrowding); the resulting figures for 1983 were 36.5 months and 24.3 months.[17] By a different measure, Minnesota sentencing patterns also showed some increase in severity. Felony convictions resulting in prison sentences increased from 15 percent in 1981 to 18.6 percent in 1982 and 20.5 percent in 1983 (in 1978, 20.4 percent of convicted felons received prison sentences, so the apparent increase in prison use between 1981 and 1983 may instead be a reversion to preguideline levels).

The Extent of Sentencing Disparities
In all three jurisdictions there was evidence that sentencing became more consistent under guidelines than before. In Minnesota, the evaluation concluded, "disparity in sentencing decreased under the sentencing guidelines. This reduction in disparity is indicated by increased sentence uniformity and proportionality. . . . Although sentencing practices were still more uniform and proportional in 1982 and 1983 than sentencing practices prior to the guidelines, there was less uniformity and proportionality in 1982 and 1983 than there was in 1981."[18] Authors of a statistical analysis of the first eighteen months under guidelines in Minnesota similarly concluded that Minnesota "was largely successful in reducing preguideline disparities in those decisions that fall within the scope of the guidelines."[19]

One major weakness of the Minnesota guidelines is that they deal only with felonies and then primarily with sentences to state prison. Although the enabling legislation provided that "the commission may also establish appropriate sanctions for offenders for whom imprisonment is not proper," the commission elected not to do so. As a consequence, the guidelines create guidance as to who goes to prison and for how long, but not concerning the disposition of persons not receiving state prison sentences. Inasmuch as up to one year's jail incarceration may be imposed as a condition of probation, the absence of guidance could well have produced considerable disparity. Moreover, for those repetitive property offenders who the commission preferred not to receive prison sentences, jail remains an available option. The foreseeable confusion resulted. The commission's three-year evaluation concluded, "nonconformity of [jail] use is found for every racial and gender group, and there has been very little improvement in uniformity of jail use from 1978 to jail use in 1981, 1982, and 1983."[20]

The extent of uniformity and proportionality in Washington is difficult to assess because the preliminary evaluation report does not break down sentenced offenders by criminal history scores. Insofar as very high compliance rates were obtained, however, it is likely that substantial consistency was achieved.

The Pennsylvania evidence is also difficult to assess. The commission's evaluation of 1983 sentencing asserts: "it appears that Pennsylvania's guidelines are accomplishing their intended goal of reducing unwarranted disparity," and in the 1984 evaluation, they note, "sentences became more uniform throughout the state."[21] These conclusions presumably are inferences drawn from high rates of "conformity with guideline." As such rates may for reasons stated already, be less impressive than they appear to be, it is not clear that disparities have been reduced.

It is difficult to know how to assess Pennsylvania's shift. Less has been published about the experience in Pennsylvania than about that in Minnesota. One of the goals of the Pennsylvania guidelines was to lessen differences in sentencing patterns between rural and urban courts. An analysis by the executive and research directors of the Pennsylvania commission indicates much greater similarity in urban and rural sentencing patterns after guidelines than before.[22]

Plea Bargaining

The former chairman of the Minnesota commission has written about the need for prosecutors to develop prosecutorial guidelines because of "the potential of the prosecutor to undermine the uniformity desired by the guidelines."[23] It has often been suggested that the greater predictability that accompanies determinate sentencing will serve to increase the potential power of prosecutors.

Experience has validated that prediction, as is shown by direct evidence from Minnesota and indirect evidence from Pennsylvania and Washington.

The Minnesota evaluation investigated plea bargaining under the guidelines in a number of ways. The overall conclusion was that under guidelines "[t]here were more charge negotiations and fewer sentence negotiations. There were more charge reductions that affected the severity level of the offense and an increase in the number of conviction offenses which affected the criminal history score of the offender."[24]

Table 2–8 shows the findings of the commission's study of dispositions in eight counties for 1978 and the first two years under guidelines. Compared with 1978, cases resolved by charge negotiations in 1982 increased from 21.1 percent to 31.3 percent. Those resolved by sentence negotiations fell from 34.3 percent in 1978 to 25.7 percent in 1982.

The increase in charge bargaining should be no surprise. The Minnesota guidelines are based on the charge of conviction and, assuming the judge will impose a sentence from within the applicable guideline range, the sentencing ramifications of a "vertical" charge reduction are explicit and predictable. This is particularly true when the charge reduction moves the case across the in-out line from the area of presumptive prison sentences to the area of presumptive nonprison sentences. Compared with 1978, cases in which there were charge reductions across offense severity levels in 1983 increased from 12 percent to 27 percent.[25]

Table 2–8

Method of obtaining conviction in eight counties in Minnesota

Method	1978 (%)	1981 (%)	1982 (%)
Trial	5.8	4.7	5.6
Straight plea	17.1	25.8	15.7
Charge negotiation	21.1	27.6	31.3
Sentence negotiation	34.3	23.4	25.7
Plea negotiation charge and sentence	21.7	18.5	21.6
Total	100.0	100.0	99.9

Note: Percentages do not total 100 because of rounding.
Source: Minnesota Sentencing Guidelines Commission, *The Impact of the Minnesota Sentencing Guidelines,* table 27.

The increase in vertical charge bargaining is thus explicable in terms of case dispositions. A change in Minnesota "horizontal" charging and bargaining practices resulted from an effort by prosecutors to manipulate the guidelines. Many prosecutors apparently disagreed with the commission's policy decision to decrease the use of state prison incarceration as a sanction for property offenses. Under the guidelines, an offender convicted of a minor property offense had to accumulate a substantial criminal record before prison became the presumptive sentence. In a deliberate effort to increase the criminal history scores of property offenders, prosecutors required such offenders to plead guilty to multiple charges more often than in the past. Prior to the guidelines' implementation, a person believed to have committed three burglaries might be convicted of one, which would yield a criminal history score of one when next he came before the court for sentencing. After the guidelines took effect, however, this same first-time offender might be required to plead guilty to three counts of burglary, which, the next time he came before a court for sentencing, would give him a criminal history score of three. Prosecutors apparently intentionally attempted to undermine the commission's policies in this way, and the commission has, to some extent, changed the criminal history scoring system to offset this prosecutorial tactic.[26]

The survival of sentence negotiations is somewhat more surprising. Although, as noted in Table 2–8, cases disposed by sentence negotiations fell from 34.3 percent in 1978 to 25.7 percent in 1982, the latter figure remains substantial (Dale Parent, the first director of the Minnesota commission, has informed me that these statistics are misleading because 90 percent of the sentence bargains concern sentences *within* the guideline range, conditions of probation, or "bogus" bargains not to seek aggravation of the sentence). The Minnesota Supreme Court has held that a sentence negotiation is not a "substantial and compelling reason" for departing from guidelines. Despite that prohibition, the single most common reason provided by judges for departures from guidelines is "pursuant to plea negotiations." Reconciling this pattern with the supreme court's decision is difficult. In practice, such a case would come before the court only if one of the parties appealed the sentence imposed pursuant to the negotiation, and neither party is likely to do so.

The evidence on plea bargaining under the Washington and Pennsylvania guidelines is much more ambiguous. As noted earlier, the patterns of conviction offenses and sentencing outcomes in

Pennsylvania suggest that plea bargaining has adapted to the guidelines.

In Washington, the initial evaluation report comparing sentencing outcomes for 1982 and the first six months of 1985 suggests that charge bargaining around the guidelines is playing a prominent role. Table 2–9 shows the offense seriousness levels by conviction offenses in Washington State during the two periods. The almost invariant shift downward in the percentages of cases disposed at each of severity levels 7 to 14 supports the inference that many cases that would have been sentenced in 1982 at one level are being sentenced in 1985 at a lower level as a result of charge bargains. The increase in cases at level 6 (the presumptive prison sentence level) may indicate that regardless of charge concessions, prosecutors in some cases insisted on pleas to charges calling for prison sentences. These

Table 2–9
Offense seriousness levels by conviction offenses in Washington

Level	Fiscal Year 1982 (%)	Jan.–June 1985 (%)	Difference (%)
14	0.2	0.1	−0.1
13	0.5	0.3	−0.2
12	0.3	0.2	−0.1
11	0.1	0.2	+0.1
10	0.9	0.4	−0.5
9	5.6	3.6	−2.0
8	1.4	0.6	−0.8
7	3.4	2.0	−1.4
6	4.7	5.7	+1.0
5	0.8	0.7	−0.1
4	10.6	9.7	−0.9
3	8.3	10.1	+1.8
2	34.5	33.3	−1.2
1	28.7	31.1	+2.4
Unranked	0.0	1.9	+1.9
Total	100.0	99.9	

Note: Level 14 is the most serious category (aggravated murder). First-time offenders who commit a level 6 offense and above have a guideline prison term. Figures do not equal 100 percent because of rounding.
Source: Washington Sentencing Commission, *Sentencing Practices under the Sentencing Reform Act*, p. 3.

analyses, however, are no more than inferences and little more can be said until more exhaustive evaluations have been completed.

Trial and Appeal Rates

Opponents of determinate sentencing and sentencing guidelines, especially judicial opponents, have often argued that determinate sentencing reduces the incentives for offenders to plead guilty. As a consequence, it was argued, offenders would insist on jury or bench trials, confident that their sentences would not be increased significantly were they convicted at trial instead of being sentenced after a guilty plea. If that hypothesis were sound, trial rates should increase in the jurisdictions that have sentencing guidelines. In Washington the rates were stable. In 1982, before guidelines, 90.1 percent of cases were disposed of by pleas, 7.8 percent by jury trials, and 2.1 percent by bench trials. During the first six months of 1985, under guidelines, the plea rate declined slightly to 89.2 percent, the jury trial rate remained essentially stable at 7.9 percent, and the bench trial rate increased slightly to 2.7 percent.[27] In Minnesota in 1978, before guidelines, and in 1981 and 1982, under guidelines, the percentages of felony cases disposed of after trials, rather than by guilty pleas, were 5.8 percent, 4.7 percent, and 5.6 percent.[28] In neither Washington nor Minnesota, notwithstanding their narrow sentencing guidelines, does the evidence suggest that large numbers of defendants chose to plead not guilty because of the lessened jeopardy they might feel concerning penalties that would be imposed after a conviction at a trial.

Nor has the recognition of appellate sentence review resulted in flooded appellate dockets. While no data are available from Washington and Pennsylvania, fewer than 1 percent of Minnesota sentences have been appealed. As Kay Knapp's analysis of the case law demonstrates, the Minnesota appellate courts have taken sentence appeals seriously.[29] The appeals courts have decided more than three hundred appeals and in general have upheld the guidelines. They have established standards for departures and for the extent to which sentences can be increased in aggravated cases. Minnesota may become the first American jurisdiction to have a meaningful system of appellate sentence review.

The Future

The sentencing commission model is the most promising of the recent sentencing innovations. Although Connecticut, New York,

Maine, South Carolina, and Pennsylvania provide illustrations of instances in which sentencing commissions did not realize their promise, Washington and Minnesota tell a different story. The Minnesota and Washington stories show that guidelines can accomplish substantial alterations in sentencing practices, that they can obtain support from the officials whose discretions they affect, and that they can reduce sentencing disparities and achieve high levels of compliance with the sentencing standards they set out.

Minnesota has experienced declining levels of compliance with guidelines as time has passed. Sentencing disparities are increasing as are rates of departure from guidelines and the prevalence of plea bargaining manipulations. Nonetheless, the contrast between sentencing before guidelines took effect, and after, remains dramatic. Sentencing is more open and officials are more accountable for their decisions in Minnesota than in most other states and than in Minnesota during earlier periods. Without guidelines, the extensive common law of sentencing in Minnesota would not have evolved, nor would the extensive system of monitoring sentencing decisions.

PART 2

Writing Sentencing Guidelines

Numerical Grids
or Guiding Principles?

Andrew von Hirsch

Sentencing guidelines of the kind described in the last two chapters are numerical. They prescribe definite quanta, or ranges, of sentence as the normally indicated penalties. To most American scholars, this numerical approach has seemed the technique par excellence for structuring a jurisdiction's sentencing policy. Particular guidelines in particular jurisdictions have been criticized, and some observers seem to doubt the value of restricting sentencing discretion at all.[1] But *if* control of discretion is desired, and *if* the politics of the jurisdiction permit the writing of reasonable standards, it is seldom questioned that numerical guidelines are the preferred technique.

Can guidance, however, best be provided through detailed, numerical standards? Judges in the United States had enormous sentencing discretion for years, including vast ranges of permitted punishment; no requirement that they give *reasons* for the sentence; and, usually, no appellate review of the sentences they imposed. From such unregulated sanctioning, is it necessary to go to the opposite extreme of adopting guidelines providing that a convicted armed robber with two prior felony convictions should receive between, say, thirty-eight and forty-four months confinement, except in exceptional circumstances? Are there not stopping points between unfettered discretion and such specific constraints?

Certainly there could be such stopping points, and some European countries are trying them. Perhaps it is worth considering these approaches so that we may better assess the relative merits of numerical and more generalized forms of guidance.

Andrew von Hirsch

The Limitations of Numerical Guidelines

To identify the limitations of numerical sentencing guidelines, it might be helpful to examine some of the shortcomings of Minnesota's standards. The Minnesota Sentencing Guidelines Commission did perform a commission's most important functions: it drew the dispositional line on the grid with reference to an explicit rationale; and it took prison populations systematically into account in fashioning its standards. It is precisely the quality of the Minnesota commission's efforts that makes it worthwhile to see where it ran into difficulty, since that might suggest the limitations even of carefully crafted numerical guidelines.

The Minnesota guidelines have two significant anomalies, detailed later. The first of these concerns the slope of the dispositional line in the right-hand portion of the grid for offenders having lengthy criminal records. On the basis of the commission's "modified" desert rationale, the line should have sloped modestly downward, so that repeat offenders convicted of lesser felonies would not have been imprisoned. The commission, however, decided to be quite severe with multiple recidivists and to prescribe imprisonment for most cells in the grid's right-hand portion. The data available to the commission suggested that there would be few offenders with high criminal history scores and that the impact of imprisoning such offenders would therefore be small. Taking a tough line with these repeat offenders seemed also to increase the political acceptability of the guidelines. The other anomaly concerned the scoring of the prior record. The general rule was that each prior felony conviction counted one point on the prior-record score that constitutes the guideline grid's horizontal axis. Conviction on multiple charges, however, was, under certain circumstances, treated as though each charge was a separate felony, so the offender could, in a single sentencing proceeding, run up a considerable score through accumulation of counts (see chapter 5).

Both these deficiencies have come back to haunt the commission. Prosecutors in Minnesota have been "building up" certain offenders' records by obtaining multiple convictions, thus pushing such cases more quickly toward the right-hand portion of the grid, where imprisonment is prescribed for most cells. As a result an increasing number of persons convicted of routine property crimes are being sent to prison—contrary to the commission's original intent of reserving imprisonment chiefly for the more serious offenses—that is, those against the person (see chapter 8).

These anomalies are remediable. By reducing the steepness of the dispositional line in the right-hand portion of the grid and by changing the method of scoring multiple-count convictions, the commission could reduce the rate of prison commitments for lesser felons. That, however, would require the commission to make substantial changes in the guidelines, which it so far has been reluctant to do.

Numerical guidelines, as we saw in the first chapter, require a commission to undertake *two* difficult tasks. The first is to select and to elaborate a rationale, establishing the system's primary aim to be, say, desert or incapacitation, and then to identify the features of the offense or of the offender that should principally be relied upon, given that rationale. The second is to construct the tariff; that is, to select the penalties normally to be imposed in various types of cases. The danger in this process—one illustrated by Minnesota's just-mentioned difficulties—is that construction of the tariff can, so to speak, overshadow the rationale. Filling in the numbers on the grid takes on a life of its own and produces results inconsistent with the principles of sentencing supposedly chosen. The inconsistency can happen through inadvertence—as probably was true of Minnesota's scoring scheme for previous multiple-count convictions. Or it can happen through efforts to make the grid seem politically more attractive, as was true with the slope of Minnesota's dispositional line in the grid's right-hand portion.

A sentencing commission writing numerical guidelines must produce a table of sentences that will be accepted (or at least not rejected) by the legislature. Commissioners may thus become preoccupied with producing an "acceptable" set of numbers that can survive such scrutiny. Once the numbers have been selected and the guidelines have gone into effect, moreover, there are disincentives to making substantial changes in the absence of pressing practical problems, as amendments risk reopening debate over the guidelines as a whole. It is thus not surprising that the Minnesota commission has changed its grid mainly where changes have been necessary to prevent prison populations from rising above capacity (see chapter 8).

Numbers or Guiding Principles?

Might it not be better to separate the function of selecting a rationale from that of constructing a tariff? Perhaps the commission should concentrate its efforts on its first mission: determining the general direction of sentencing policy. Its standards would comprise a statement of sentencing principles. These principles would specify the primary rationale for sentencing, identify the features of the offender or offense chiefly to be relied upon in deciding sentence, and, perhaps, provide broad policy guidance about when imprisonment is and is not a suitable sanction. The courts would then be called upon to evolve the details of the sentencing tariff.

Let us imagine how a rule-making commission might implement, in narrative form, the "modified desert" rationale purportedly sought to be achieved by Minnesota. Instead of a grid, the standards would be in words. They might begin with a statement of purpose, to the general effect that sentences should be fairly proportionate with the seriousness of offenders' criminal conduct. Then might come an identification of primary factors. This might consist of a statement that the principal determinant of the sentence should be the seriousness of the offender's current crime, and that previous convictions may be considered but must be given less weight than the current conviction.[2] Finally might come general policy directives concerning the use of imprisonment. A system of appellate review of sentences would be instituted, if not in existence already. The appellate court would be directed to decide appeals in accordance with these principles and to develop an informal tariff through the case law to implement these principles further.

This approach might, conceivably, make it easier to avoid the difficulties Minnesota encountered. Because no table of numbers is presented, the politics might be less contentious. It should be easier to gain assent to the general proposition that lesser felons (even with long records) ought ordinarily not to be imprisoned than to defend a grid in which the car thief convicted for the tenth time would escape a prison sentence. Unintended consequences are more easily avoided, also. If prosecutors start obtaining multiple convictions to "build up" offenders' records, these would not automatically turn into high criminal-history ratings. It would be easy enough for the appellate courts to decide according to the underlying principle: to insist that a long record means a record of truly repeated convictions, not merely an artifact of multiple-count counting. Let me, then, examine whether existing or proposed law outside the United States provides any models for developing such guiding principles.

"Principles" Established by Case Law Alone?

American appeals courts have not been notably successful on their own in developing principles for sentencing. In most U.S. jurisdictions, the sentence was not appealable at all. In those few places where the sentence could be appealed, appellate judges were reluctant to do much more than reverse the more manifestly outrageous dispositions.[3]

Some English commentators, most notably David Thomas, have asserted this reluctance to be a peculiar American difficulty, stemming from the lack of a strong tradition of appellate sentence review. Where sentence review has been institutionalized, he argues, the appeals courts themselves can develop guidance for individual sentencing judges. England is succeeding in this effort, he asserts. The Court of Appeal, Criminal Division, has been developing sentencing principles—most recently in the form of "guideline" sentences that specify how particular classes of defendants should be punished.[4]

The English sentence-review mechanism has specific procedural weaknesses that have been noted by several observers.[5] My objections are more fundamental, however. An appellate court, acting without external policy guidance, might begin to develop some kind of tariff—imprisonment ordinarily prescribed for this kind of case, probation for that kind. What it is unlikely to be able to produce, however, is a *principled* resolution of sentencing issues: a tariff undergirded by a systematic and thought-through rationale.

Let me give an example. Martin Wasik has collected and examined all English appellate cases concerning perjury. The cases, considered together, furnish a kind of rule: perjurers almost invariably are to be imprisoned. What remains opaque, however, is the rationale. The Court of Appeal's stated rationale is deterrence,[6] but this brings a number of questions immediately to mind. Do we know enough about deterrent effects to say that routine imposition of imprisonment will deter perjury better than a more selective imprisonment policy would? Even a cursory examination of today's deterrence research suggests how limited our ability is to gauge the magnitude of deterrent effects, but the court seemed unaware of such limitations of knowledge.[7] Perjury, moreover, is not the only crime we might wish to deter. Do we not also want to stop burglary and car theft and insurance fraud? Should those crimes also have their penalties decided on the basis of deterrence, and should they also routinely be punishable by imprisonment? Without serious inquiry into such issues, merely seizing upon deterrence (or, for that matter, dangerousness or treatment) tells us very little indeed.

My thoughts about perjury extend more broadly to the present English scheme. The Court of Appeal, according to Thomas, has evolved an informal scale of penalties for various crimes, based on deterrence and allied notions, and then permits deviations from this "tariff" on rehabilitative and predictive grounds.[8] Conceivably, the English cases do reveal this pattern. The pattern does not seem, however, to be the result of sustained critical analysis of what the direction of sentencing policy ought to be.

Could another jurisdiction do better with the English technique? That is, could an appellate court succeed in developing a tariff based on a carefully developed rationale? Conceivably, but there are impediments. The court is not likely to possess the requisite information. Sentencing is a somewhat arcane subject. Commonsense beliefs about deterrence or treatment or dangerousness are not necessarily correct; questions about fair distribution of penalties do not necessarily resolve themselves easily. This makes it essential for the policy maker to be familiar both with the sentencing literature and with sentencing regulation in other jurisdictions. A sentencing commission is in a position to obtain this information: even if the members initially are not expert, they can obtain the assistance of a specialized staff and consultants. Appellate court judges, given the press of other court business, are not likely to be or become particularly knowledgeable about the intricacies of sentencing theory and policy. The litigants—absorbed as they are in their particular case rather than in wider policy ramifications—are not likely to provide judges with much assistance.

More troublesome still is the question of perspective. Setting sentencing policy requires the taking of a comprehensive view: deciding what rationale should predominate and comparing different types of crimes and of sanctions. A sentencing commission can take such a view because of the systematic nature of its task. An appellate court, however, deals serially with particular cases, arising in no predictable order. The incentive is to decide the particular case or type of case, rather than to examine the wider reasons underlying a comprehensive sentencing policy.

Where does that leave the appellate courts? On a sentencing-principles approach, they would have a crucial role in developing the tariff. But they should do so pursuant to explicit general policy directives established by law. Such an approach is being developed in two Scandinavian countries, Finland and Sweden. Let me examine those countries' efforts.

Statutory Statements of Purpose: The Finnish Model

Statutory statements of purpose have had a deservedly bad reputation. Customarily they list several potentially conflicting aims, thereby providing the appellate courts with little guidance. An example is section 46 of the German Penal Code. It is the product of two competing drafts, one of which emphasized proportionality and desert, and the other, special prevention. The two conflicting versions were combined to yield the following language:

> The guilt of the offender shall be the basis of the measurement of sentence. However, the expected effect of the sentence on the future life and conduct of the actor is to be taken into account.[9]

The problem should be apparent. The first sentence is consistent with a desert philosophy and focuses on the seriousness of the offender's criminal acts. The second is predictive and rehabilitative in emphasis. There is, notoriously, a tension between these concepts: the sentence that would be fairly commensurate with the gravity of the offender's criminal conduct is not necessarily the same as the sentence that optimally would forestall future offending on his part. The paragraph does not clearly indicate the relative priority that should be given these conflicting ideas. The German doctrine on sentencing has suffered from these ambiguities.[10]

Statements of purpose are potentially useful only if the stated principles are coherent and are not in potential conflict with one another. One aim must be chosen as primary. The utility of such statements is that they can help appellate courts choose which of the conflicting aims—desert, deterrence, incapacitation, or treatment—should be given emphasis. That can be accomplished only if the drafters of the statement are willing to make the choice.

One European country—Finland—has, however, adopted a reasonably coherent statement of sentencing purpose. In 1976, the Finnish penal code was amended to add a new chapter dealing with the choice of sentence. The most important provision reads:

> The punishment shall be measured so that it is in just proportion to the damage and danger caused by the offense and to the guilt of the offender manifested in the offense.[11]

This provision states a single guiding principle for choice of sentence: that which is termed the principle of "proportionality" in Scandinavia and the principle of "commensurate-deserts" in the United States. The sentence is to be proportionate to the gravity of the offense for which the offender stands convicted. The section also specifies the main factors that should be relied upon in gauging the offense's gravity, namely: the harmfulness of the conduct and the culpability of the actor. Risk should be considered only insofar as it relates to the potential injuriousness of the conduct. Risk of *future* misconduct by the defendant (the positivist's preferred criterion) is, quite intentionally, omitted. If I am convicted of driving dangerously, the risk of injury I create through my act of bad driving is part of the harmfulness of the conduct that may properly be taken into account. Not included, however, would be the risk of recidivism: the danger that I might after conviction *again* decide to climb into my car and drive badly.[12]

Other provisions of Finland's sentencing statute deal with aggravating and mitigating circumstances. Several of the listed factors concern special circumstances relating to harm or culpability and thus square with a desert-oriented rationale.[13] Somewhat puzzling, however, is the provision relating to prior criminal record. It makes previous convictions an aggravating factor if they suggest that "the offender is apparently heedless of the prohibitions of law."[14] While a desert rationale would permit limited weight to be given to the offender's record,[15] it is not clear how much importance this provision permits the prior record to be assigned, or how the elusive quality of "heedlessness" should be judged. The Finnish penologists with whom I have spoken regard this to be the weakest point in the law.

How helpful is this Finnish statute? Studies of its impact on sentencing practice are not yet available.[16] On its face, however, it is clearer than the German law. Courts, it suggests, should be making their sentencing judgments primarily in terms of the gravity of the criminal conduct rather than on the basis of an indeterminate combination of desert and treatability or dangerousness.

Nevertheless, the statute leaves much, perhaps too much, unspecified. The role of the prior criminal record is uncertain, as just mentioned. Little also is said on the crucial issue of the use of imprisonment. Should a large variety of crimes be punished by imprisonment, albeit with appropriately graded durations? Or should imprisonment be a sanction of last resort, reserved only for serious felonies? Perhaps sentencing principles can give the courts guidance on such important matters while still remaining principles rather than a table of numbers. To see how that might be done, it is worth examining legislation that is being proposed in Sweden.

A Fuller Statement of Principles: The Proposed Swedish Law

The Swedish provisions, yet to be enacted, were proposed early in 1986 by the Committee on Prison Sanctions (*Fängelsestraffkom-*

mittèn), a government-appointed study commission.[17] The committee's main proposals are embodied in two draft chapters of the penal code, dealing with choice of sentence.[18] Those chapters were largely written for the Committee by a consultative working group, which included several of the country's leading authorities on sentencing.[19]

The basic idea is similar to the Finnish, emphasizing punishments proportionate to the gravity of the criminal conduct. The provisions, however, are more sophisticated. The measurement of the punishment is to depend ordinarily on the "penal value" of the actor's offense. Penal value—what Americans would term the "seriousness" of an offense—is determined by the harmfulness of the conduct and the "guilt" (culpability) of the actor manifested in the offense. This general principle is followed by more specific criteria—including those on use of imprisonment.

The proposed Swedish provisions give the courts more guidance than the Finnish law does, because the steps for determining the sentence are more clearly spelled out. First, the penal value of the crime category is to be determined, reflecting the harmfulness and culpability that is typical for such conduct. Next, the penal value of the offender's particular criminal act is ascertained, by considering the presence and extent of any aggravating and mitigating factors— and these are defined in the statute in some detail.[20] Next comes the choice of type of sanction, which depends on whether the penal value thus ascertained is high, or low. Crimes of high penal value would generally result in imprisonment; those of low penal value would draw fines. For offenses in the middle range of gravity, the disposition would depend on the criminal record: imprisonment would be invoked if the offender's record was substantial; otherwise, probation or conditional release (possibly coupled with fines) would be used.[21] The prior record is not, however, supposed to have much impact on duration of imprisonment. Likelihood of future offending may be considered in the choice of sanction only in limited circumstances, which the statute spells out.[22]

Swedish law provides already for appellate review of sentences.[23] The proposed statute is designed to provide the appeals courts with guidance in their sentence-review decisions. The law would spell out the penal aims to be achieved and would offer a broad framework for deciding which type of sanction would be appropriate. The tariff would then be evolved by the courts over time. The courts would not, however, be working in a vacuum. They would receive guidance as to aims, the general shape of the sentencing structure, and the steps to be considered when a sentence is imposed. That would put them in a better position than the English courts to decide how much punishment various kinds of crimes should normally receive.

Suppose, for example, that the issue were the one I touched upon already, the appropriate punishment for perjury. The Swedish courts would not need to select, as the English appellate court had to, the purpose to be achieved: it would not be necessary to decide (on scant penological knowledge) whether the goal was to deter perjurers or treat them or whatever. The statute would already have established the aim: the imposition of punishment, proportionate to the reprehensibleness of the criminal conduct. It would also supply the principal criterion for deciding the quantum of the penalty—namely, the penal value (i.e., seriousness) of the offense. The court's job, therefore, would be to assess perjury's penal value. How much harm does perjury do or threaten to do? How culpable is the conduct? What grounds for extenuation might various kinds of perjurers have? Deciding this is concededly no easy task, but the court and the litigants would at least have the issues framed for them. There would be an incentive to begin to break down perjury into different types and to distinguish among their respective penal values. Since not all types of perjury would be likely to be rated high in penal value, not all would routinely receive sentences of imprisonment. The courts would retain their primary responsibility for deciding sentence severity but now would have assistance in reasoning through such decisions. The drafters of the statute would be doing what rule makers are well positioned to do: establishing aims and general policy directions for the system as a whole, which the courts would then implement in greater specificity.

The Prerequisites for Sentencing Principles

The Swedish legislation is still only a proposal—although its chances of enactment have recently improved, because the Ministry of Justice has tentatively decided to give it support. Whether or not it becomes law in Sweden, it represents an alternative to numerical guidelines for policy makers to consider. The approach, however, is likely to work only where the following prerequisites are satisfied.

A Competent, Specialized Rule Maker   There needs to be a sufficiently skilled body to draft the standards. Drafting sentencing principles is as exacting work as devising numerical guidelines. True, one need not undertake the time-consuming task of filling in the numbers in a grid. But that makes it necessary, all the more, to state the intended policies with care. If desert, for example, is selected as the primary rationale, it cannot be expressed merely by drawing a flat or flattish dispositional line on a grid (see chapter 5); one needs to state the principle of proportionate sanctions, and its criteria for application, with reasonable precision.[24]

The drafting body thus needs to have the time and the expertise comparable to those possessed by a sentencing commission. The proposed Swedish standards are in statutory form and call for eventual parliamentary enactment. The process of drafting the standards, however, was not unlike a sentencing commission's process. The work was done over a considerable period of time by a study commission specially organized for the purpose and aided by a working group of penologists who were familiar with the sentencing literature and with sentencing reform in other jurisdictions. The more routine methods of drafting legislation—for example, a bill written in a ministry—would have yielded less satisfactory results.

Active Involvement of Appellate Courts A sentencing-principles approach demands more from the appellate courts. With numerical guidelines, the articulation of policy and construction of the tariff is done by the sentencing commission. The appellate courts' primary role is that of making sure that trial courts ordinarily impose the penalties prescribed in the grid. Adoption of sentencing principles, instead of numerical guidelines, increases the responsibility of appellate judges, since the standards merely point the direction of sentencing policy. The work of constructing the tariff, of determining the punishments for various crimes, needs to be spelled out through case law. The courts need the competence and the willingness to undertake this work. The proposed Swedish statement of principles will, it is true, provide assistance; it indicates not only the rationale but the faint outlines of the tariff (through the recommendations concerning types of dispositions for crimes with high, medium, and low penal value). This, however, still leaves judges who develop the case law with much of the labor; and means the opportunity for failure—for ignoring the stated rationale or for simply not developing any real tariff at all—is considerable.

An episode from Minnesota illustrates the results. That state's supreme court has had a degree of success in enforcing the commission's numerical guidelines, and has shown no hesitation in reversing noncomplying lower-court decisions. In one area, however—that of aggravation and mitigation—the court's function is closer to that of implementing sentencing principles. The guidelines provide a nonexclusive list of aggravating and mitigating circumstances thus leaving it to the court to decide what other circumstances of extenuation or exacerbation might be grounds for departing from the grid ranges. The circumstances listed in the guidelines chiefly are desert-related and concern special situations of increased or reduced harmfulness or culpability.[25] Given the character of the listed circumstances and the stated overall purpose of the guidelines, it would be reasonable to expect any unlisted factors to relate also to the offender's blameworthiness in a broad sense (see chapter 5). Nevertheless, the state supreme court decided that "amenability" or "unamenability" to probation qualifies as grounds for departure from the grid's prescriptions on whether or not to imprison.[26] Whatever "amenability to probation" may mean (and I do not understand its precise meaning), it is plainly rehabilitative or predictive in character and has no visible bearing on the offender's degree of blameworthiness. This factor has since been used by lower courts to reduce sentences for persons convicted of crimes against the person. Its use has been making it harder to achieve the guidelines' original intent of shifting the use of imprisonment to those convicted for serious crimes (see chapter 8). To remedy the problem, the sentencing commission would probably need to intervene to amend its definition of aggravation and mitigation. What this suggests, however, is how much more difficult it may be for courts to interpret and extend a stated rationale than to enforce a table of sanctions.

Technical Assistance to the Courts   A drawback of the proposed Swedish law is that the appellate courts are not provided with a source of assistance in applying the principles and developing the tariff. Even with the statutory principles and their legislative history[27] as a guide, the courts may thus have some difficulty determining the penal value of various classes of crimes.

The courts could be provided with a source of specialized technical assistance, in the form of an advisory body that would assist in classifying the penal value of different crime categories. This laborious task of comparison and assessment of the harm and culpability of various criminal acts is one the courts may have little time and inclination to undertake themselves. This body's guidelines could be advisory only, and the courts would have final responsibility for deciding the sentence that crimes of a given penal value ordinarily should receive. But the penal-value recommendations would constitute an important start toward development of a sentencing tariff. The body might also provide advisory guidelines on the assessment of aggravating and mitigating factors, or on the assessment of the prior criminal record. Depending on the jurisdiction, that body could, in addition, be empowered to issue nonbinding advisory opinions on selected hypothetical cases.

While such an advisory body might resemble a sentencing commission in its composition and organization, there would be an important difference in its functions: it would be grading crimes (and possibly criminal records), not establishing the resulting punishments. Because it is not confronted with having to develop an "acceptable" tariff of penalties, this body could pay more heed to developing crime-seriousness rankings that comport with the stated statutory rationale.

The utility of such an advisory body depends, crucially, on its personnel. Its members and staff must be knowledgeable, sympathetic to the task of structuring sentencing discretion, and supportive of the rationale embodied in the statutory sentencing principles. If the advisory body consists of persons without the requisite sympathy and understanding for the task, it will be useless or worse.

Cooperative Lower Courts   A sentencing-principles approach also requires responsive lower courts. The tariff developed through case law by the appellate courts, if it is to have any value, should specify whether imprisonment is or is not recommended for given types of cases and, if it is, suggest durations of confinement. But the tariff cannot be as specific as numerical guidelines; it will not have the sharp-edged ranges that are found in a grid. While this provides advantages of flexibility, it requires cooperative sentencing judges, ones who are willing to be guided by a light rein. In some jurisdictions, certainly many in the United States, such a tradition of judicial "legalism" is weak or nonexistent. Trial judges are inclined to follow their own practice, and appellate courts are reluctant to reverse save for "clear" error. Here, numerical guidelines can provide more authoritative guidance. The normal range for a given grid cell is clearly specified as X to Y months; and grounds for permitted deviation can be stated with considerable specificity. The trial judge is given to understand that he or she *must* sentence within the applicable grid range or else come forward with permissible reasons for departure, or face reversal.

Sentencing principles, therefore, are not simply a middle way—a compromise between breadth of unregulated discretion and the specificity of numerical sentencing guidelines. It is a mistake to suppose that—if there is too much resistance to numerical guidelines to permit their enactment—statutory principles will necessarily be a workable alternative. Sentencing principles are potentially useful only in a certain kind of environment: one in which there is considerable judicial support for regulating and guiding sentencing discretion but where a flexible instrument for guidance is being sought. In less propitious environments, the choice may be the starker one between poorly regulated sentencing discretion and the more forceful modes of intervention that numerical guidelines represent.

The Prison Overcrowding   Narrative standards are not as suited as numerical guidelines to addressing the problem of prison overcrowding. The reason should be evident: their greater open-endedness. The impact on use and duration of confinement will become apparent only over time, as the courts use the statutory principles to develop the tariff. Numerical guidelines, with fairly narrow cell ranges, allow impact on populations to be projected and are more amenable to being drafted with population targets in mind.

Many jurisdictions face crowding problems, either now or in the foreseeable future, but the extent of the problem varies. In some places, population pressures are modest or can be alleviated by identifiable policy changes. In Sweden, for example, some penologists are beginning to advocate changing the practice of routinely imprisoning drivers who drink, in part because these cases now occupy so large a proportion of prison facilities.[27] There, sentencing principles might prove quite helpful by providing guidance about when drinking-and-driving cases should receive a sentence of confinement and when not.

In other jurisdictions, however, crowding is persistent and virulent. Here, standards with definite population targets may become a necessity. Concerns about prison costs, moreover, may be the one available political antidote to the lock-them-up sentiment that motivates high commitment rates (see chapter 4). As crowding thus comes to occupy the more central role in sentencing policy, numerical guidelines may be the necessary response.

Emergence of a Tariff:
The Test of Success

If sentencing principles are enacted, how does one tell whether they are working? The most important test, perhaps, is whether a case-law tariff is beginning to emerge. What sentencing judges require, in their everyday cases, is a yardstick. They need definite, consistent norms for what the various crimes they frequently confront are worth. Numerical guidelines provide such norms in the grid itself. With sentencing principles, those norms may or may not begin to become apparent in the case law. If they do emerge, progress is being made. How well the emerging tariff sentences comport with the stated principles and their rationale will still need to be considered, as will the questions of whether and to what extent trial court judges pay heed to the tariff in their everyday sentencing decisions. If, however, the case law does not begin to suggest definite yardsticks, the experiment is failing. No tariff is emerging, and the statutory principles are not being systematically implemented.

A final note: I am not optimistic that the narrative-principle approach would succeed in most U.S. jurisdictions. It requires, as I have indicated, strong appellate review of sentence, a willingness of the appellate courts to involve themselves actively, cooperative lower courts, and no major prison overcrowding crisis. The American distrust of theory—and the weak or nonexistent tradition of appellate sentence review—will make it difficult for appellate courts to take the statutory principles seriously and use them to develop definite yardsticks in the case law. Trial courts are apt to be reluctant to relinquish their broad sentencing discretion unless compelled to do so. Prison overcrowding is likely to be a pressing problem, and sentencing policy is likely to be considerably politicized. If sentencing discretion can be regulated at all in such a difficult environment, numerical guidelines will probably be more effective. They, at least, set forth a tariff clearly, require the appellate courts to scrutinize noncomplying sentences, and can be designed to take prison-capacity constraints into account. Under the best of circumstances, I would prefer the flexibility of the narrative-principles approach. But circumstances are much less than optimal for American sentencing policy and may require guidelines that have more teeth.

CHAPTER 4

The Enabling Legislation

Andrew von Hirsch

A sentencing commission is created by statute and derives its powers from the enabling legislation. This makes the legislation important. Whether the commission has a policy-making mission, whether its guidelines are binding or merely advisory, how specific the guidelines should be, and how the guidelines are to be enforced through judicial review all depend on the law creating the commission. How, then, should such legislation be written? What political impediments may there be?

Drafting the Enabling Statute

Deciding on the contents of the enabling legislation is a matter of judgment: one must reflect on the functions of a sentencing commission and then choose the legislative mandate that would promote those functions. I shall therefore be unabashedly judgmental. My method will be to examine how existing enabling statutes[1] handle a series of issues; to suggest reasons why I think those solutions are or are not useful; and, at various points, to propose alternatives myself. Some readers, inevitably, will not agree with my judgments. For them, my only defense is that this chapter may help them identify the issues that need to be addressed.

One important issue which I will pass by is the composition of the commission. The legislation needs to specify the size of the sentencing commission and the manner of its members' appointment. Kay Knapp will address this question in chapter 7. Let me, then, proceed to the other major elements of the legislation.

The Policy-making Role of the Commission
The enabling statute should make clear that the commission's role is a *policy-making* one. The commission should not be called upon

to reflect existing sentencing practice in its guidelines but be authorized to develop its own policy for sentencing—one that may entail changes in existing practice. The reason this is important has already been explained in chapter 1. What chiefly is missing in a discretionary sentencing system is, precisely, systematic, reflected-upon policy choices. Making those choices explicitly is a commission's chief utility.

In Minnesota the enabling law left the question of the commission's role open. The statute called upon the commission to take historical sentencing and paroling practice "into substantial consideration," but it did not specify how much weight that practice should be given. Considerable debate developed within the commission over whether it should write guidelines that reflected past sentencing practice or develop its own policy. The latter view prevailed, happily.[2] But the matter might have been settled more easily had the statute expressly granted the commission a policy-making mission. This could have been accomplished by inserting language in the statute calling upon the commission "to develop and reflect in its guidelines a systematic policy for criminal sentencing in the state."

The Reach of the Guidelines

Sentencing guidelines should, at a minimum, address judges' decisions on whether to imprison and on the duration of prison terms. The question is, What other sentencing choices should the guidelines regulate?

The Minnesota enabling statute requires the guidelines to deal with the use and duration of imprisonment. However, it merely authorizes, and does not require, that the guidelines regulate the choice among nonprison sanctions, where prison is not prescribed.[3] The commission has never used the latter authority. Imprisonment, in Minnesota as in most of the states, is confinement in a *state* facility for more than a year. Thus the use of jail (that is, confinement in a county or regional facility for a year or less) has remained unregulated. Here, Minnesota has no consistent policy, and disparity in the use of jail apparently remains considerable.[4]

Washington has been more ambitious. The commission was required from the outset to address not only the use of imprisonment but of jail sentences as well.[5]

Which approach is preferable? Because jail guidelines involve the use of locally funded facilities of varying capacity, such guidelines can be somewhat more difficult to write. In Pennsylvania the commission's effort to deal with jail use in its initial guidelines drew opposition from rural judges and prosecutors jealous of their local powers.[6] It might thus be practical (in some states, at least) to write guidelines on use of state imprisonment first and develop the guidelines on jail use later, after judges have had a chance to become familiar with the imprisonment guidelines.

There is no reason, however, why a commission should be permitted to postpone guidelines on jail use indefinitely. A substantial portion (in some places, the bulk) of incarcerated offenders are jailed, not imprisoned. Confinement in a county facility is too onerous a sanction to remain permanently unregulated. If the statute does not require the guidelines to address the choice between jail and lesser sanctions at the outset, it should provide a later deadline—perhaps five years later—for promulgating guidelines on jail sentences. This deadline would give the commission extra time for developing the jail guidelines but would not allow the matter to be deferred indefinitely.

The Binding Effect of Guidelines

Sentencing guidelines, even if in numerical form, are not meant to be applied mechanically; judges should deviate from the prescribed ranges in exceptional aggravating and mitigating circumstances. Nevertheless the guidelines should be legally binding standards: only for certain *appropriate* reasons should departures be permissible—and what those reasons are should depend on the structure and rationale of the guidelines themselves. The enabling statute, therefore, should make the binding character of the guidelines clear. If the guidelines are described merely as norms that judges should "consider" in their decisions—as in Pennsylvania's enabling statute—such language could invite their being disregarded.[7]

A number of alternative formulations are possible to establish the guidelines' binding character. The most straightforward, in my judgment, would be to declare that the applicable standard ranges have "presumptive applicability."[8] The commission then could, in its guidelines, define the nature of this presumption more precisely— for example, by declaring (as the Minnesota commission did) that departures may be invoked only in "substantial and compelling" circumstances; or by devising some appropriate alternative formula.[9]

The Structure and Definiteness of Guidelines

Should the guidelines be numerical and definite, or be narrative and couched as broader principles? I addressed the question in the preceding chapter, and concluded that for most American jurisdictions, only numerical standards are likely to have much impact. If numerical standards are desired, the enabling legislation should make it clear—otherwise, much of the commission's time may be absorbed in discussion of how much guidance to provide.

To make the guidelines take numerical form, the legislation can call upon the commission to develop definite sentences or ranges of sentence as its presumptive dispositions. Those dispositions thus could, as the commission chose, either take the form of a particular amount, such as X years, or else a range, such as X to Y years.[10] This statutory provision would also permit the commission, if it wished, to utilize a format for the guidelines other than a grid— say, a multistep formula (see chapter 1)—so long as the eventual recommended sentences or ranges were numerical.

Another issue is the breadth of the ranges (in the event that the commission chooses to use ranges instead of definite terms). The Minnesota law provides, with respect to prison sentences, a maximum range width of 15 percent above or below the range midpoint, and the federal statute has a comparable provision. The precise formula is a matter for judgment, but it may well be desirable to impose a limit on range breadth. Such a limit would bar the very broad ranges that have appeared in some guidelines: Pennsylvania has some ranges as wide as 48–120 months, and New York's proposed standards provide a range of three to nearly seven years for a first armed robbery offense. Ranges of such width would leave discretion in large part unregulated.[11]

The Selection of the Rationale

The selection of a coherent rationale for the guidelines is, for reasons explained in chapter 1, an essential task. How, and to what extent, should the enabling legislation assist in this choice?

Some enabling statutes attempt to supply a guiding rationale. The Washington law, for example, has a statement of purpose which emphasizes desert.[12] Other statutes do not. The Minnesota law suggests no particular rationale; the standard ranges are to be based on "appropriate" offender and offense characteristics, and it is left to the commission to determine which characteristics are appropriate and on what rationale.[13]

As an advocate of a desert rationale,[14] I initially preferred Washington's approach. Ultimately, the Washington commission's guidelines did give primacy to desert, and the statutory statement of purpose may, perhaps, have facilitated that choice (see chapter 2).

Now, however, I have come to doubt the wisdom of the legislature's selecting a particular rationale in the enabling legislation. Choosing a rationale requires some understanding of the extent and limitations of existing knowledge of deterrent, incapacitative and rehabilitative effects, and a grasp of desert principles and their implications for sentencing. The rationale needs to be chosen with care, as that choice substantially affects the guidelines' structure. A sentencing commission is designed precisely to examine such matters. A legislature—confronted with the press of other business—is not likely to have the time or the requisite specialized knowledge.

When creating rule-making commissions, legislatures often set forth certain policy objectives in the enabling law. These objectives are supposed to supply overall guidance while leaving the details to commissioners' expertise. The practice assumes that the definition of the objectives does not itself call for specialized knowledge and can be accomplished using sound judgment and generally available information. That assumption does not hold true, however, for selection of a sentencing rationale. To illustrate, let us consider New York's enabling statute, which includes a statement of "principles of sentencing" which the commission should follow. The first part of that statement seems to emphasize desert: penalties should be "directly related" to the seriousness of the criminal conduct, and similar crimes committed under similar circumstances should receive similar sanctions. A later part, however, seems to emphasize prediction and deterrence: incarceration is declared appropriate "to protect society by restraining a defendant who has a history of conviction for serious criminal conduct" or "to provide an effective deterrent to others likely to commit similar offenses."[15] The relation between these apparently divergent rationales is not made clear—and having such a mandate did not make the commission's search for a coherent rationale any easier.

Conceivably, a commission might resolve the ambiguity in such a statutory directive through arguments of statutory interpretation. It might, for example, treat the mandate as calling for a hybrid rationale, in which desert sets the outer limits of the sentence, within which deterrent and incapacitative considerations would apply. Some penologists have been urging such a mixed rationale.[16] Others (including myself), however, have challenged such a hybrid rationale's coherence and fairness—charging that it leaves the desert limits vague and unspecified and that it results in the unequal condemnation of equally reprehensible conduct.[17] Who is right? That can best be decided by a body that has the leisure and the understanding to weigh such issues—that is, by the commission itself. If the commission opts for a mixed rationale, it should be because it has become convinced it is right—not because it feels it has been given no choice.

If the choice or rationale is best left to the commission, it should be required to develop a rationale and state it explicitly. Otherwise, the commission might fail to develop any coherent and explicit conception of its aims. (That occurred, in fact, in Pennsylvania. The guidelines do not purport to be based on any particular rationale; they seem neither plainly desert-based nor plainly incapacitative in character, and they have been characterized by the commission's chairman and staff director as having no single consistent aim.[18]) The enabling legislation thus should call upon the commission to develop an explicit, internally consistent rationale. The language might read something as follows:

> The commission shall develop a rationale for its guidelines and
> state that rationale explicitly in the guidelines or in its initial
> report to the legislature. Where that rationale involves more than
> a single purpose of punishment, the relations and priorities among
> the various purposes shall be explained.

Such a provision is no guarantee of a well-thought-out rationale, but it might help discourage purely ad hoc decision making by the commission.

Mandated Dispositions

Some enabling statutes contain mandates to the commission that particular types of cases should receive, or normally receive, particular types of dispositions. The federal law creating the U.S. Sentencing Commission, for example, directs that the commission prescribe a "substantial" term of imprisonment for offenders with two prior felony convictions and, generally, prescribe nonprison sentences for first offenders whose crime is not violent.[19] The Minnesota enabling law has no such provisions, although the few previously enacted mandatory minimums were permitted to stand (see chapter 5).

Such directives may be of two kinds. Some may be fairly specific, calling for a particular type of disposition for a particular type of case. The federal provision on two prior felonies is an example. The objection to such provisions is that they defeat the whole point of a sentencing commission, which is to have *that* body write the tariff, not the legislature itself. Until the structure and aims of the guidelines are decided upon, one cannot intelligibly decide particular dispositions. By making such specific mandates, the legislature may force anomalous results. The federal rule for two prior felonies, for example, could mean prison terms of many months for offenders convicted of repetitive lesser offenses. On a desert rationale, such terms are patently inappropriate—for reasons to be elaborated in chapter 5.[20] Even on an incapacitative rationale, such sanctions may be a mistake: repeat property offenders may have high probabilities of recidivism, but the degree of harmfulness of their predicted conduct does not seem sufficient to make it worthwhile invoking the drastic and costly measure of imprisonment.[21]

There also are political hazards. An important raison d'etre of a commission is to permit decisions about the tariff to be made by a body that is more insulated from law-and-order pressures than the legislature. Once the legislature begins mandating particular dispositions, it involves itself in debates over the guidelines' detailed contents. Such prescriptions can easily multiply, and become progressively severer, as legislators compete to show their "toughness" on crime. Even without specific mandates, the commission should be aware enough of legislative concerns—in view of the legislature's power to disapprove guidelines it deems politically unacceptable.

The other kind of legislative directives may be broader—that is, be statements of policy preference. An example is the federal provision stating a preference for not imprisoning nonviolent first offenders. Such general statements are less likely to produce anomalous specific results; the federal provision presumably still would allow the commission to prescribe imprisonment for first offenders convicted of nonviolent but nevertheless serious offenses, such as major white-collar crimes. Such provisions trouble me, nevertheless, for much the same reason that legislative prescriptions concerning the guidelines' rationale would. To create a policy on first offenders presupposes that the person's criminal record or lack of it should play a central role in determining punishments. What the criminal record's appropriate role should be, however, depends on the rationale chosen. Incapacitative, deterrent, and desert rationales each place quite different degrees of emphasis on the offender's prior record.[22] It seems better to let the commission decide the rationale first, before deciding how much importance to assign to the fact that the defendant is a first offender.

Consideration of Prison Capacity

A sentencing commission should (for reasons described already in chapter 1) take prison capacity into account in writing its guidelines. Prison overcrowding can be alleviated by regulating prison commitments and durations with capacity constraints in mind. And such constraints are the best way of prompting realism in debates over how severely to punish—to compel recognition that if one wishes to confine one group of offenders one may need to refrain from confining another group.

The legislation should provide the commission with authority to take prison capacities into account in writing its guidelines. Some enabling statutes—notably, Pennsylvania's—failed to do this. Because the law was silent on the capacity question, some members of Pennsylvania's sentencing commission questioned that body's power to consider space availability—and the commission chose to skirt the prison-population issue in writing its guidelines. The absence of firm projections of prison populations made it difficult for the commission to defend its initial guidelines against charges of leniency when they were made public.[23]

How should that authority be drafted? The Minnesota, New York, and federal enabling statutes direct the commission to take prison capacities into "consideration" or "substantial consideration."[24] Such a broad directive authorizes the commission to give attention to capacity but does not state how much weight that factor should be given. The commission could interpret such a provision either as calling for a firm capacity constraint in deciding the aggregate amount of imprisonment the guidelines prescribe or as requiring that prison populations be merely one of several factors used in deciding the guidelines' overall severity levels.

The Minnesota commission interpreted the statutory directive to call for a firm capacity constraint (see chapter 5). This interpretation had much influence on the commission's ultimate decisions. For each alternative guideline model the commission considered, its staff had developed population projections. The guidelines it eventually approved were designed to leave prison populations a small margin below capacity.[25]

New York, however, interpreted its comparable statutory language as making prison capacity only *one* factor the commission might bear in mind. The commission did not direct its staff to begin making estimates of population impact until a late stage in its proceedings, and those estimates were not completed when the proposed guidelines were published. While those guidelines probably would have increased populations substantially over existing levels, the commission could not demonstrate that fact in response to criticisms of the guidelines' supposed mildness.[26]

These experiences suggest that a directive to "consider" (or even "substantially" consider) prison populations does not suffice. The statute should explicitly require population estimates to be an integral part of constructing the guidelines. A useful place to begin, perhaps, is with Washington's law. It provides that the commission shall project whether its proposed guidelines exceed available prison capacity. If they do exceed capacity, then the commission must submit, along with its proposed guidelines, a schedule of proposed sentences that are consistent with estimated available capacity.[27]

Washington's provision is designed for a system where the commission proposes the guidelines to the legislature, which then must give its approval before they take effect. This means that, if the proposed guidelines exceed capacity, the legislature can choose: it can approve the guidelines and finance additional space; or it can reject the guidelines and approve the commission's alternative sentence schedule that comports with existing prison space. Such a provision is not suited, however, for a jurisdiction in which the guidelines automatically take effect in the absence of contrary action by the legislature.

A variant of the Washington provision could be used in such a jurisdiction, however. The commission should, as in Washington, be required to project whether its guidelines are within or exceed available capacity. There should be a further requirement that the guidelines *not* exceed available capacity unless the commission (1) finds "compelling" reasons to do so and explains those reasons, and (2) informs the legislature how much additional prison space would be required for implementing its guidelines. The aim of such a provision would be to ensure that population impact estimates are made and to create an incentive for adopting a Minnesota-style constraint of not exceeding current capacity. The provision gives the commission an escape clause, however, should it find existing capacities manifestly insufficient.

Deviating Sentences

A sentencing guideline system contemplates departures from the presumptive terms or ranges in special circumstances of aggravation and mitigation. Should the legislation require the commission to furnish a list of aggravating or mitigating factors? The Minnesota, Washington, and Pennsylvania statutes have no such requirement. Pennsylvania's guidelines do not list the factors at all—the individual judge is free to decide what grounds qualify as aggravating or mitigating. The Minnesota commission initially considered having no list, but then changed its mind: the guidelines contain a nonexclusive list of aggravators and mitigators. The Washington guidelines likewise provide such a list.[28]

Adequate guidelines should address the grounds for departures. If they do not, judges can choose grounds wholly at variance with the underlying rationale of the guidelines. The statute thus should require the commission to address this area. On the other hand, it does not seem desirable for the enabling statute to specify aggravating and mitigating factors itself. What should qualify as grounds of departure cannot be determined until the rationale, and the factors used in determining the standard ranges, have been chosen.

The preferable solution, therefore, would be a legislative directive that the commission address the grounds for departure in its guidelines. Such a directive could be a simple statement in the enabling statute that "the commission shall address the grounds of aggravation and mitigation warranting departures from the standard sentence ranges."

Under Minnesota's guidelines, a deviating sentence could fall anywhere short of the applicable statutory maximum. This wide leeway proved a source of contention, and some judges, in cases of aggravation, imposed sentences that were several times the applicable guideline range. The state supreme court responded to this practice by ruling that aggravated terms may, in general, not exceed twice the presumptive term,[29] but that ruling initially was met with considerable criticism.

This problem might have been alleviated had the commission addressed the issue at the outset in its guidelines. It could have done so in a variety of ways. One way would have been to impose numerical limits upon upward and downward departures. An alternative would have been to establish a general principle. Minnesota, for example, has amended its guidelines to provide that departures should be "proportionate" to the weight of the aggravating or mitigating factors involved.[30] Which device is preferable should be left to the commission, as it may depend on the guidelines' rationale and structure. What the enabling statute should contain, again, is a directive that the commission address the matter.

Legislative Review of the Guidelines

There are two models for review of the guidelines by the legislature: legislative approval and legislative veto. Washington opted for the first, as did New York.[31] The proposed guidelines were to be submitted to the legislature, and would not take effect until affirmatively approved. Washington's legislature approved its commission's proposed guidelines; New York's did not. The drawback of this technique is that it may do what the commission device was intended to avoid: namely, shift debate over specific sentencing norms back to a legislative forum, where temptations to posture—and to add a host of toughening amendments that could destroy the guidelines' rationale and consistency—may be considerable. True, this did not occur in Washington, but the hazard remains nevertheless. (The one possible advantage of the legislative approval device is that, should the legislature decide to grant its approval, it may become more committed to the guidelines than were the guidelines merely promulgated by the commission and permitted to survive. As a result, the legislature might be more reluctant to pass mandatory-minimum or other subsequent legislation that conflicts with the rationale of the guidelines.)

Minnesota's and Pennsylvania's laws took the alternative approach of the legislative veto. The Minnesota statute required the guidelines to be submitted by a specified date and provided they would take effect on a subsequent date four months hence "unless the legislature provides otherwise."[32] The legislative veto is a familiar device in American regulatory practice. Some jurisdictions have now imposed constitutional restrictions on its form: a procedure which permits one house, or both houses, to reject the rule-making agency's standards may be impermissible if the rejection decision is not sent to the chief executive for signature or nonacquiesence in accordance with normal legislative procedures.[33] A provision that the guidelines take effect within a specified period unless disapproved by law, however, should be unproblematic.

The legislative veto device permits the legislature, if it wishes, to avoid having to debate and vote upon the guidelines' particular set of penalties. If the legislative leadership is reasonably satisfied with the guidelines as a whole, they can be allowed to survive without a floor debate and vote, simply by the taking of no action to block them. The principle of legislative supremacy is retained, however. If there is strong legislative sentiment against the guidelines, they can be blocked. Pennsylvania's legislature did exercise its veto power and rejected the commission's initially proposed guidelines. Those eventually permitted to take effect were considerably revised to meet legislators' objections.[34]

Appellate Review of Sentences

Adequate provisions on appellate review of sentence are essential. Sentencing guidelines depend on the appellate courts for their enforcement. Absent the authority to test compliance with the guidelines on appeal, and to reverse noncomplying sentences, the guidelines become only precatory.

The Minnesota provision on appellate review is surprisingly ambiguous. The reviewing tribunal—at the time of the statute's enactment, the Minnesota Supreme Court—is authorized to review the sentence to determine whether the sentence is "unreasonable, inappropriate, excessive, [or] unjustifiably disparate."[35] The quoted language does not make compliance or noncompliance with the guidelines grounds per se for review; a further finding is necessary that noncompliance renders the sentence unreasonable, inappropriate, or unduly disparate. Thus it is largely left up to the reviewing court to decide what weight to give the guidelines. Fortunately, the state's supreme court has given them a great deal of weight: sentences that disregard the guidelines are treated as unreasonable or inappropriate and hence reversible. But had the supreme court been differently inclined, it could have treated the guidelines as only one possible factor in deciding on the "reasonableness" of the sentence. That could have reduced the force of the guidelines to almost nil.

The Washington statute is less ambiguous. Sentences that are outside the applicable standard range are appealable per se. Such deviating sentences may be reversed if the reasons specified by the judge for deviating "do not justify a sentence outside the standard range."[36] This language has the advantage of tying appellate review expressly to compliance with the guidelines. It does, however, permit sentences deviating from the standard range to be upheld if adequate reasons for deviation are cited.

Still, the Washington provisions might be improved on two points. First, it should be made explicit that misapplication of the guidelines is itself grounds for review and reversal. If the judge purports to apply the guidelines but, say, selects the wrong seriousness-rating on the grid, the case should be appealable without need to consider his or her other reasons for the sentence. The Pennsylvania law has such a clause, directing reversal if "the sentencing court purported to sentence within the sentencing guidelines but applied the guideline erroneously."[37]

Second, sentences *within* the standard ranges should be reversible in exceptional cases where the court disregarded clearly convincing aggravating or mitigating circumstances. The Washington statute does not permit this.[38] But if the aggravating or mitigating grounds are sufficiently strong, it does not seem fair to allow them to be ignored without review. Pennsylvania does permit such appeals, if failure to depart was "clearly unreasonable." An alternative formulation would be to authorize appeals if the trial court disregarded "clearly convincing" grounds for departure, "within the purposes of the guidelines."[39]

Another important issue is the choice of the appellate tribunal. When the enabling act became law in 1978, Minnesota had no intermediate appellate court. The act thus provided for direct appeals to the state supreme court.[40] Now, such an intermediate appeals court has been created, and sentence appeal goes to that court— with discretionary further review by the supreme court. Washington's scheme resembles Minnesota's present system.[41] Other states might make different choices, depending on their court structure. The appeal, however, should be to true appellate court, accustomed to reviewing trial court decisions and developing a case law. It does not suffice to have review merely by ad hoc review panels of trial judges. Such panels—having no regular appellate functions—may be unduly deferential to the sentencing judge and will be unaccustomed to developing the case law that is needed to interpret the guidelines.

Parole Release and Supervision
Existing enabling statutes have various provisions about parole. The most radical is Washington's; not only is the parole board's discretionary releasing power eliminated, but so is parole supervision.[42] Minnesota does not go quite so far; it has eliminated discretionary parole release but has retained parole supervision. The offender is released from prison after serving two-thirds of his term and (subject to loss of "good time" credits for misconduct in prison) serves the

last one-third under supervised release.[43] Pennsylvania retains parole release *and* parole supervision. Each offender is sentenced to a minimum sentence, denoting his or her eligibility for parole, and to a maximum sentence, denoting the latest permissible time for release. Within the minimum and maximum, the parole board decides release and administers supervision. The guidelines govern only the determination of the minimum sentence.[44]

I shall not here try to analyze which solution is preferable, having written at length on that subject elsewhere.[45] Let me merely make a few simple points:

- The enabling statute *must* address the future status of parole release. If not, no one knows what the guideline sentences mean in actual duration of confinement.

- Retaining discretionary parole release will, obviously, complicate any effort to estimate the impact of the guidelines on prison populations. Minnesota could make firm prison population projections because the duration of confinement was a predictable two-thirds of the prison sentence (see chapter 6 for methods of making such projections). Pennsylvania, by retaining discretionary parole release, would have had much more difficulty making comparable projections.

- If parole supervision is retained, as it is in Minnesota for the final one-third of the term, then the enabling statute should empower the commission to issue supplemental guidelines for duration of reconfinement upon revocation of parole.[46] If length of reimprisonment is left to the discretion of the parole or correctional authorities, then offenders may be confined for substantial periods on account of technical violations of release conditions or lesser criminal offenses which would not qualify for prison sentences under the guidelines. Such reconfinements frustrate the guidelines' stated policy of limiting the use of imprisonment to specified types of cases that are deemed more serious, and if they occur in substantial numbers, they can raise prison populations above the targets which the guidelines presuppose. Giving the commission authority to regulate duration of reconfinements can help ensure that they comport with the general policy reflected in the guidelines.

Political Constraints

Can sentencing guidelines be established everywhere? Perhaps not. Political constraints will make the task particularly difficult in some jurisdictions.

Shortly after Minnesota's guidelines took effect, New York State created its sentencing commission.[47] Although the effort was generously funded and staffed, New York's commission never succeeded in developing a firm consensus. The proposed guidelines embodied no coherent rationale and did not systematically take prison populations into account. Instead of developing a new policy, the commission simply resorted to previous averages of time served when filling in the sentencing grid.[48] When the guidelines were published, they were assailed as too lenient, although in fact they would have resulted in substantially increased prison commitments. Without reliable projections of impact on prison populations at its disposal, the commission was unable to respond to these charges of leniency. The guidelines have not been approved by the legislature.

Some of the responsibility for the failure can be laid to New York's commission itself. The lack of a consistent rationale and the absence of projections of the effect on prison populations were avoidable mistakes—ones that Minnesota and Washington had already avoided. One wonders, however, whether the guidelines would have survived had they been better crafted. A hostile political environment in that state may well have frustrated even a sophisticated effort.

Can potential political impediments to a commission's work be identified? There has been no systematic effort to do so. Political scientists have not devoted much attention to the politics of sentencing reform. Case studies are rare—save for one comparative study of the commissions in Minnesota and Pennsylvania.[49] Useful theoretical models on the political dynamics of such reforms are virtually nonexistent.

Reformers cannot, however, afford to wait for the scholars to address the question. In various jurisdictions, they are confronted *now* with deciding whether to proceed with a sentencing commission. What can be said to assist them? While I am not a political scientist and have not studied the politics of sentencing commissions in systematic fashion, I have had the opportunity to follow the development of guidelines in a number of states. This experience has suggested to me a few suppositions about potential political obstacles. I claim no scientific validity for my suppositions, only that they strike me as plausible.

The political impediments will not necessarily present themselves when the proposed enabling statute is before the legislature. In New York and in Pennsylvania, for example, the statute creating the commission sailed through without much organized opposition.[50] Mere creation of that body did not commit the interested constituencies to much; they could wait to see if the product was to their liking. The objections emerged when the commission started work and the guidelines began to take shape. The drafters of the enabling legislation would be wise, however, to ask themselves at the outset about the potential political impediments to the approval of the guidelines. If those impediments are great, they might reconsider the wisdom of going forward, or at least think of what special strategies may be needed. Let me, then, proceed with my suppositions.

▪ *A criminal justice constituency can be expected to oppose the guidelines if they would significantly diminish its existing powers. Where that constituency is politically active and influential, that suggests trouble.*

The role of prosecutors illustrates this point. In a system that has wide sentencing discretion, prosecution as well as defense may profit from sentencing guidelines: the prosecution, by the greater assurance provided of imprisonment for serious cases; the defense, by the greater assurance of prison's being avoided for lesser cases. Once a state has enacted an extensive system of mandatory minimums, however, the incentives change. The mandatories give prosecutors the bargaining leverage they desire, since these provide substantial minimum penalties while allowing wide discretion for them to seek still tougher sanctions. Replacing mandatories with guidelines is thus potentially disadvantageous to the prosecution: it offers both less flexibility to propose sentences above the prescribed norm and somewhat more flexibility for judges to deviate below the norm in mitigated cases. In a state having numerous mandatory minimum sentences, therefore, one can expect prosecutorial opposition to their replacement by sentencing guidelines. If the prosecutors are politically well organized (as they are likely to be in states that have resorted heavily to mandatories), the guidelines may be defeated.

Minnesota, before the guidelines, still had a largely discretionary sentencing system. The commission's studies disclosed that judges often granted probation for offenses against the person when the offender did not have an extensive criminal record (see chapter 5). The guidelines thus had something to offer prosecutors: namely, to facilitate the imprisonment of persons convicted of violent offenses. While some prosecutors may have preferred mandatories, existing law provided only a few of these, and a significant expansion of mandatory sentences did not have much prospect for enactment. The prosecution bar did not oppose the guidelines.[51]

New York, by contrast, had an elaborate system of mandatory minimum sentences in place when the commission started its work. This included a "predicate felony" law, which prescribed a prison sentence for almost any second felony conviction. The leverage this gave the prosecution was enhanced by appellate court decisions entitling a prosecutor to take back a plea offer if the sentence proposed by the judge was not to his liking.[52] Since prosecutors already had the power to imprison most convicted felons, guidelines did not have much to offer them. In fact, the guidelines could only dilute prosecutorial power—by eliminating mandatory imprisonment for lesser second felonies and by permitting downward deviations from the ranges on account of mitigating circumstances. It is thus not surprising that New York prosecutors took an intransigent position. The district attorneys association submitted a paper opposing any dilution of the existing mandatories and virtually any power to deviate below the guidelines.[53] The prosecution member of the commission (who was the influential Manhattan district attorney) dissented from the commission's report.[54]

The interests of the judiciary are less readily identifiable than those of prosecutors. Sentencing guidelines limit (albeit by no means eliminate) judicial discretion. They have, however, the countervailing advantage of relieving judges of some of the onus for unpopular sentencing policies. The guidelines may add to judges' work in cases where they wish to deviate, as these decisions must be explained in writing. By the same token, however, they make sentencing simpler in normal cases, since the decision can be made by consulting the grid.

In Minnesota, judges suffered some restriction of their discretion over whether to imprison, but they gained new authority to adjudicate duration of confinement—a matter that hitherto had largely been within the parole board's discretion. The judiciary did not oppose the guidelines.[55]

The situation might be different, however, in a jurisdiction in which judges had extensive discretionary authority over duration as well as over the "in-out" decision. There, guidelines could be perceived primarily as narrowing the powers of judges. If the judiciary's views are influential in the legislature, this perception may bode ill for guidelines. A case in point seems to be Maine, where legislation enacted a decade ago eliminated parole release, giving judges wide authority over duration of confinement as well as over the decision to confine. When a legislatively appointed study group recently recommended that a sentencing commission be created for the state, judicial opposition was strong, as noted already in chapter 2; the group lost its funding before it could even spell out the details of its proposals.[56]

▪ *An atmosphere of escalating punitiveness is an impediment.*

State sentencing systems deal with street crimes that evoke public anxiety. In almost any such system, politicians may be tempted to adopt postures of toughness. The more pervasive the law-and-order rhetoric becomes, however, the more difficult the sentencing commission's job will be.

Sentencing guidelines require legislative and gubernatorial support. The legislature must enact the statute creating the commission and resist proposals for more draconian alternatives. The governor must refrain from vetoing the enabling law and, usually, help round up legislative support for it as well. Once the commission publishes its guidelines, the legislature must let them survive. These political actors may need incentives to provide the requisite support.

Guidelines are supposed to make sentences more predictable and fair. While a limited reduction in crime rates might conceivably also be achievable, major breakthroughs in crime prevention cannot be.[57] The most obvious incentive for support—being able to promise and deliver improved public safety—will thus be lacking. Predictability and fairness are important desiderata in themselves but they have, in the view of many politicians, little public appeal when the bulk of voters fear and loathe criminals and few convicted criminals do or may vote.

What other incentive can there be? One is limiting the expense of prisons. Prisons can cost as much as $75,000 per cell to build and $15,000 per cell per year to maintain. Rising commitment rates can have substantial budgetary effects and crowd out other desired expenditures. Sentencing guidelines can help control this expense by setting population targets. If the population target reflects present capacity, new prison construction can be avoided and maintenance costs kept at or near current levels. Even if the commission sets a population target which exceeds present capacity, the expansion of space can be held within affordable levels. The Minnesota commission skillfully responded to the concern over rising prison costs in order to generate political support for the guidelines.[58]

The mere fact of rising prison outlays may not be a sufficient incentive for support, however. In New York the state's prison populations have continued to rise, more than doubling in a decade. Yet, as James Jacobs has pointed out, the state corrections department has been successful in obtaining expanded prison space (in part, through conversion of that space from other uses), and legislators have willingly appropriated the necessary funds.[59] New York politicians have not, by and large, shown much interest in braking prison costs. Why not? The state's budgetary situation might be part of the explanation. Prisons are expensive everywhere, but their affordability depends on how tight the budget is in the particular state. New York (whose financial picture had been improving since the 1975 fiscal crisis) may have been better able to absorb prison expansion than Minnesota was. The difference in degree of financial constraint in the two states would be worth exploring.

Another factor seems to be involved, however, and that is the extent of politicization of punishment issues. To resist added prison costs is a matter of priorities; it is to say that outlays for other purposes are more worthwhile than outlays for more cells. Giving prison spending this lower priority involves some measure of risk for a politician—of seeming insufficiently tough on crime.

The risk seems manageable in a state where punishment has not become a major focus of political advocacy. That was so in Minnesota, where no statewide figure had recently campaigned for a general toughening of penalties. It is not so much present levels of severity that count, however, as the extent of pressures for *increasing* those levels. A conservative state might have larger prison capacities than Minnesota's and a correspondingly sterner sentencing practice. Still, legislators might feel they could safely question the expense of *further* expansion in prison capacity when there has not been much agitation for inflating penalties more. Such a state would have more severe guidelines than Minnesota's, but an environment that nevertheless may favor the adoption of guidelines.

It is *escalating* punishments, and rhetoric about punishment, that create the problem. Consider New York: sentencing has been a contentious issue there, ever since the famous (or infamous) Rockefeller drug law of the early 1970s. Gubernatorial campaigns have witnessed competitions in toughness, with each candidate featuring proposals for increased penalties. In such an environment, a legislator is wise to assign spending on prisons a rather high priority. The willingness of New York legislators to approve large additional prison expenditures may reflect the political hazardousness of publicly questioning such spending.

Aside from reducing the concern over prison costs, such an environment can directly hinder the sentencing commission's work. Sentencing guidelines can promise a more rational scheme of penalties and tough punishments for those convicted of serious crimes. What responsible guidelines cannot do is offer vast increases in overall punishment levels, because they should be based on current prison capacity or on realistic targets for expanded capacity. Lesser offenders, inevitably, will have to receive comparatively mild sanctions. In an atmosphere in which politicians compete to show their ferocity about crime issues, such standards will not be easy to support.

New York, again, is a case in point. To any detached observer, the New York sentencing commission's proposed guidelines scarcely are lenient. Imprisonment or jail is recommended for most cells in the grid; and the guidelines, if implemented, probably would produce a considerable increase in prison populations.[60] The commission's proposals, however, quite appropriately dismantle some of the more draconian mandatory minimum sentences of current law and provide modest penalties for offenses having low seriousness scores.[61] The comparative moderation of the guidelines made them vulnerable to charges of leniency. Such charges were not long in coming. Several of the state's principal elected officials denounced the proposed guidelines.[62] The governor—who had initially proposed establishment of the commission—chose not to come to the guidelines' rescue.[63] Public defense of the guidelines was seen as imprudent politics.

Do New York politicians demand increasing punishments because that is what the voters want? I doubt there can be a confident answer. While there is evidence that the public tends to favor punishments that exceed the levels the courts generally impose, it is not known how strong this sentiment is or how voters' preferences on these sentencing issues affect their voting decisions.[64] What is apparent is not citizen attitudes so much as politicians' *perceptions* of those attitudes. The visibility of the crime issue in political campaigns suggests, at least, that New York politicians have believed their constituents to be in a law-and-order frame of mind. It is that belief which directly affects sentencing guidelines' chances for survival.

- *A jurisdiction's "political style" counts.*

I have been speaking thus far of the interests of various criminal justice constituencies. Adequate guidelines cannot be written, however, on the basis of institutional self-interest alone. The members of a commission need to adopt a "policy perspective" of concern about the guidelines' broader merits, rather than merely the perspective of representing their respective constituencies. In chapter 8, Kay Knapp suggests that the members of the Minnesota commission did adopt such a policy perspective in the initial development of the guidelines. In New York, however, institutional self-interest dominated from the outset. Members of the commission tended to respond in predictable ways that reflected the concerns of their respective constituencies; public comment about the guidelines seldom addressed their merits or offered constructive suggestions for improvement.

Why this difference? Personalities have something to do with it. The Minnesota commission benefited from the initiative and seriousness of its first chairperson, and of its most important judicial member, as well as from the competence of its staff (see chapter 2, above). That kind of leadership was lacking in New York.

Yet there may be something more: a difference in political style and tradition. In an influential study, Daniel Elazar differentiates styles of state government.[65] An "individualistic" style of politics, he asserts, is tied to a history of political machines. Government is seen chiefly as a marketplace, and office as a means for securing favors, perquisites, and power. In such an environment, it is scarcely surprising that various groups' perceived self-interest dominate over the pursuit of larger, programmatic concerns. A "moralistic" style emphasizes programmatic ends. Politics is seen less as purely a market for allocating power among defined interests. Concern about the merits of policies is consistent with such a style. Not surprisingly, Elazar singles out New York and Minnesota as paradigms of the two styles.

Elazar's distinctions are far from precise. They confirm, however, my own impressions of guideline development in the two states. In my (admittedly limited) contacts with Minnesota, I was struck by the fact that public officials—not only commission members but interested others—had at least *some* concern about the broader merits of the guidelines. In New York, my impression was otherwise: the dominant theme was how the guidelines might help or hurt the participants' respective interests as judges, prosecutors, defense counsel, and so on.

Elazar has classified other states according to their political styles.[66] The proponents of guidelines in a particular jurisdiction should examine his classification and then check it against their own judgment and experience concerning the prevailing manner of decision making. If, in their judgment, the prevailing style does not favor programmatic concerns, they should expect difficulties ahead.

It is easy to be wise after the event. We now may think that Minnesota's political environment was more favorable than it in fact was, because the guidelines were approved; and we may perceive New York's as more unpropitious than it was, because the guidelines were repudiated. Nevertheless, I am convinced that the prospects for the survival of guidelines do vary with the state's institutional structure and political atmosphere. Political scientists should begin to explore the politics of the sentencing commission. Proponents of this reform in a particular state should, from the beginning, think seriously about the political incentives and disincentives to approval. Politics may be messy to think about and have to deal with, but only a politically informed effort has prospects for success.

CHAPTER 5

Structure and Rationale:
Minnesota's Critical Choices

Andrew von Hirsch

$\mathbf{C}$hoosing an explicit rationale is one of the chief functions of a sentencing commission, for reasons explained already. How should a commission make this choice? How should it fashion its guidelines to comport with that rationale? To help answer these questions, it may be instructive to examine Minnesota's guidelines, and the reasoning process involved in their construction.

The Overall Structure and Rationale

Let me begin with the overall structure of the Minnesota guidelines: the slope and elevation of the dispositional line, separating prison from nonprison sanctions; and the prescribed durations of imprisonment.

The Slope of the Dispositional Line: Desert and Incapacitation Models

The Minnesota commission treated as its first major policy choice that of deciding the *slope* of the dispositional line.[1] At the outset, the commission had its staff examine the pattern of previous sentencing decisions and found that the factor which statistically best accounted for judges' decisions whether to imprison was the extent of the prior criminal record. Defendants who had felony records tended to be imprisoned even if their current crimes were not so serious, whereas first offenders tended to receive probation even if their current crime was a substantial one.[2] The commission needed to decide whether to continue to emphasize prior criminality or instead stress the gravity of the current crime.

The commission chose the latter course, of giving emphasis to the gravity of the current offense. Persons convicted of serious crimes

84

are to be imprisoned even if they are first offenders, and those convicted of lesser offenses are to receive nonprison sentences unless their criminal records are lengthy. This change constituted a major shift in the emphasis of sentencing policy in Minnesota.

The commission gave two reasons for its decision. The first concerned existing sentencing legislation. Minnesota had enacted mandatory prison sentences for certain crimes involving possession of firearms. The state also had a Community Corrections Act, which created financial incentives for not imprisoning persons convicted of crimes (generally, property crimes) carrying a less-than-five-year statutory maximum. A flatter dispositional line, it was argued, would mean that crimes committed with firearms, being more serious, would receive prison sentences—whereas property crimes would generally receive nonprison dispositions.[3]

This reason, standing alone, does not seem dispositive. While the legislature had prescribed a few mandatory minimum sentences, it had not done so extensively. And although the Community Corrections Act created incentives for use of probation for "lesser" crimes, it did not provide specific criteria for sentencing decisions. A steeper dispositional line might arguably have been devised so as to accord still with the existing legislation.

The second reason supplied by the commission for emphasizing the gravity of the offender's crime is more plausible; it relates to the rationale for punishment. A steep dispositional line stressing the prior criminal record, the commission asserted, would reflect an incapacitative philosophy. A dispositional line with a flat slope, making the offense of conviction the determining factor, would reflect a desert rationale. Considering these two philosophies the commission opted for a compromise solution, but one which was closer to the desert philosophy and which the commission termed a "modified" just deserts approach. This solution was reflected in a dispositional line that placed more weight on the gravity of the current crime than on the criminal record.[4]

The commission's account leaves much unanswered. Why did the commission regard a steep line as incapacitative and a flatter one as desert-oriented? When the commission spoke of a "modified" desert rationale, how and to what extent were desert principles being modified? To answer such questions, let me briefly compare desert and incapacitation as described in today's sentencing literature, and then discuss how these two philosophies might affect the slope of a dispositional line.

A desert rationale requires that punishments be proportionate to the comparative blameworthiness of defendants' criminal conduct. That conduct is, in the first instance, the crime for which the defendant has currently been convicted and is being sentenced. What significance, if any, prior convictions should have in a desert model has been a matter of debate among desert theorists. George Fletcher and Richard Singer have argued that prior criminality should not be considered at all in determining how much punishment an offender deserves. I have contended that the absence of prior convictions should be extenuating to a limited extent. Space does not allow me to rehearse the arguments for these respective positions here, but they are readily available to the interested reader.[5] For present purposes, it suffices that the proponents of these two interpretations of desert theory agree that *if* prior criminal record is utilized, it should carry considerably less weight than the gravity of the current offense. This conclusion coincides with the view stated in the commission's report, that a desert model would yield a relatively flat dispositional line, one that relies primarily on current offense seriousness.

An incapacitative rationale aims at reducing future criminality by restraining offenders, for a period, from being able to commit new crimes in the community. There are two main strategies of incapacitation. One is through *selective* restraint; that is, seeking to identify those convicted offenders who have higher probabilities of future criminality and separating such persons from the community. The other is through general incapacitative strategies; that is, restraining *all* those convicted of felonies—or particular types of felonies—for predetermined periods, without trying to identify which of these felons are the worse risks.[6] As long as some (even if by no means all) of such felons would have committed new crimes, the sanction could have an incapacitative effect.

Selective restraint has been the more familiar incapacitative strategy and the one about which we possess some empirical knowledge. There exists an extensive prediction literature, whose conclusions may roughly be summarized as follows.[7]

- A limited capacity to predict criminality exists. Statistical prediction methods have had some success in identifying groups of offenders who are more likely than others to return to crime—"success," that is, in the sense that these methods perform better than random selection would.
- Prediction methods, however, are not very accurate. While not failing entirely, they account for only a small portion of

the variability in subsequent behavior. They are also plagued with problems of overprediction: most of those identified as potential recidivists will be "false positives" who are not in fact found to return to crime.

- Statistical prediction methods rely on several kinds of offender characteristics: chiefly, their criminal records, employment histories, and drug histories. Of these, the dimension that carries the greatest predictive weight is prior criminal record. That does not mean that prior criminal record predicts well, for nothing does. Relying only on factors concerning the criminal record and omitting the other predictive factors will result in some loss of predictive power. But if a single set of factors were relied upon to predict recidivism, they would relate to the criminal record.

This summary supports the commission's assertion that a dispositional line emphasizing the criminal record would suggest an incapacitative rationale. It would do so, that is, if the following qualifications are borne in mind: (1) the incapacitative strategy is one of selective restraint, and (2) a single offender variable is being sought that facilitates comparisons on the grid between a predictive and a desert scheme.

The second point deserves a brief elaboration. The grid permits comparisons to be made between the effects of a more desert-oriented and a more predictively oriented rationale, *provided* that common variables—offense and prior record—are used. Utilizing prior record as a proxy for risk permits this to be done. Using a more complex risk indicator that includes the offender's social history would spoil the comparison, as the latter factors are germane only to incapacitation, not to desert. Had the commission, after making this initial comparison, decided that it wished to emphasize incapacitation, then it would have become appropriate to use a *tested* measure of risk—and that measure might include social as well as prior-record factors.

The result would be different were general incapacitation used rather than selective restraint. General incapacitation strategies do not rely upon the offender's prior criminal record or his or her social history and thus could be consistent with a quite flat dispositional line.[8] To date, however, research has not advanced far enough to warrant reliance upon such strategies.

Let us assume, for the foregoing reasons, that the choice is between a predictive rationale (that is, one of selective restraint) and a desert rationale. Was the commission justified in leaning toward the desert?

The issue of desert and prediction has been extensively debated in today's sentencing literature. As I have examined that debate at length in my recent book, *Past or Future Crimes,* let me only summarize some of the contentions here. Desert advocates, myself included, assert that it is a requirement of elementary justice that penalties be scaled commensurately with the gravity of the offenses. Prediction advocates reply that desert should, instead, merely serve as an outer limit barring gross disproportion in leniency and severity; and that within those broad limits, the sentence should be determined by the predicted likelihood of the offender's returning to crime. Desert advocates retort that such theories, by treating the blameworthiness of the conduct as mere outer bounds, would lead to substantial disparity in punishment of those whose criminal conduct is equally reprehensible. Severities of punishment would not even be rank-ordered according to the seriousness of the crime: the defendant who commits the lesser crime may receive the larger penalty—if his crime or criminal record happens to be of the kind associated with higher recidivism rates—subject only to the limitation that the penalty may not be manifestly excessive in relation to the gravity of the crime.[9]

Was the commission right in deciding to emphasize the blameworthiness of the criminal conduct? That depends, ultimately, on one's conception of the nature of punishment. In my view, the distinguishing feature of punishment—what separates it from taxes, conscription, civil commitment, and other state impositions on citizens—is that it *condemns:* it treats the act as reprehensible and the actor as someone to be blamed. The sterner the penalty, the greater the implicit reproof. That is why the severity of punishment should comport with the comparative seriousness of crimes. The more one downgrades the role of the gravity of the defendant's criminal conduct—and the more one relies instead on predictive factors associated with the offender's social or previous criminal history—the more the censure being visited through punishment will fail fairly to reflect the blameworthiness of the crime for which the offender is being sentenced.[10]

There is also an important practical reason supporting the commission's choice, one that concerns fostering realistic expectations for a sentencing system. Sentencing policy can have only limited influence, if any at all, on aggregate crime rates. Insofar as anything is known about the etiology of crime, levels of criminality appear to respond primarily to demographic, economic, and social factors: the percentage of youthful males in the population (since this group is responsible for so large a share of the crimes commonly committed); the economic incentives people have to seek legitimate versus criminal activity; the amount of intergroup tension in the community; and the degree of alienation felt by less-privileged groups. These are matters which cannot easily be influenced by a state's criminal justice policy. If changes in sentencing policy can affect the incidence of common crimes at all, its impact is likely to be slight as compared with the impact of these major, uncontrollable factors.

A predictive sentencing scheme offers itself as a crime-prevention technique—and therein lies its vulnerability. If a commission presents its policies as crime preventive, it is asking to be judged by its effectiveness in reducing criminality. Yet there is little that a commission can do to make certain that the crime rate will fall, since that rate is largely beyond the control of sentencing policy. Predictions, moreover, have a substantial incidence of "false negatives" as well as false positives: many defendants classified as good risks will, in fact, offend again.[11] As the misclassified good risks begin to return to crime in significant numbers, the commission will appear to have failed its mission by its own definition. The search will then proceed for tougher, more costly (but, alas, not necessarily more effective) sentencing schemes.

A rationale emphasizing desert has a different mission: that of scaling punishments so as to reflect differences in the reprehensibleness of the criminal conduct. Such a system may have collateral preventive payoffs, even if not fashioned with crime prevention primarily in mind. Those convicted of the more serious crimes would, under the guidelines, be more likely to be imprisoned than was previously the case. Increasing the likelihood of imprisonment in this fashion could have some general-incapacitative effects and possibly some modest deterrent benefits as well. Even if those benefits do not materialize, however, a desert-oriented sentencing scheme remains defensible on grounds of equity. Because the scheme aims chiefly at proportionality and consistency, disappointed hopes for crime prevention (always a risk in any criminal justice strategy) would not be quite so devastating.

The next question for the commission was, *how* flat the dispositional line should be. Assuming that the seriousness of the current offense should carry more weight than the criminal record, to what extent should the record play any role at all?

The dispositional line, as the commission drew it, is flat at the left, and hinges down at the right, as is shown in Table 5–1. (In this table, I use the customary format for sentencing grids, in which seriousness of crimes is arrayed in *ascending* order on the vertical axis, so that the highest ratings, that is, worst crimes, are on top. Imprisonment (denoted "IN") is thus *above* the dispositional line, and nonprison sanctions (denoted "OUT") are below it. This reverses the actual format of Minnesota's grid, in which crime seriousness is arrayed in descending order. I make the transposition because Minnesota's format is unusual, and possibly confusing.)

The dispositional line is entirely horizontal for offenders with a criminal history score of 2 or less, that is, who have two or fewer felony convictions. Only the seriousness of the offense counts, and the criminal record (to wit, whether the offender is a first offender, has one prior felony, or has two) carries no weight at all. This portion of the grid, therefore, reflects a desert rationale: one which follows Fletcher and Singer's view of not considering prior criminality at all. The bulk of the caseload of Minnesota courts was expected to lie in this portion of the grid. Before implementation of the guidelines, about 87 percent of Minnesota's criminal caseload involved persons who would have had criminal history scores of 2 or less, and whose cases would thus have fallen in the part of the grid where the dispositional line is flat.[12]

The right-hand portion of the grid looks quite different: it slopes sharply downward. Starting with offenders having a criminal history score of 3 or more (that is, who had three or more prior felonies), the line moves six cells downward on the grid as it moves four cells to the right. Here, the criminal history has more dispositive power than the gravity of the current offense.

To account for the downward shift on the right, the commission suggested it was not adopting a pure desert rationale but a modified desert model instead.[13] In the literature the modified desert model has been defined as a scheme in which desert plays the dominant role in determining the relative severities of punishment, but modest deviations are permitted for incapacitative (or other utilitarian) ends.[14] It is thus a compromise, but one emphasizing commensurability: the basic structure of the system would be shaped by the desert principle, but predictive considerations would be allowed a limited scope in the choice of penalties. A modified desert model

Table 5–1
The dispositional line on Minnesota's grid

Seriousness of Conviction Offense	Criminal History Score					
	0	1	2	3	4	5	6 or more
10 (e.g., 2d-degree murder)							
9 (e.g., felony-murder)							
8 (e.g., rape)				IN			
7 (e.g., armed robbery)							
6 (e.g., burglary of occupied dwelling)							
5 (e.g., burglary of unoccupied dwelling)							
4 (e.g., nonresidential burglary)							
3 (e.g., theft of $250 to $2,500)			OUT				
2 (e.g., lesser forgeries)							
1 (e.g., marijuana possession)							

91

thus would permit somewhat more reliance on the criminal record than would be allowed on a pure desert model and could arguably support tilting the dispositional line more steeply on the right.

There also were practical reasons for the shift. With its flat or flattish dispositional line, a desert model would limit the use of imprisonment to those convicted of the more serious crimes. Lesser felons would have to receive nonprison sanctions, even if they were recidivists. This is a policy which the commission could readily defend for normal cases but would find much harder to defend publicly for offenders having *very* long criminal records. If a car thief convicted for the ninth or tenth time would still receive a sentence other than imprisonment, the credibility of the guidelines could suffer. With the line dropped at the right, the guidelines ensure imprisonment for cases of frequent recidivism. Yet only a small minority of offenders were expected to be involved. On the basis of its statistics on previous sentencing practice, the commission could expect there to be few cases in which the highest criminal history scores (scores of 5 and 6) would be obtained. Those convicted of lesser felonies would be imprisoned only if they obtained these high scores. The commission could thus make the grid more publicly acceptable while retaining the desert emphasis for the bulk of cases.

In principle, however, the commission's solution is troublesome. If an offender has run up a high criminal history score, the guidelines call for his imprisonment even when his current crime is a property offense in the lowest seriousness grade. This includes routine thefts, since Minnesota law classifies as a felony any theft of $250 or more.[15] Even if these cases were intended to be the exception, persons convicted of such minor crimes do not seem to deserve, or even come close to deserving, the severe sanction of imprisonment. Giving the record substantially more emphasis than the gravity of the current crime, as the right-hand portion of the grid does, hardly seems consistent with desert, even in modified form.[16]

The imprisonment of lesser felons has also proven less unusual than the commission had hoped. The steep drop-off of the dispositional line has created an incentive for prosecutors to try to imprison property offenders by building up their previous records of convictions. As described in chapter 8, that is precisely what prosecutors have been doing. As a result, the commission has had greater difficulty than anticipated in keeping prison commitments within available space and has been confronted with imprisonment for many more nonserious cases than it had anticipated or hoped for.

Would a prediction advocate be satisfied with steepness of the right-hand portion of the line? Not necessarily. Criminal record tends generally to be associated with risk: enough, as we saw, to treat it as a proxy for risk for heuristic purposes, when initially modeling the guidelines under different rationales. But how accurate is Minnesota's *particular* criminal history score as a predictor? The score depends on the number of previous felony and misdemeanor convictions.[17] To the extent that such a scoring system picks out older offenders who are losing their criminal initiative, it might prove to be merely an indifferent predictor. The predictive efficacy of the grid's criminal history score was not tested empirically by the commission or by independent researchers. It is thus not known whether the downward angulation of the dispositional line on the right significantly enhances the guidelines' incapacitative effect, even were one prepared to sacrifice desert constraints.

The discussion above illustrates the hazards a commission can encounter when it disregards its own purported rationale in fashioning the guidelines. By hinging the dispositional line down so steeply on the right, the Minnesota commission failed to implement the modified desert rationale it was claiming to follow. This departure from the rationale, however, does not necessarily mean that another rationale is being furthered. A prediction rationale, systematically implemented, would not merely call for steepness on the right-hand portion of the dispositional line: the entire line would need to be tilted down. And the grid's offender score then should consist of a *validated* prediction score, if there is to be any confidence that the guidelines provide enhanced incapacitation. The sharp downward tilt at the right seems to have involved a loss of commensurability in the desert sense, without any verified gain in achieving ulterior ends.

The Elevation of the Dispositional Line:
Population Constraints

The commission's next major decision concerned the aggregate use of imprisonment. This would have a considerable impact on the *elevation* of the dispositional line. With a line that is flat on the left-hand side of the grid, where most cases fall, increasing the aggregate person-years in prison would mean drawing the line lower across the grid, to include more cells that call for imprisonment. Conversely, restricting the permissible total use of imprisonment would require the line to be drawn closer to the top of the grid, so that fewer grid cells would prescribe imprisonment.

The commission decided to adopt a firm constraint on aggregate imprisonment. The guidelines, it determined, should be written so that with present or foreseeable rates of conviction, the rated capacity of the state's prison system would not be exceeded.[18] This meant that for the bulk of convicts not having long records, imprisonment could be invoked only if the crime of conviction was fairly serious: there was room to imprison those convicted of armed robbery or worse crimes on their first offense; but there was not room to imprison convicted burglars routinely. The dispositional line was drawn so that it imprisoned first offenders with crimes rated "7" or higher in seriousness, thus including the robbers but excluding most burglars, the seriousness rating of whose crimes was lower.

By relying on space availability to decide the aggregate use of imprisonment, the commission made its main normative questions those of allocation: which classes of convicted prisoners, for how long, and for what reasons, should be allocated to the existing prison bedspace. The commission did not make a normative judgment about how much, apart from the availability of resources, the state *ought* to rely upon the prison sanction.

As it happens, Minnesota has relied upon imprisonment sparingly: its per capita use of state penal institutions has been among the lowest in the country, and the state's prison capacities reflect this low rate.[19] Thus for reformers favoring restraint in the utilization of imprisonment, the commission's procedure led to desirable results. A rule about staying within existing prison capacities does not, however, always guarantee this outcome: applied in a jurisdiction that has historically been prodigal with imprisonment, it could lead to quite severe overall punishment levels.

The issue of aggregate use of imprisonment, therefore, must ultimately be decided on its merits. If one favors Minnesota's modest use levels, it does not suffice to point to the state's prison capacities. The judgment must be made that Minnesota has acted appropriately in not using imprisonment more than it historically has, and hence that prison capacities ought not to be increased. Only by making such judgments can one explain why one might favor basing the guidelines' overall severity levels on existing prison capacities in Minnesota, but not necessarily so in another state that has different traditions regarding imprisonment—where one might wish to argue that imprisonment has historically been over- or underused.

Is relying on available prison space consistent with the desert rationale which the commission purported to implement? Desert imposes its most stringent constraints in deciding *comparative* punishments. Persons convicted of similar criminal conduct should receive similar punishments; those convicted of conduct of differing gravity should suffer punishments correspondingly ranked in severity; and the current crime of conviction should receive substantially more weight than prior convictions (if the latter are considered at all). These requirements of *ordinal* proportionality would be infringed were one to allocate relative severities on the basis of prison capacity—for example, to confine some armed robbers but release others because there was not enough space for them.[20]

Desert is less restrictive, however, when it comes to deciding the overall magnitude and anchoring points of a penalty scale. If the penalties have been decided for some other crimes, then the penalty for robbery can be fixed by comparing its seriousness with those crimes. Such judgments, however, require a starting point. There seems to be no quantum of punishment that can readily be identified as the uniquely deserved penalty for the crime or crimes with which the construction of the scale begins. The reason why such a uniquely deserved penalty cannot be found is that the extent of censure expressed through penal deprivation is, to some degree, a convention. When a penalty scale has been devised to reflect the comparative gravity of crimes, altering the scale's magnitude and anchoring points by making modest pro rata increases or decreases in all the prescribed sanctions would represent simply a change in that convention.[21]

This means that *cardinal* proportionality, unlike ordinal, provides only limits.[22] The penalty scale as a whole should not be so much inflated that it begins to visit substantial deprivations on nonserious criminal conduct, for that would overstate the blame for the conduct or else undervalue the importance of the rights of which the defendant is being deprived. Similar reasoning militates against deflating the penalty scale as a whole so much that the most serious crimes are visited with mild punishments.

The leeway thus allowed by cardinal proportionality explains why prison space may be considered in writing the guidelines. What prison space affects is the aggregate use of imprisonment under the guidelines. Permitting somewhat more or somewhat less aggregate imprisonment is, in effect, a pro rata adjustment in punishment levels throughout the scale. Such adjustments are permissible, within reasonable limits, provided the guidelines continue to observe ordinal proportionality by scaling the comparative severity of punishment according to the gravity of the criminal conduct.[23]

Durations of Imprisonment

Having decided the slope and elevation of the dispositional line, the commission needed next to decide durations of confinement for the grid cells above the line. The durations fixed by the commission fall in a recognizable progression, increasing as one moves toward more serious crimes and longer records. In an analysis of the guidelines, Richard Sparks and his associates were able to "predict" the durations in the cells through use of a multiplicative progression formula. His study suggests that while the criminal record carries substantial weight throughout the grid, it has slightly less influence on durations than does the seriousness of the offense.[24]

Nevertheless the increases in lengths of prison terms are quite large as one goes across the rows, with offenders having long records receiving more than double and sometimes treble the terms of first offenders. This raises the question: What rationale was the commission trying to achieve in fixing durations? Was it also a modified desert rationale, and if so, does the weight given the record comport with such a theory? Or was some other purpose sought?

The rationale, unfortunately, cannot be definitively identified. The commission considered its most important decision to be the drawing of the dispositional line and felt that durations should be fixed in a manner that (when population impact was taken into account) would not disturb the location of the line. It did not, however, make an effort to develop a conceptual basis for its decisions about durations comparable to its efforts to identify a rationale for the slope of its dispositional line.

That was an opportunity missed. Much of the criticisms I have made about the steepness of the right-hand side of the dispositional line carry over to the grid's durations. A modified desert rationale could scarcely support as much as a trebling of penalties for offenders with long records. Nor does this emphasis necessarily serve incapacitative ends, since the predictive efficacy of the criminal history score was (as noted earlier) never verified. This aspect of guidelines could have been better had the commission been willing to sustain interest in the purpose served by its prescriptions.

Rating Crimes and Criminal Records

The vertical axis of the grid grades the seriousness of crimes; the horizontal axis, criminal records. The commission therefore needed to establish rating systems for these two dimensions—and that involved a number of important policy choices.

The Breadth of Offense Classifications

The Minnesota guidelines base the seriousness ratings of crimes on their statutory definitions. The commission generally refrained from trying to subcategorize the gravity of criminal conduct within statutory offense categories.[25]

Using the statutory offense definitions can create problems when those definitions are broad. Under the California Penal Code, for example, there is a single statutory robbery category embracing all takings of property by force or threat of force, and a single first-degree burglary category involving all residential burglaries, whether or not the occupant was present or was confronted in the course of the crime. California's decision to use these broad categories as the basis of its presumptive sentencing system meant giving conduct of substantially varying gravity the same normally recommended sanction.[26]

In Minnesota, the statutory categories are less broadly drawn. When the commission wrote its guidelines, there were different statutory categories for different subspecies of robbery and burglary. The categories were given different seriousness ratings by the commission, as shown in Table 5–2. These categories are still somewhat crude. Because the statute did not have a separate category for commercial burglary, it was included with most residential burglaries, even though, arguably, commercial burglaries are less serious because the elements of personal insecurity and invasion of privacy are not typically present. Nevertheless, the problem was not as great as in California; the statute drew at least some significant distinctions which the commission was able to use in its offense ratings.

An alternative would have been for the commission to devise its own subcategories within existing statutory offense classifications and to assign separate seriousness ratings to those subcategories.[27] It could, for example, have assigned separate seriousness ratings to commercial and residential burglaries, although the statute treated them as a single offense category. However, only the offense of conviction is, in litigated cases, determined by the high evidentiary standard of proof beyond reasonable doubt. Had the commission subcategorized in this fashion, the sentencing hearing—with its lower evidentiary standards and lack of a jury—would have had to determine the facts about the offense subcategory that had not been determined through the conviction itself.[28] A tension thus exists between the desiderata of substantive and procedural fairness. Substantive fairness, in the desert sense, calls for separate seriousness ratings to be assigned to different types of burglaries (or other

Table 5–2
Seriousness ratings assigned by the Minnesota Sentencing Commission to
robberies and burglaries

Statutory Reference	Conduct	Sentencing Commission's Seriousness Grade
§ 609.24	Ordinary unarmed robbery (taking by force or threat of force)	5
§ 609.245	Robbery where defendant is armed with a dangerous weapon or inflicts bodily harm	7
§ 609.58(1)(b)	Burglary of dwelling when armed with dangerous weapon or when assault is committed	7
§ 609.58(2)	Burglary of a dwelling with occupant present	6
Other subdivisions of § 609.58	Other burglaries	4

crimes) that differ significantly in the harmfulness or culpability
they typically involve. Attempts by the commission to refine the
seriousness categories by going beyond the statutory definitions,
however, would result in use of a lower evidentiary standard to
determine what the offender did.[29] Since Minnesota's statutory categories were not excessively broad, the commission's decision to
uphold the high evidentiary standard seems sensible.

It is possible, moreover, to seek amendment of statutory definitions. The commission's enabling statute expressly states that it
"shall from time to time make recommendations to the legislature
regarding changes in the criminal code."[30] The commission has
sought, and obtained, refinement of some offense classifications. In
1982, this was done with burglary. The statute now differentiates
burglary of an occupied dwelling from burglary of an unoccupied
dwelling and from nonresidential burglaries.[31] After these recodi-
fications took effect, the commission assigned separate seriousness
gradations to the different subspecies of burglary.[32]

The Number of Offense Seriousness Grades

The commission decided to use a ten-point scale for rating the seriousness of offenses. Are ten grades of seriousness enough? Are they too many?

It has sometimes been suggested that a grading system might have very few gradations of seriousness, and I once mentioned the possibility of having only five grades.[33] I now think this number does not suffice. A five-grade system would not even allow one to distinguish between the lower and upper ranges of, respectively, lesser, intermediate, and serious offenses. Yet, surely, we are capable of making judgments that, say, armed robbery and rape are both serious crimes but that rape is more heinous; or that bad checks and common auto theft are both lesser crimes, but that the former should rank lower. On the other hand, seriousness gradations cannot be indefinitely multiplied. After a certain rather modest number, the gradations would become too refined for making understandable distinctions in gravity.[34]

A ten-category grading system seems a sensible compromise. It permits the making of basic distinctions between lesser, intermediate, and serious crimes, and the division of the first two of these groups into three subcategories and the last into four. Significant distinctions in gravity can thus be made: the four-fold distinction among serious crimes, for example, allows differentiation in ascending order of gravity among the following crimes of violence: armed robbery, rape, reckless homicide, and unpremeditated but intentional homicide.[35] Yet the gradations do not become so numerous as to evade common sense.

Assigning Seriousness Ratings to Crimes

The commission treated judging the seriousness of crimes as an issue of policy which it was required to resolve. The commission's technique for assigning seriousness ratings consisted, essentially, of having each commission member rate offenses according to his or her best judgment of their seriousness and then having the members resolve disagreements in ratings through discussion.[36]

In adopting its rating techniques, the commission implicitly rejected suggestions that it should rely on someone else's estimation of the seriousness of crimes. One form of using other people's judgments would have been to rate crimes on the basis of the comparative severity of the various statutory maximum penalties assigned by the legislature. Although sentencing schemes in other jurisdictions have taken this approach, I do not think it is helpful. Legislatures may make rough-and-ready judgments of seriousness in the maximum penalties they set (especially where the legislature has created felony and misdemeanor classes). But those legislative judgments are directed to the *worst* possible case of a given type of crime instead of to the typical case with which guidelines' presumptive sentences deal.[37] Moreover, considerations other than seriousness may, to an unknown degree, have entered into the determination of the statutory maximum. If the legislature sets the maximum penalty for certain narcotics offenses very high, one cannot be certain whether it did so because it regarded narcotics crimes as particularly serious or because it thought long terms might be useful as a deterrent or incapacitant, irrespective of the crime's seriousness.

Another form of relying on others' judgment, also implicitly rejected by the commission, would have been to base the ratings on popular perceptions of the seriousness of crimes, as shown by opinion survey research.[38] The difficulty of relying on such popular judgments is that they prevent *reasoned* judgments to be made. The surveys simply ask people to rate the gravity of certain crimes, without asking them for their reasons or holding those reasons up to critical scrutiny. Rating seriousness of crimes in part involves factual judgments about the typical risks or consequences of various species of criminal conduct. Popular judgments of crimes may, to a greater or lesser extent, be based on factually inaccurate beliefs about their consequences. Rating seriousness also involves moral judgments about the relative importance of the rights and interests that are concerned and of the degree of culpability attached to the offender's choices. These judgments, likewise, need to be supported by reasons.[39]

If a reasoned assessment of seriousness is called for, the commission appropriately treated the rating of crimes as a policy matter which it should decide. The rating technique the commission used is also a step toward the making of reasoned judgments: it compelled the commission members, where divergent initial ratings had been assigned, to explain to each other why they gave their individual ratings and to debate those reasons until consensus was reached. The method also worked in the sense that the commission was able to reach consensus on the ratings.

My reservation with the commission's technique is that it does not go far enough. It supplies no *systematic* rationale for the ratings that were adopted. When the members initially agreed about the rating assigned to a crime, moreover, there was no discussion—so no reasons emerged why it was given that rating.

Could any systematic rationale have been used? Seriousness depends both on the harmfulness of the conduct and on the actor's culpability. One could begin by looking at harmfulness—holding the culpability variable constant for the moment by considering only the foreseeable consequences of intentional crimes. Harms, I have suggested recently, can be graded according to the degree to which they characteristically restrict people's ability to direct the course of their own lives.[40] The gravest harms are those which interfere with almost any choice a person might wish to make. This accounts for our sense of the gravity of violence, for violence restricts victims' choices so drastically. (The person who is murdered has no choices left at all; the person who is seriously injured has his choices sharply curtailed.) The theory explains why certain economic crimes can also be serious. A person cannot order his or her own life if deprived of the means of subsistence. Economic crimes that typically destroy or curtail peoples' livelihood (for example, swindling persons of their savings) therefore involve grave harm. Such a criterion cannot be applied automatically, and we will need a supplemental theory to deal with crimes which primarily injure collective interests, such as corruption or tax evasion. But it may be a start. A commission could utilize this criterion when rating various species of intentional criminal acts. It could then compare the seriousness ratings, thus derived, with those assigned by commissioners using their own unaided judgments. The commission could debate any divergences between the formally derived and the informal ratings and give reasons for the rankings eventually decided upon.

The Omission of "Enhancements"

The Minnesota guidelines do not contain "enhancements." No separate seriousness points are assigned to being armed, inflicting bodily injury, or other special features of criminal conduct beyond the seriousness rating assigned to the crime category itself. This differs from Washington State's guidelines, which provide added terms for being armed with a deadly weapon.[41]

The problem with enhancements is that it is difficult to rate the importance of a given feature of an offense without knowing what its other features are. How much more serious, for example, does possession of a weapon render an offense? The theory is that risk of injury or death is higher when a weapon is carried. But how much added risk is involved depends upon the nature of the offense, on whether, for example, it typically involves direct confrontation with its victim. It thus makes better sense, rather than adding a uniform number of seriousness points for arming across the board, to take this factor into account in rating particular types of crimes. Thus, the Minnesota commission gave separate seriousness rankings to armed robbery and strongarm robbery; to burglary while armed and other species of burglary.[42] These separate rankings also enable the sentencing court to rely on the offense of conviction in rating the gravity of the crime and not have to establish additional elements in a separate sentencing hearing with its lower standard of proof.

Scoring the Criminal Record

The criminal history score adopted by the Minnesota commission focuses chiefly on the number, not the quality, of prior convictions. The only distinction the score makes is between felonies and misdemeanors: each prior felony conviction counts one point on the score, each gross misdemeanor counts one-half point, and each misdemeanor one-quarter point.

I need not comment at length on this scoring system, as my earlier comments should suggest its problem: the commission failed to suit the score properly to the structure of the guidelines. If the commission felt compelled to angle the dispositional line sharply downward at the right to increase the guidelines' public acceptability, and if it wished nevertheless to emphasize desert, then it should have recast criminal history scores accordingly. The scoring system should have been designed so that only very few offenders, with the very worst records, could qualify for the highest offender scores—and hence find themselves in the rightmost cells, where the line falls at its lowest. Had that been done carefully, prosecutors could not evade the intent of the guidelines as they have been doing: obtaining prison sentences for property offenders by building up their records through multiple-count convictions (see chapter 8). For most cases, if not all, the seriousness of the offense would remain the principal determinant of the punishment.

Aggravation and Mitigation

The penalties prescribed in the grid are presumptive only. A judge may deviate from the cell range—or even shift from a prison to a nonprison disposition or vice versa—in appropriate aggravating or mitigating circumstances.

Should the guidelines furnish a list of aggravating and mitigating factors? The commission had difficulty with this issue. Its aim was to encourage judges to give thoughtful, specific reasons in cases where they wish to depart from the grid ranges. Two possible strategies were considered toward this end.

One strategy, initially discussed, would be to refrain from specifying such a list. Certain factors—notably age, sex, race, employment, education, marital status, residence, and living arrangements—would expressly be ruled out because of their close association with social and economic status.[43] Aside from these excluded factors, however, judges would determine the grounds for departure. That, it was suggested, might induce judges to develop their own reasons, rather than citing one of a list of factors in a possibly mechanical fashion.[44]

The drawback of such a broadly permissive approach was that it would provide judges with no policy direction. As one of the commission's consultants, I argued that "if the Commission is silent about departures from the guidelines, [there may] well emerge [a case law] jurisprudence for departing from the guidelines that is at odds in principle with the rationale for the guidelines themselves."[45] The commission agreed and dropped this option.

I then urged a substantially more ambitious alternative—that the guidelines provide not only a list of suggested aggravating or mitigating factors but a general statement of principle governing departures:

> I don't think the Commission can totally control what reasons
> may be used to depart from the guidelines, nor should it try to do
> so. But some policy directions from the Commission might be
> useful. The Commission's guidelines might state that an ordinarily
> acceptable reason for varying from the guidelines ranges is that
> the harmfulness of the criminal conduct or the culpability of the
> actor in committing such conduct is substantially greater or less
> than is characteristic for that kind of criminal conduct. That is, of
> course, classic desert-based aggravation or mitigation, and squares
> with the overall philosophy of the guidelines. The guidelines might
> then give a non-exclusive list of specific aggravating and
> mitigating factors that are based on this rationale.[46]

The commission, however, did not wish to go so far. It decided, instead, on a compromise. The guidelines would, in addition to prohibiting the use of factors relating to race and social status, provide a *nonexclusive* list of permissible aggravating and mitigating factors. It would not, however, furnish any general principles to guide judges in deciding on additional grounds for departure. The commission listed the following factors:[47]

Aggravating factors:

- Victim vulnerability, where that was known or should have been known by the offender
- Victim treated with particular cruelty
- Victim injured, and a prior felony conviction also involving injury
- Offense was a "major" economic or drug offense.

Mitigating factors:

- Victim was the aggressor in the incident
- Offender played a minor or passive role or became involved under circumstances of coercion or duress
- Offender lacked substantial capacity for judgment because of physical or mental impairment
- Other substantial grounds tending to excuse or mitigate the offender's culpability, although not amounting to a complete defense.

This is a short list. Perhaps the fact that the list is designed to be suggestive and nonexclusive permitted its brevity.

The list accords generally with a desert rationale. Most of the factors relate to the harm involved in the current offense or to the actor's culpability in committing it. Prior criminal record is introduced only to a limited extent, in aggravating factors relating to victim injury and economic or drug crimes. None of the factors constitutes predictions of future good or bad behavior, as is the case in some other jurisdictions.[48] The list might thus be read as suggesting that departures from the ranges should normally be based on desert grounds—that is, based on the greater or lesser harm or culpability than is normal for the offense.

How successful has the commission's compromise been? Generally, the Minnesota Supreme Court has followed the apparent rationale of the listed aggravating and mitigating factors by overruling departures from the guidelines based on the offender's dangerousness, need for treatment, or the like. As noted in chapter 3, however, there has been one conspicuous exception: the supreme court has accepted "amenability" or "unamenability" to probation as an additional mitigating or aggravating factor—although this has little or no bearing upon the blameworthiness of the offender's criminal conduct.[49] The result has been, contrary to the commission's original intent, to increase the number of property offenders given prison terms and the number of offenders against the person given nonprison dispositions (see chapter 8). Had the guidelines set forth general principles on the grounds of departure, this outcome might have been avoided.

How Much to Limit Judicial Discretion

In adopting its presumptive-sentence ranges, the commission imposed substantial limits upon judicial discretion. There were, however, a number of important decisions to be faced on just how extensive the control over that discretion should be.

The enabling statute, in addition to requiring the commission to develop guidelines on whether to imprison and on duration of prison sentences, states that the commission "may also establish appropriate sanctions for offenders for whom imprisonment is not proper."[50] Unfortunately, the commission has not exercised this power. In March 1982 the Criminal Justice Committee of the state House of Representatives adopted a resolution requesting the commission to report on the feasibility of developing an additional grid for nonprison dispositions. Such a project, however, has never got under way. Where the guidelines prescribe a sentence other than prison, there are no standards on whether that sentence should be a jail term or a sentence to probation. A recent commission report suggests that considerable disparity persists in this area, and the state still lacks a policy on when jail terms are appropriate and when lesser sanctions are.[51]

Where a prison sentence is prescribed, the Minnesota guidelines call for a specified number of months' confinement, and a range surrounding that number. The ranges are narrow—usually about 5 to 8 percent above and below the midpoint—compared with the maximum permissible variation of 15 percent above and below.[52] The narrowness of the ranges, among other things, facilitated the commission's population projections. The expected variations were small enough to permit an estimate of how long offenders convicted of various crimes were likely to serve. A range of as much as 15 percent above and below the midpoint would have impeded the making of reliable estimates (see chapter 6).

A final decision before the commission was the strictness of the presumption in favor of the normal ranges—or in other words, the burden that had to be sustained for departures. Incapacitatively oriented guidelines could require little or no leeway for departures. Historically it has been claimed that judges need wide discretion in order to determine which defendants constitute higher risks, but this claim seems erroneous. If, according to the available prediction tables, a defendant is in a given risk category, he or she could be given the disposition which the guidelines deem appropriate to that level of risk. Little attention might have to be given to individual circumstances that ostensibly bear upon a defendant's likelihood of recidivism, since such clinical estimates of risk tend not to enhance the accuracy of the statistical forecast.[53]

Departures become more important, however, when a sentencing scheme emphasizes desert. A presumptive sentencing system such as Minnesota's takes various crime categories, assigns seriousness ratings to them, and then prescribes recommended penalties ostensibly commensurate with those levels of seriousness. Yet, inevitably, there will be variations in blameworthiness among individual cases within those crime categories. To the extent there are, the principle of commensurate deserts calls for deviation from the normally prescribed sentence. This means the guidelines should authorize variations from the presumptive sentence on account of aggravation and mitigation. There need to be significant constraints on these variations, however; otherwise the guidelines become little more than precatory.

The commission opted for a seemingly stringent standard for departure: the normal guideline range must be imposed unless the individual case involves *substantial* and *compelling* circumstances, explained by the judge in writing.[54] The standard has, however, afforded a measure of flexibility in practice. Departures from the ranges have been occurring at a rate somewhat under 10 percent as far as the choice of whether or not to imprison is concerned (see chapter 8).

CHAPTER 6

The Sentencing Commission's Empirical Research

Kay A. Knapp

To write and maintain its guidelines, the sentencing commission must undertake certain empirical research.[1] Experience suggests that guidelines written without adequate and timely empirical support are likely to fail.[2] Four main research areas are involved.

- A study of preguideline sentencing patterns is needed, so that existing sentencing practices can be compared with the new policies proposed in the guidelines—to see how much change the latter involves. To that end, the offense and offender variables used in the study should reflect characteristics relied upon, or likely to be relied upon, in the proposed guidelines.
- A study of the impact of the guidelines on correctional resources (particularly, prison populations) is required. If the guidelines' sentencing policy would exceed the available resources, and if additional resources cannot be provided in timely fashion, the policy cannot be implemented as written.
- Baseline data need to be obtained as the guidelines are being written, to facilitate the commission's evaluation of the guidelines' effects on sentencing practice after they are implemented.
- An information system should be established to enable the commission continuously to monitor the guidelines' use.

These four areas represent the minimum empirical study required for a successful guideline system, and they need to be addressed by the commission itself. Other research on the guidelines, their impact, and effects can be undertaken by outside researchers.

Kay A. Knapp

The Study of Preguideline Practice

To reach a destination, it helps to know where one is starting from. That, in essence, is the reason for the preguideline practice study: it tells the commission what present sentencing patterns are so the commission can know how much change in policy the guidelines would represent.

In the early 1970s "descriptive" guidelines were briefly in vogue and were used in judicially generated standards in a number of jurisdictions.[3] Because such guidelines were designed to reflect current sentencing patterns, a multivariate analysis of existing practice was required, which identified the factors most closely associated with sentencing decisions and determined the weights accorded those factors.

Guideline development has now come to be understood as a normative process, however (see chapter 1). It involves decisions about what *should* be the state's sentencing policy, not merely what the sentencing patterns happen to be today. The function of empirical research on current practice has therefore changed. It is not to "explain" that practice in order to incorporate it into explicit policy. Rather, it is to show what *changes* the new policy would involve. Knowing how much change is involved is essential for the commission to be able to assess how easy or difficult it will be to put the proposed policy into practice. Moreover, the first question likely to be posed when the proposed guidelines are made public is, How will the guidelines alter what courts do now? The commission needs to be able to identify the nature and extent of any change so that it can explain why it is desirable.

The key design feature in such a study is inclusion of the variables incorporated, or likely to be incorporated, in the guidelines themselves. Every individual offender included in the study should be scored according to the criteria in the guidelines—so that the sentences called for by the guidelines can be compared with those which would have been imposed in similar cases before.

In Minnesota the guidelines' principal variables were the offense score, which scaled the seriousness of the current conviction offense, and a criminal history score, which rated the number of prior felony and misdemeanor convictions. The commission's study therefore measured preguideline practice according to these same variables, enabling a comparison to be made. One could then say how long a sentence defendants with serious current crimes and short criminal records—or with lesser current crimes and long records—would be likely to be given before and after the guidelines were implemented. These data revealed that the guidelines, if implemented as written, would shift the emphasis from the offender's previous criminal record to the seriousness of his or her current crime (see chapter 5).

Existing data sets are unlikely to include the criminal history measures and the offense differentiations proposed in the guidelines. A separate data collection effort from court files and presentence investigation reports generally is necessary. The data collection effort ordinarily would have to begin before the guidelines' criteria are finally decided upon, so that the elements to be included will have to be based on speculation regarding the final policy. The variables used in the study need to be overinclusive in order to cover the various policy options before the commission.

The study of preguideline practice should encompass at least a year of that practice, so that it is not biased by seasonal variations. The period should be reasonably current—otherwise the pre- versus postguideline comparison will be invalid because the study has measured practices that were disappearing. Generally, a period shortly before the commission begins its work is suitable. It gives time for the study to be conducted and still assures that the data represent genuine preguideline practice, that is, that judges are not yet changing their behavior to anticipate what they expect to be contained in the guidelines.

The sample will need to be stratified to ensure that adequate numbers of cases are included on all relevant factors. Obvious candidates for stratification include offense, criminal history, gender, and race. Infrequently occurring offenses may have to be oversampled, if those types of conduct are important to the commission. On the other hand, a relatively small sample of cases will provide representation for an offense type that occurs fairly frequently and varies little among cases.

Geography is another candidate for stratification. Two obvious geographical concerns are regional representation and district size representation. At a minimum it is desirable to represent every region and every category of size. In some states, regional sentencing patterns vary considerably so that the proposed new policy represents a greater change for some regions than others. The commission needs to be aware of such differences, so that it can target its persuasive efforts on the representatives of the regions most affected.

Policy concerns may also dictate oversampling females in order to determine the impact of the guidelines on them. Correctional resources are often gender-specific, requiring an adequate analysis of the guidelines' impact on correctional resources for women. It may also be necessary to oversample other racial, ethnic, or social groups.

Because the data in the preguideline sentencing practice study must serve the multiple purposes of describing existing practice, supporting impact analysis, and serving as a baseline for evaluating sentencing guidelines, the size of the sample generally needs to be larger than it would be if any single purpose were being served. The size of the sample will be determined in part by how much information seems necessary for these various purposes and by the variability likely to be found when the sample is stratified. Generally, the more the variability, the larger the sample must be.

The analysis of the data, once collected, need not be complicated. The data tend in any case to be too crude for sophisticated analytic methods, and a simple model will be easier for commission members to understand and work with. Whereas "descriptive" guidelines might require an analytic model that fits the data as closely as possible, the type of guidelines discussed here require only an understandable general picture of existing practice with which the proposed policy can be compared.[4] Simple descriptive statistics and bivariate displays of data should generally suffice for most questions. The difficulty is obtaining the data on the relevant offense and offender characteristics, not analyzing the data once they have been obtained.

The Study of the Guidelines' Impact on Correctional Resources

The commission must examine the effect of its proposed guidelines on correctional resources, particularly prison populations. The reasons why have been described already (chapters 1 and 5). Such an impact study will give the commission a sense of its realistic options by informing it of how much imprisonment it has at its disposal to allocate. With such information, it can begin to decide priorities. Should the available prison space be used principally for those with serious current crimes or for those with extensive records? Should such a finite resource be used to imprison more offenders for longer periods or fewer offenders for shorter periods? Do existing prison facilities suffice to imprison those whom the commission urgently feels ought to be confined, and if not, how much additional space should the commission recommend that the legislature finance? If such a recommendation is made, the legislature can be informed of what it is "buying" by funding additional space and can better compare that with competing claims in such areas as health, education, highways, and parks. Regardless of whether it is eventually decided that prison populations be maintained, expanded, or reduced, such impact analysis can make decisions more rational.

Such a study assumes that policy drives prison populations. While crime and conviction rates may fluctuate, officials decide how much prison space there is—and the kinds of offenders who occupy that space. There are no more prison cells than the legislature and correctional authorities decide to build; no one is confined in those cells except by decisions of sentencing judges, decisions which it is the commission's role to guide. The purpose of the study is to aid in making such decisions.

Given this assumption, projections of impact are not predictions about what has already been determined and is waiting to unfold. The projections are, instead, policy-based contingency statements taking the form: "if the guidelines direct X should occur, then Y amount of prison space is called for." If, for example, the commission amends its proposed guidelines to raise the seriousness-rating assigned to armed robbery, a given increase in the number of months armed robbers serve may be anticipated; and such an increase—considering the number of convicted armed robbers—will have such-and-such an impact on the use of prison resources.

In making projections, it will probably be better to engage in multiple projections or simulations with different scenarios than to choose one scenario and project on that basis alone. Suppose, for example, that the commission is deciding the guideline for imposition of consecutive sentences. It will need an impact projection for each option it is considering in order to estimate the respective use of prison space. Some options, moreover, may leave sentencing judges a residue of choice—for example, discretion on the imposition of concurrent versus consecutive sentences. The researchers should project the likely effects of judges' exercising that discretion sparingly, more regularly, or as frequently as permitted. Such multiple scenarios will give the commission a better sense of what its realistic policy choices are.

The projections of impact should be for a short term—perhaps for the ensuing year or two. The system will continue to change. Its inputs (that is, the frequency of convictions for various crimes) cannot be expected to remain stable over long periods, nor can the legal definitions within which the guidelines operate. However, the potential impact of long prison terms should also be considered.

The projections themselves are not so difficult to make. One needs a data set that distributes offenders across the relevant offense and offender characteristics—that is, a data set such as the one used for the preguideline-practice study. The projections are then made by simple modeling techniques using probabilities.

The Minnesota Sentencing Guidelines Commission developed such a projection model. It used micro-level data—that is, data on individual offenders—obtained from the preguideline-practice data set. For example, an offender convicted of armed robbery with no prior record would, under a given proposed guideline, be assigned an 80 percent probability of being sentenced to prison and a 20 percent probability of receiving probation. (These would be the estimated probabilities, were prison made the presumptive sentence and a 20 percent dispositional departure rate assumed.) The case would then be fractionalized into two parts. The "prison part"— that is, .80 of the case, including such personal characteristics as sex, race, and age—would be routed through the prison part of the model. The "probation part"—that is, the remaining .20 of the case—would be routed through the probation part of the model. There, further probabilities would be specified as the case moved forward, including work release, supervised release, and the probability of probation revocations. The length of time spent at each status point would be specified. Individual characteristics associated with a case are thus maintained throughout the system, with the fractions aggregated at various outcome points.

The Minnesota commission examined the impact on prison populations of virtually all of its major decisions. Particular attention was paid to the impact of its two most important decisions: the slope of its dispositional line, and the durations of imprisonment (see chapter 5). Other policies, such as the criminal history score computations, consecutive sentencing, probation revocations, and sentences for attempts and conspiracies, were also informed by impact analysis. The commission decided to write guidelines that would fit within 95 percent of the prison capacity of 2,072 beds. Population projections indicated that under the guidelines finally adopted, the average prison population would be between 1,943 and 1,982. These projections proved quite near the mark when the guidelines began to be implemented (see chapter 8).

The one prerequisite for making such projections is significant limits on sentencing discretion. The Minnesota commission could make reasonably accurate projections because guideline ranges were narrow, the dispositional line firm, and authority to depart from the guidelines limited. With broad ranges such as these in Pennsylvania's guidelines or New York's proposed guidelines, projections would be almost impossible to make with any degree of accuracy.[5]

Designing the Evaluation Research

After the guidelines are adopted, their effects on sentencing practice need to be evaluated. The groundwork for such evaluation studies should be laid early, while the guidelines are being written. As the evaluation will compare preguideline practice with practice after the guidelines take effect, the data base concerning preguideline practice must be adequate for the purpose. To avoid possible duplication of data-collecting effort, it is best to consider the design for the evaluation study simultaneously with the design for the study of preguideline practice. To some extent, the evaluation issues will be specific to the type of guideline system chosen, depending on its goals. There are, however, several topics that should be covered.

Implementation of New Sentencing Policies The guidelines probably will, in one respect or another, establish a new policy for sentencing. That new policy will involve changes of varying extent and type from preguideline practice. The most important topic of the evaluation, then, is to examine whether the intended changes are, indeed, occurring. Does postguideline practice implement the new policy embodied in the guidelines, or is there a reversion to sentencing practice before the guidelines?

Minnesota's most important policy change, designated "proportionality," involved giving more emphasis in sentencing to the seriousness of the current crime. In its evaluation the Minnesota commission found that in the initial stage of implementation this shift of emphasis was being realized: a much larger proportion of persons convicted of serious crimes were being imprisoned, and a correspondingly increased proportion of those convicted of lesser crimes were receiving nonprison sentences. In later years, however, these proportions have been changing, suggesting a regression toward preguideline practice. (These findings, and their implications, are discussed more fully in chapters 2 and 8.)

Disparity   A common goal of sentencing guidelines is reduction of disparity. As discussed at some length in chapter 1, however, disparity cannot be defined without a specification of rationale—for it is that rationale that identifies which factors in the sentence should and should not be permitted to vary. Prior to guideline implementation, an explicit sentencing policy is usually missing. The lack of explicit policy, coupled with multiple sentencing goals (including rehabilitation, incapacitation, deterrence, and desert), create a situation in which almost any sentence could be justified.

Once the commission has established a rationale and defined its policy goals, however, "disparity" becomes definable. It consists of unwarranted variation in factors which, under the applicable rationale, should remain constant. On a rationale emphasizing desert, for example, the concern over disparity should focus on how much variation there is in the disposition of offenders whose criminal conduct is of similar gravity. An analysis of how such variation may be assessed has been supplied in a recent article by one of my co-authors, and I need not rehearse the details here.[6]

In a state such as Minnesota, where the principal dimensions of the guidelines are the gravity of the current crime and the extent of the criminal record, a study of disparity can use the same data base as the study of preguideline practice. The question to be addressed is how much variation in dispositions exists that cannot be accounted for by the seriousness of the current crime and the extent of the criminal record.

Prosecutorial Practice   An evaluation of changes in prosecutorial charging and negotiating practice is needed. It is of particular importance when the guideline sentence is based on the offense of conviction rather than on alleged behavior (sometimes called "total" or "real" offense behavior). Sentencing guidelines generally replace an indeterminate sentencing system in which there is wide latitude to consider unadjudicated behavior in deciding the sentence. Charging and negotiating patterns under an indeterminate system often include charge reductions which are essentially bogus, in the sense that the reduction does not affect the disposition of the case. Reducing an armed robbery charge to an unarmed robbery charge matters little if the sentencing judge can and will consider the allegation of gun use in setting sentence. When the conviction offense determines the guideline sentence and unadjudicated elements cannot be used at sentencing, however, charge reductions result in reduced sentences. The prosecutor has more power to affect the sentence, and charge reductions are more visible in their effects. (These possible impacts are examined more fully in chapter 9.) The different results that can occur from given prosecutorial practice before and after implementation of the guidelines suggest that practice may well change once the guidelines take effect. To make such an evaluation, the commission will require baseline data on initial charges and charge dispositions.

Prison Populations   In the evaluation, the accuracy of the projections of impact on prison populations should be ascertained. If added prison space is not expected to become available, unanticipated rises in the prison population may call for changes in the guidelines. As discussed in chapter 8, the Minnesota evaluation efforts have continually examined changes in populations over time.

Case Processing   Issues of case processing emerge at several points. The proportion of cases that go to trial is probably the most significant such issue: the concern is often stated that guidelines will result in more trials, since the certainty of the guideline sentence reduces the defendant's incentive to plead guilty. The evaluation can determine whether, and to what extent, such an increase is occurring. A second processing issue is the length of time it takes following conviction to compile the information needed for sentencing. Guidelines generally do not require more information for sentencing than is required under an indeterminate system, but information about the offender's crime, criminal record, and other relevant variables needs to be more carefully verified. A third issue is the number and proportion of sentences appealed and the length of time between filing and judgment. The baseline data must include processing times and method of case disposition for the commission to evaluate these issues.

The Monitoring System

The monitoring system is an information system which follows each case and registers the charges, the relevant offense and offender characteristics, and the disposition. It is a continuous source of data on how judges are applying the guidelines. Normally, the monitoring system should use the same forms as those relied upon in the actual sentencing process. The probation officer or other person responsible for calculating the guideline sentence for the judge's consideration can then, with little additional effort or risk of inaccuracy, supply the same information to the commission for monitoring purposes. The monitoring system serves a number of purposes:

- It continually informs the commission of sentencing practice under the guidelines. By doing so, it can enable the commission to identify problem areas. An increased rate of departure for a particular kind of case, for example, may suggest the need for amendments that either change the guideline norm to make that disposition appropriate within the guidelines or that reaffirm the existing norm and make it clear that frequent departures are inappropriate.
- It helps rectify errors in applying the guidelines. The monitoring system, by permitting commission staff to calculate the appropriate guideline sentences, can flag calculation errors in individual cases. The commission then can inform those involved of the errors and seek rectification.
- It provides the data on postguideline practice for the evaluations the commission wishes to conduct.
- It can be of assistance in training probation officers in how to calculate guideline sentences.
- It enables the commission to answer queries from the legislature, corrections department, judiciary, prosecution, defense, or the media concerning the operation of the guidelines. That service may be of assistance in maintaining support for the guidelines.

It should now be apparent that much of the work in designing empirical research—research that will support the commission's efforts for years to come—had best be accomplished in the initial stages of developing the guidelines. The study of preguideline sentencing practices, in particular, must carry a heavy burden in that it must support the formulation of guideline policy, the analysis of the impact on correctional resources, and the evaluation of the guidelines after implementation. Accomplishing this empirical research is not an easy task, given the time constraints within which the commission ordinarily must work. Failure to accomplish the research, however, bodes ill for the guidelines' future.

CHAPTER 7

Organization and Staffing

Kay A. Knapp

The staffs of existing state sentencing commissions are frequently queried by legislators and planners in other jurisdictions who are considering sentencing guideline proposals. The most common inquiries relate to the composition and organization of the commission and to its staffing and funding. There is probably no "best" configuration for organizing and staffing a state guidelines commission. A number of patterns and compositions can work, depending on local political constraints and the talent available to do the task. My purpose here is to share information about organizational and staffing issues based on the Minnesota experience and that of several other states that have developed guidelines or have attempted to do so.[1]

The Composition of the Commission

The size of the sentencing commission and the manner of choosing its members are commonly specified in the enabling statute. The appointment procedure should resemble that followed for other independent rule-making bodies. Usually members are nominated by the chief executive, with senatorial advice and consent.

Membership

Three models of commission membership—a judicial model, an elite model, and a representative model—have been discussed in the literature on sentencing commissions.[2] A judicial model of membership would contain only judges and is the model that was used in the development of several descriptive sentencing guideline projects in the 1970s.[3] Since judges play a central role in the sentencing process, a commission composed of judges might have more credibility with the judiciary than one composed differently. It risks, however, becoming unduly deferential to judges' sensitivities about restrictions on their discretion.

The judiciary is not the only actor in sentencing. Prosecutors and defense attorneys play a critical role. Corrections officials need to have input to ensure that the sentencing policy can operate within available correctional resources. To exclude such other actors, and rely only on the judiciary, risks narrowing the commission's perspective excessively.

A second possibility is an elite model, in which the commission would be composed of highly authoritative experts. Such a commission might include criminologists, political scientists, and jurists drawn from the universities, foundations, and private practice. Such a commission might bring more imagination to the task, being less socialized to current institutions. The independence and autonomy that comes with an elite membership, however, also means that the members are less likely to appreciate institutional needs and constraints and would have less credibility among criminal justice groups which must implement the policy. It also may be difficult to find an entire slate of acceptable elite members that would be willing to serve. Although it might be desirable to include some experts—some commissions have a member who is an academic criminologist or legal scholar—an entire commission of experts seldom seems feasible or desirable. The necessary expertise can largely be obtained by using consultants from inside and outside the state and by hiring staff with specific areas of relevant knowledge.

The third possibility—a more representative membership structure—has been the model utilized by the state sentencing commissions established by law to date. Even in Florida, where the sentencing commission began as a judicially oriented structure within the judicial system, the membership became more representative when the legislature "adopted" the project. Judges, prosecutors, defense attorneys, corrections administrators, law enforcement officials, parole administrators, and private citizens are common generic categories of membership. Such a representative membership can greatly facilitate input from and involvement of the various criminal justice constituencies. Members drawn from these groups can provide practical knowledge, from a variety of perspectives, on how guidelines might be implemented and on where the potential obstacles lie. Commission members from the various criminal justice constituencies also can serve a liaison function in communicating commission policy to their groups, aiding in the work of generating support for the guidelines.[4] The disadvantage of a representative membership is the danger that a narrow interest-group perspective will emerge, with each member primarily interested in protecting his or her constituent group rather than focusing on general sentencing policy (see chapter 8 for a discussion regarding this issue in Minnesota).

While recognizing the dangers of parochialism that a representative commission membership can pose, I would recommend that model for state sentencing commissions. Those dangers can be lessened by careful selection of members who are experienced in public policy and who are not overly wedded to the status quo. The alternatives—judicial or elite models—seem less desirable for the reasons discussed.

There is general agreement that judges, prosecutors, defenders, and corrections officials should be included in a representative model. There is less agreement over the inclusion of legislators. Legislator-members can act as liaisons with the legislature and can warn the commission of political constraints. They may, however, be unable to participate as fully as other members because of the press of other business while the legislature is in session. To the extent that the rationale for a sentencing commission is the insulation of sentencing policy making from the political pressures that prevail in legislatures, moreover, appointing legislators might well be self-defeating. Ultimately, the choice to include or not to include legislators may depend on the state's political environment and culture.

The appointees—while drawn from various criminal justice constituencies—should have a background in and understanding of broader public policy. A judge or prosecutor will be a less useful member if his or her previous experience consists merely in judging or prosecuting cases and participating in that constituency's professional organization. Wider experience is called for, that which involves the formulation of law, rules, or policies. The judge or prosecutor will be a better member if he or she has previously worked with members of other criminal justice constituencies in formulating and seeing through to adoption a major legislative proposal or a set of rules. The commission should not have to provide on-the-job training in practical civics.

Size

The size of the commission depends to some extent on how many interests it is deemed important to represent. The commission must be of manageable size, however, in terms of both scheduling commission activities and having a small enough group that the members can grapple with issues and work with each other. It is not necessary to create a mini-legislature to obtain the knowledge and experience of major segments of the criminal justice system, and it would probably be well to sacrifice some representation in order to have a manageable working group. The commissions have ranged in size from approximately nine to fifteen. Probably anything over eleven members is too large to be manageable, and fewer members than seven is too small to provide the knowledge, experience, and representation needed. Most of the commissions have four-year terms with staggered membership so that there is some continuity over time.

Part-Time or Full-Time?

Sentencing commission members at the state level have all been part-time. Members are reimbursed for travel expenses by the commission and generally receive a per diem payment if they are not already government employees. The chairperson is usually designated by the appointing authority—that is, the governor. The chair may have specific authorities, such as calling meetings, signing contracts, and accepting and expending funds.

There would be some value to having a full-time chairman at least during the development and initial implementation stages. The tasks of generating support for the guidelines are substantial and are better performed by commission members than staff. It may be difficult, however, to find someone of the right experience and stature who would be willing to leave his or her current work to chair a commission full-time. One possibility would be to recruit a respected retired judge or prosecutor or a retired citizen (for example, a former newspaper editor) who would be willing to take on the challenge. It would probably not be wise, however, to trade experience and stature for the sake of full-time status.

Frequency of Meetings

The meeting schedule for a commission varies with the task at hand. The usual schedule tends to be one meeting a month. During the writing of the guidelines, particularly in the latter stages when most of the decision making occurs, commissions tend to meet more frequently, such as every two weeks. Establishing subcommittees with frequent meetings has worked well during periods of intense analysis and decision making. This method enables staff to perform the necessary analysis and still receive frequent input and direction from commission members. Also helpful during periods of intense work are one- or two-day work retreats for staff and commission members.

In addition to regularly scheduled meetings to take care of commission business, commission members need to interact regularly in order to establish and maintain the necessary esprit de corps. As I discuss in chapter 8, constituent groups compete with the commission for the loyalty of its members. Commission meetings should be as frequent as can be justified by meaningful activity. Time for informal interaction, such as dinners together before or after commission meetings, provides an opportunity for members to get to know one another better and share information which may not surface in a more formal setting.

Staffing and Funding

Staffing

With the exception of that of the New York commission, the staffing configurations of the commission during the writing of guidelines were very similar. Staff positions included an executive director, a research director, an administrative assistant, a secretary, and research assistants. The specific responsibilities of each staff position varied somewhat among the commissions, depending on the particular skills of those filling the positions. Generally, however, the executive director exercised responsibility for general administration of the agency and organized commission meetings, the research director dealt with the empirical research, and the rest of the staff worked with one director or both of them. This configuration covers two of the three major areas—administration and empirical research—needing staff. The third area is policy analysis; like the commission members themselves, senior staff must have an understanding of policy development and the political process. These individuals should have previous experience—as participants, staff, or consultants—in the formulation of legislation or of agency rules.

The staffs of state sentencing commissions have primarily come from social science fields—in particular, political science and criminal justice—and have generally had some training in social science methodology. Political science training is more likely to be accompanied by sensitivity to policy and political process, whereas criminal justice training provides a good substantive background. Lawyers have not been recruited to staff state sentencing commissions except in New York and Florida. Most state criminal codes and sentencing provisions are fairly straightforward and do not require special training or expertise to understand. The Minnesota criminal code, for example, can be perused in an afternoon, leaving the reader with a good understanding of felony crimes and sentencing provisions. On the rare occasions that legal research is needed on specific issues that arise, attorney-general staffs or law clerks have been consulted. This approach allows full-time commission positions to be filled with staff possessing more general substantive, methodological, and policy analysis skills.

In chapter 6, I outlined the empirical research which the commission needs to undertake. The staff should possess the empirical and methodological skills to perform these tasks. Without such skills, crucial work—such as estimating the impact of the proposed guidelines on prison populations—cannot properly be undertaken. The research director, particularly, needs such qualifications.

New York's experience illustrates the hazards of not having an adequate research capability. It took approximately six months to hire a research director, and there were subsequent turnovers in research directors because of various difficulties. Ultimately a descriptive study was made of judicial sentence dispositions that included about one-sixth of the approximately 33,000 felony convictions sentenced in 1983. Existing data sets were used to estimate the duration of sentence. The durational study did not have good measures for classifying cases according to the criteria selected by the sentencing commission. Very late in the writing of the guidelines, a model was developed to simulate the impact of the proposals on correctional resources. The data that had been collected, however, were viewed by many as insufficient from which to project the impact on correctional resources. South Carolina had comparable difficulties. There was staff turnover in the research director position, and it took approximately a year before the research effort became well organized. Eventually, an adequate study of previous sentencing practice was developed, but delays in completing research findings required the commission to postpone decision making for significant periods of time, causing loss of momentum and allowing time for opposition to solidify against the guideline effort.

Once the guidelines have been written and take effect, staffing needs may change. There will be less intensive drafting work, but the empirical tasks may increase as the guidelines' implementation is evaluated and the monitoring system put into operation (see chapter 6). Training the probation officers to calculate the normally applicable sentence in individual cases for a judge's consideration will become an important function. Some continuity in staff, as well as in commission members, should be encouraged. As I shall discuss at greater length in chapter 8, maintaining the conceptual integrity and momentum of the guidelines over time is perhaps the most difficult task of all.

Funding

The funding for establishing a sentencing commission and instituting its guidelines has varied significantly, depending upon the budget of the state. The allocation for the New York sentencing commission for the first full year (1984–85) was $900,000, of which the commission expended approximately $830,000. The budget for South Carolina, on the other hand, was much smaller, and relied on federal grants as well as state-appropriated funds. The South Carolina commission had approximately $120,000 for 1982–83 in the form of a grant from the National Institute of Corrections. The budget was approximately $104,000 in 1983–84, the funds of which were equally contributed by the National Institute of Corrections and the state. The 1984–85 budget was funded with a state appropriation of approximately $158,000.

The allocations in the state of Washington were $391,000 for the 1981–83 biennium and $558,000 for the 1983–85 biennium. The commission in Minnesota was allocated approximately $200,000 per year in 1979, 1980, 1981, and 1982. The annual allocation dropped to approximately $150,000 in 1983, 1984, and 1985. In addition, the Minnesota commission received several grants—including a $12,500 grant from the National Institute of Corrections to aid in the development of a prison population projection model, a $65,000 grant from the same agency to aid in the evaluation of the sentencing guidelines, and approximately $100,000 in grants from the MacArthur Foundation to supplement the guideline evaluation study. The annual appropriation for the Pennsylvania commission was approximately $200,000 from 1979 through 1984. The Florida commission expends approximately $130,000 a year.

These figures do not represent a total picture of the costs of running a commission. For example, the Florida commission obtained much of its computer and data processing support from the state court administrator's office, and those costs are not budgeted by the commission. Similarly, the South Carolina commission received computer support from the University of South Carolina at little or no cost, and "rap sheets" were provided gratis by law enforcement offices during data collection. The Pennsylvania commission is housed in the Pennsylvania State University campus and receives substantial support from the university, including data-processing support and office space. Increasingly, even large data analysis projects are being processed on microcomputers—and in the future, commission budgets will undoubtedly include more computer hardware and less purchasing of processing time than was the case several years ago. That trend also means that there will be less opportunity to accept computer support from universities and other agencies.

The major proportion of the budgets (approximately two-thirds) are for personnel costs for staffing the commission. The remainder of the budget is used for various administrative costs, including printing, data processing, office space, travel, and meeting expenses. The size of the staffs during guideline development varied along the order of the budgets. The New York commission had approximately twenty-two full-time employees and approximately twenty temporary data coders. The South Carolina commission had a staff of three full-time and several part-time employees. The Washington and Pennsylvania commissions had approximately five and a half full-time employees during development and the Minnesota commission had seven. All three staffs were supplemented with temporary coders for data collection.

A sentencing commission is only as good as its personnel. The best-drafted enabling act and the most generous funding will not help if competent and committed individuals are not recruited for the commission and its staff. A big budget did not save New York's commission, because the members became more concerned with representing their various constituencies than with agreeing upon a workable policy and because of continuing turnover and difficulty in staffing (see chapters 2 and 4). Washington and Minnesota were more successful in writing workable guidelines, despite much smaller budgets, in part because the commission members were able to work together to produce a common policy and had the requisite staff support.

PART 3

The Implementation of Guidelines

Implementation of the Minnesota Guidelines: Can the Innovative Spirit Be Preserved?

Kay A. Knapp

The Minnesota Sentencing Guidelines, which became effective May 1, 1980, have been hailed as innovative and successful. The primary goals were to increase uniformity and proportionality in sentencing. In order to achieve these objectives, it was necessary to adopt the additional goal of coordinating sentencing policy with correctional resources, because proportionality and uniformity cannot be achieved unless adequate resources exist to implement the sentencing guidelines as written.

The preliminary evaluation of the Minnesota Sentencing Guidelines revealed considerable success in achieving the stated goals.[1] In 1981 there was a 6.2 percent "dispositional" departure rate (that is, a departure from the guidelines' presumptions of who should go to prison and who should not). This was a significant increase in uniformity: during the preguideline period, approximately 17–18 percent of dispositions differed from that which the guidelines would have prescribed had they been in effect. Sentencing practice in 1981 substantially conformed also to the stated policy of sending to prison more offenders against the person and fewer property offenders. There was a 73 percent increase in imprisonment of offenders convicted of high-seriousness crimes who had low criminal histories, and there was a corresponding 72 percent reduction in imprisonment of offenders convicted of low-seriousness crimes who had moderate to high criminal histories. Prison populations remained within the state's prison capacity of 2,072 beds during 1980 and 1981, with commitments close to the level projected.

The next stage of program life—institutionalization—is seldom documented as thoroughly as a program's initial stages. That is unfortunate because it is the program as institutionalized that will eventually have the greatest effect. The reality of the institutionalized program tends to differ from the programs as launched,

Seymour Sarason warns.[2] A RAND Corporation study notes that most criminal justice innovations change over time as they are adapted to their institutional environment and that initial characteristics of the innovation itself rarely provide useful information about ultimate success.[3]

The Minnesota Sentencing Guidelines have entered the institutionalized stage. They have become a major feature of felony processing in the state. The sentencing guidelines commission has substantial influence in the legislature on criminal justice matters. As of 1985 three additional years of data on sentencing practices under the guidelines have been amassed, and four additional years of policy decisions have occurred since the preliminary evaluation of the guidelines. Recent sentencing practices indicate less success in achieving the goals of sentence uniformity and proportionality than was the case initially.[4] Sentence uniformity and proportionality also have not been stressed as much in recent policy decisions of the commission. While developments are still too recent to provide a definitive answer to the nature of the institutionalized guidelines, the following review of sentencing practice and of the current setting can provide clues.

Sentencing Practice, 1982–1984

Proportionality in Sentencing

During the first year, as just noted, Minnesota largely achieved the goal of reserving imprisonment for more serious offenders and using nonprison sanctions for offenses assigned low seriousness ratings (such as routine property offenses). Sentencing practices have, however, been shifting toward preguideline patterns in the later years. An increasing proportion of commitments to prison during 1982–84 were of property offenders; and a concomitant decreasing proportion of commitments were of offenders against the person. In 1981, 37 percent of offenders committed to prison were property offenders. In 1982 the percentage increased to 43; and in 1983 and 1984 it increased further to 50. The last percentage is similar to the 47 percent of property offenders committed to prison before the guidelines were implemented. The percentage of commitments for person offenses has similarly diminished. In 1981 the rate of commitments for person offenses was 57 percent. The rate was 50 percent in 1982 and 43 percent in 1983 and 1984, contrasted with a 39 percent prior to implementation of the guidelines.

Several factors contributed to this change. One was a change in prosecutorial practice. Prosecutors began bringing multiple charges against common property offenders and dismissing fewer of those charges, which resulted in higher criminal history scores and therefore more presumptive commitments.[5] Prosecutors apparently began "targeting" to the dispositional line in 1982. The guidelines ordinarily presume nonimprisonment for offenses having a seriousness-rating of 4 on the grid's ten-point seriousness scale, such as commercial burglary. Because the dispositional line slopes more steeply on the right-hand portion of the grid (as discussed in chapter 5), however, a prison sentence is presumed once the offender accumulates a criminal history score of 4 (that is, has four prior felonies or an equivalent number of misdemeanors). Under the scoring system, each concurrently obtained felony conviction counts for a point. Prosecutors thus can target to the imprisonment side of the dispositional line by obtaining separate convictions for several burglaries rather than just one in cases where the offender is charged with multiple burglaries, thereby increasing the offender's criminal history score toward a level that would provide for presumptive imprisonment.

Another contributing factor has been that the courts are finding aggravating factors present in property crime cases and are departing from the standard range to impose a prison sentence. Such "aggravated dispositional departures" occurred in 1981 at a rate of only 3.1 percent. They rose, however, to 3.5 percent in 1982, 4.5 percent in 1983, and 4.0 percent in 1984. Because of Minnesota's relatively low rate of imprisonment (approximately 20 percent of all convicted felons), a change in this departure rate of 1 or 2 percent can have a substantial impact on the number of prison commitments. For example, the difference from 1981 to 1983 of 1.4 percent in aggravated dispositional departures constitutes approximately eighty additional commitments to prison. With approximately one thousand annual commitments, the eighty additional commitments results in an 8 percent increase.

A third contributor has been some defendants' own preference for prison sentences over a nonprison sanction. A short prison sentence may be less onerous than a nonprison punishment—which can include incarceration for up to a year in a local jail or workhouse, restitution, community service, treatment, and long periods of probationary supervision, all at the discretion of the judge. The case law has supported defendants' requests to have their sentences "executed" (that is, to be committed to prison), in effect requiring the judge to depart from the applicable presumptive sentence.[6] Such departures numbered 38 in 1981, 73 in 1982, 111 in 1983, and 86 in 1984.

This last group of cases, where property offenders are imprisoned at their own request, can be viewed from another perspective, however. The policy underlying the guidelines is one that (1) assumes that imprisonment is the system's most severe sanction, and (2) calls for that sanction's use primarily for offenses having the higher seriousness ratings. The assumption about the greater severity of imprisonment does not hold here: a short stint in prison is *less* onerous (or so defendants believe) than the possible alternative of a longer jail term. The departures thus become appropriate when judged by the guidelines' policy of punishing such property offenders less severely. As Michael Tonry suggests in chapter 2, these hundred-or-so cases per year (representing about 8 to 10 percent of the additional commitments to prison) might be viewed as constituting no real slippage. The reversion toward tougher sentences for property offenders may therefore be less marked than the departure figures indicate on their face.

There has, in addition, been an increase in departures from the guidelines *against* the presumption of imprisonment. The increase has involved cases with serious conviction offenses but a low criminal history score. Certain intrafamilial offenses have particularly been involved, as I shall discuss later.

Uniformity in Sentencing

Sentences were more uniform in 1981 than they had been prior to implementation of the guidelines. They were particularly more uniform in terms of disposition—that is, who goes to prison—with a 6.2 percent departure rate from the presumptive disposition. Dispositions in 1982, 1983, and 1984 were still more uniform than dispositions prior to the guidelines, but the level of uniformity decreased somewhat from that found in 1981. The rate of dispositional departures was 7.2 percent in 1982, 8.9 percent in 1983, and 9.9 percent in 1984. The higher departure rates reflect the increase in property offenders' going to prison and the decrease in person offenders' going to prison.

The degree of uniformity in the duration of imprisonment is more difficult to assess because no stable durational practice existed prior to the guidelines. Durational uniformity, however, appears to have increased in 1983 and 1984 in one important respect over 1981 and 1982. When the guidelines were first implemented, judges who were unused to pronouncing "real-time" sentences would, if they departed from the guidelines, extend durations to the statutory maximum sentence (for example, from a twenty-four-month presumptive sentence to up to twenty years). In very rare cases, the statutory maximum sentence was appropriate to the extraordinary degree of seriousness of the offense, but in many of the cases such severe sentences were plainly disproportionate. In *State v. Evans*, the state supreme court established a standard of double the presumptive sentence as the general limit for aggravating durational departures.[7] The average increase above the prescribed guideline sentence dropped from fifty-six months in 1981 to forty-six, twenty-eight, and twenty-five months in the ensuing three years.

Prison Populations

The guidelines as written attempt to coordinate sentencing policy with available correctional resources. During 1981 the commission's prison-population target of 95 percent of capacity was nearly achieved: populations dropped from almost 100 percent of the capacity of 2,072 beds to approximately 93 percent of capacity.

Commitments during 1982 were higher than in 1981, and prison populations increased to capacity. Projections based on the sentencing practices in 1982 indicated that if those sentencing practices continued, prison populations would continue to grow and would result in a serious crowding problem. The imprisonment of more property offenders contributed significantly to the increased prison population. In addition, in 1981 the legislature raised the mandatory minimum sentence for felonies committed with a handgun from a year and a day to three years for the first offense, and from three to five years for the second offense. This change resulted in longer prison terms for many offenders. Finally, although the crime rate was apparently decreasing, the number of offenders moving through the system increased somewhat.

The legislature and commission worked together in 1983 to avert the projected crisis in prison populations. The legislature extended the good-time statute to mandatory minimum sentences (which had previously been excluded from earning good time) so that such sentences earned one day off for every two days of good behavior. This amendment had the effect of reducing the term of imprisonment for the longer mandatory minimums passed in 1981: from three years to two years for first offense with a weapon, and from five years to three and one-third years for second or subsequent offenses. Also, the legislature established retroactivity for such durational reductions—meaning that offenders sentenced to the longer terms during the preceding year were eligible for sentence reductions, unless the sentencing judge decided to depart from the new guideline durations.

The commission also modified the guidelines in 1983, reducing sentence lengths slightly for the least serious property offenses. The commission (in conjunction with the state supreme court, which modified the rules of criminal procedure) extended jail credit to time spent confined as a condition of probation when probation was later revoked and the offender imprisoned. In addition to legislative and commission intervention, 1983 sentencing practices changed in two respects to ease the potential problem of prison crowding. First, as noted above, there were more dispositional departures toward nonprison penalties. And second, as also noted, the extent of departures from the guidelines in the duration of imprisonment substantially decreased. A 400-bed maximum security prison was also completed, but budgetary problems in the state prevented the legislature from immediately funding its operation.

Prison populations rose as high as 2,143 in 1983 but began decreasing in November 1983 when the retroactivity provision went into effect and judges began resentencing eligible inmates. Prison population dropped to 2,012 by the end of February 1984. It soon began climbing again, however, and at the end of 1985 stood at 2,235. By then the new prison had become operational with funding generated by housing Wisconsin and federal prisoners; now Wisconsin and federal prisoners are being returned to facilities elsewhere so there is enough room for the added Minnesota offenders. All in all, the guidelines have successfully ensured that prison commitments would not exceed capacity.

The Commission's Changing Role

The setting within which the guidelines operate has altered in many ways. The terms of all commissioners expired in 1982, and the commission's composition changed. Four of the original members were reappointed, five new members joined, and one member who had served for approximately a year and a half was reappointed. The member who had served as chair of the commission for the first four years was not reappointed, and another member assumed the leadership responsibilities during 1982–86. Terms expired again in 1986. As a result, yet another chairman has taken office, and only two of the original members remain. Other changes in the political setting occurred. The long-standing chairman of the senate judiciary committee failed to be reelected in 1982. The governor's office also changed hands and parties. A new commissioner of corrections was appointed; a new attorney general was elected. My examination of these changes will focus primarily on those related to the goals of the guidelines, commission roles, and commission resources.

Guideline Goals

Discussions of sentencing cannot exclude values. Value-laden issues, that emerge in almost all discussions, include merits of retributivist versus utilitarian purposes of sentencing, the amount of unstructured discretion that should exist in sentencing, and the most appropriate locations of that discretion. No single set of positions has gained ascendancy in the country, but a fairly clear resolution of the issues had evolved within the Minnesota commission during the development and initial implementation of the guidelines. That consensus was important because achievement of sentence uniformity and proportionality depends on relatively clearly articulated policies on these matters. As Seymour Sarason notes, some degree of value agreement is necessary even if it is not sufficient for successful innovation.[8] The commission's initial policies incorporated desert as the dominant purpose of sentencing, imprisonment as appropriate primarily for persons convicted of serious crimes,[9] and restriction of discretion to depart from the guidelines (see chapter 5).

Three sentencing issues have surfaced, the responses to which suggest that this agreement on values has lessened in the current commission. The first issue concerns the growing prosecutorial practice of building up the criminal history scores of property offenders so as to send such persons to prison. Several commission members favored changing guideline provisions in some way so as to preserve the initial conceptions of proportionality and of reserving scarce correctional resources for more serious offenders against the person. Options that have been considered include revising the criminal history score so that prosecutors would be unable to increase the scores of property offenders so easily through multiple charges and similar practices. For example, the number of points that accrue for property offenses occurring during a year could be limited to two. Alternatively, or additionally, the dispositional line could be redrawn to eliminate some of its steepness on the right-hand side of the grid (see chapter 5). This would mean that low-severity property offenders would have to be handled more by local correction systems (perhaps, with some jail terms) and that imprisonment could be imposed only if their records were quite extensive. Such a change might be coupled with guidelines for sanctions other than imprisonment, which the commission may develop but has not yet done.[9]

A majority of commission members were unwilling to make such changes, however. When faced with projected prison crowding, the commission proposed reduced durations for serious person offenders rather than changes in the dispositional policy that would diminish the number of property offenders imprisoned.[10] (The commission later abandoned the proposal to reduce sentences for serious offenders against persons and reduced durations only for the least serious property offenders, effective November 1, 1983.) The commission stated its intention to address criminal history scoring procedures in the beginning of 1984 so as to weight prior offenses against persons more heavily than prior property offenses and thus to establish more proportionality in the criminal history computation. When the issue was raised early in 1984, however, the commission delayed action on the matter indefinitely. As of this writing, no action has been taken to reassert the initial goal of reserving prison space for serious offenders against persons. The judge who left the commission in 1986 after eight years of service expressed concern regarding this issue in his closing remarks as a commission member and urged the commission to take remedial action.[11]

A second sentencing issue which arose in 1984 involves appropriate sentences for sexual abuse of children. The crime of first-degree sexual abuse of children is assigned a seriousness grade of eight—that is, treated as very grave. The presumptive sentence for a first offender (with a criminal history score of zero) is incarceration for forty-three months. There has been a significant increase in convictions for first-degree sexual abuse of children and a substantial increase in mitigated departures—very few offenders are receiving prison sentences in spite of the presumption of imprisonment. Rather, they are receiving stayed sentences with a condition of jail time, treatment, or both.

The problem of sentencing practices for sexual abuse of children encompasses almost every value question contained in the sentencing reform. The comparative emphasis given to desert or to the utilitarian aim of rehabilitation is at issue, as is the goal of truth in sentencing, which is undermined if a high-severity ranking is maintained with a high departure rate in practice. The extent of judicial discretion is likewise in question: how easy or difficult it should be to depart from the standard ranges toward less severity. Distribution of authority in sentencing is also at stake, because the language in one of the child-abuse statutes has contributed to more lenient sentences for offenders than the guidelines call for.[12] The question arises whether the commission, with its authority for setting sentencing policy, monitoring sentencing practice, and recommending improvements to the legislature, should take leadership in recommending legislative change, or whether the commission should merely inform the legislature of the departures from the guidelines and wait for legislative clarification.

After studying the question, the commission decided that the severity ranking of child abuse should not be lowered. One commissioner stated that it should be left at a high level as a "moral" statement, although that statement would merely be symbolic in the absence of commission action to change prevailing practice. The commission decided to wait for direction from the legislature rather than use its own experience to recommend statutory changes. In 1985 the legislature made only minor modifications, requiring psychiatric evaluation and treatment when a nonprison sentence is imposed.[13] Nothing was done to discourage the high rate of departures from the guidelines by either the commission or the legislature.

Sentences for drug dealers have also become a problem in recent years. The drug dealers who appear in state court tend to be "user-sellers" who sell relatively small amounts of drugs to friends and acquaintances in order to support their habits. Major drug dealers have been handled in federal court for the last fifteen years or more. The commission consistently held that the appropriate punishment for first-time convictions of user-seller drug dealers was probation with a condition of local jail time, treatment, or both. In 1981 an aggravating factor for major drug dealers was added to the guidelines to cover the rare instance when a major drug dealer was prosecuted in state court.

In response to a major lobbying effort by law enforcement officials in the state, the legislature in 1986 revised the controlled-substance statute to specify amounts of drugs that presumably would indicate a major drug offense.[14] It was clear that the legislature, in defining the offenses, felt that a presumptive sentence of prison was appropriate in all cases. Most observers agree that the amounts of drugs specified did not adequately differentiate the user-seller from the major drug dealer. It is also clear that the motivation for the legislation was less to provide a proportionate punishment for major drug dealers than it was to provide law enforcement officers with leverage to induce user-sellers to inform on the next level of the drug hierarchy. While final action has not been taken by the commission as of this writing, it has proposed ranking the new offenses to presume prison, despite the disproportionality that is involved.

The shift of sentences toward preguideline patterns—with more property offenders and fewer offenders against the person being imprisoned than the original guideline policy contemplated—appears at least up to this writing to have become acceptable to many commission members, perhaps a majority. The goals of sentence proportionality, truth in sentencing, desert as the primary sentencing purpose, and an emphasis on sentence uniformity seem to have become less important to commission members than they were during the development and initial implementation stages of the guidelines. As yet, however, the commission has not articulated a new set of goals to replace the initial aims.

Commissioners' Role Definitions
Under Minnesota's enabling statute, commissioners are selected from specified constituencies: there must be two district court judges, a defense attorney, a law enforcement member, and so on.[15] Because such persons are members both of the commission and of a criminal justice interest group, a member can define his or her role on the commission in a number of ways. One role definition might be termed "commissioner as policy maker" and involves trying to fashion broad public policy that transcends the interests of the commissioner's own constituency. Here, the commissioner uses his or her experience as judge, prosecutor, defense attorney, or whatever to assist in making a more-informed public policy. A second and alternative role is "commissioner as interest-group representative"; in this case the commissioner adopts a role to further the sentencing aims of the group from which he or she was appointed—for example, more sentencing discretion for judges, harsher sentences for prosecutors, more lenient sentences for defense lawyers, and more social control for probation and parole agents.[16] Constituent groups tend to expect, or at least want, their sentencing aims furthered by

"their" representative and provide little support for commission members who adopt a more policy-oriented role.

There appears to have been a significant change in commissioners' role definitions. Almost all commission members adopted a policy-making role as the guidelines were being written. One judicial representative, in particular, became recognized for adopting a strong policy-making role rather than representing his narrower constituent interests. At one point, toward the end of guideline development, the judge cast a vote that seemed inconsistent with his earlier positions. When asked for an explanation he said that for once he was voting his interest as a judge. Commission members were sensitive to the roles that had been adopted by other members, and constituent representation was relatively rare as a dominant theme.

It appears that constituent representation has become, since 1982, the dominant role definition on the commission. For example, the commissioner of corrections has primarily been interested in the impact of guidelines on corrections and appears relatively uninterested in such other important aspects of sentencing policy as proportionality and uniformity. The probation officer zealously guards the interests of field services staff and attempts to expand social control mechanisms for those supervising offenders in the community. A policy-maker role has not entirely disappeared from the commission (the chairman during 1982–86 maintained a policy-oriented role), but it has decreased significantly. Even commission members who formerly adopted a policy-making role became primarily interest-group representatives, perhaps in self-defense.

Change in role definitions has affected the commission's dynamics. Interest-group politics generally result in allocating areas of interest and following the leadership of the member with the greatest stake in that area. During most of 1983, commission attention was focused on projected increases in prison populations. The interest-group perspective resulted in the commissioner of corrections' playing the central role in defining the problem and its solutions. The commissioner of corrections had no more information than others on the commission, since almost all data were provided by commission staff, but members tended to defer to this individual's judgment because prison population was "his" bailiwick.

The interests of the Department of Corrections, however, were not necessarily the same as those of the sentencing guidelines commission. A major concern of the Department of Corrections in 1982 and 1983 was finding funds to operate a new prison that had been constructed. Only minimal "mothball" operating funds had been appropriated for the institution, because the legislature was operating under severe budgetary constraints and because the Minnesota prison population at that time did not require its operation. The Department of Corrections had received legislative authorization in 1981 to house Wisconsin and federal inmates on a contract basis, using excess space that existed in the old institutions after the guidelines went into effect. Funds generated in this manner were used to open wings of the new institution so that more Wisconsin and federal inmates could be housed so that additional wings could be opened, and so on. As these wings opened, Minnesota prisoners began to replace the out-of-staters. The Department of Corrections was not only concerned with potential overcrowding but also with finding ways of funding and filling the new facility.

Another change, which at least partially results from a change in role definitions, is the way in which commissioners' views are communicated to the legislature and the press. With a policy-oriented role definition, members tended to unite behind the decisions the commission adopted, even if they themselves had not supported the majority position. When asked about a close decision, "losing" members were likely to report that there had been extensive debate, and to relate the reasons for the decision.

A different dynamic tends to occur with an interest-group perspective, since primary loyalty is to the constituent group rather than to the commission. Members who do not prevail on an issue are more likely to pursue their constituent goals in other arenas, such as in the media or legislature. During the 1984 legislative session, a position taken by the commission lost some credibility when a member on the losing side of the issue communicated his opposition to legislators. Similarly in 1985 and 1986, when the drug-dealer issue was under consideration by the legislature, the law enforcement member of the commission actively campaigned for mandatory sentences, which was in direct contradiction to commission views. As the interest-group approach has become more prevalent, commission members have begun to oblige both legislators and the press when asked about their positions both before and after commission decisions. This conduct has not enhanced the commission's influence.

Commission Resources

Minnesota experienced severe budgetary problems in 1982 and 1983, and the commission's resources were significantly reduced.

The RAND study previously cited identifies three deleterious outcomes for a new program in these circumstances, particularly when retrenchment is prolonged.[17] First, cuts that cannot be absorbed will probably result in a decline in performance. Second, resource shortages in other areas can have a negative spillover effect on the new program. Third, the grace period that a new program needs for learning and experimentation may be reduced.

On the whole the Minnesota Sentencing Guidelines were sufficiently established by the time funds were reduced, so the reductions did not disrupt the learning and experimental stage. In 1982, staffing was cut from six to three and one-half positions, but by that time the guidelines had been developed, implemented, monitored, and preliminarily evaluated. The resource reductions did, however, cause the commission to discontinue answering questions from probation officers, prosecutors, and defenders on the application of the guidelines in individual cases. Occasional calls were accepted, but most calls were referred to probation supervisors, the attorney general's office, and the state public defender's office. Probation officers, the "field" guideline experts who calculate the applicable presumptive sentences for judges, do a thoroughly competent job; however the guidelines are sufficiently complex to make it helpful to have someone from the commission available to answer questions. The probation officers lobbied the commission to reinstate the question-answering service, fearing that without such a resource, different probation offices would develop different interpretations of the guidelines, with consequent increases in disparity. They also argued that incorrect application of the guidelines would result in expensive appeals that might be avoidable. In 1985 the legislature increased the commission staff complement from three and one-half to four positions to allow more support for those applying the guidelines.

In addition to reducing the level of service provided to field staff, the budget cuts prevented the commission from fully absorbing the functions that had been performed by the previous chairperson. Commission members serve gratis, and most members have demanding occupations that limit the time they can devote to commission activities. The initial chairperson (from 1978 to 1982) devoted an enormous amount of time and energy to commission business. She met constantly with criminal justice groups, citizen groups, legislators, and the press; the commission essentially had a full-time chair. Because of the resource reductions that occurred when she left, many of the important functions she performed could not be absorbed. Resource reductions have thus resulted in the performance of fewer functions. The essential present functions of monitoring and evaluating the implementation of the guidelines, however, have continued.

Preserving the Innovative Spirit

It is, I have suggested, not uncommon for an institutionalized program to stray from its initial modus operandi. The slippage that occurs as a program ages is too common to be attributable to personalities. It is simply easier to create a program, given the enthusiasm and excitement that accompany the initial stages of innovation, than it is to maintain the program's substantive features year after year in the face of resistance, adaptation, and routine.

It must be stressed that not all aspects of sentencing have reverted to earlier patterns. The new procedures have gained widespread support throughout the system. Sentencing worksheets, indicating the applicable presumptive sentence, are completed in almost all felony conviction cases. Appellate review of sentences—which had been virtually nonexistent prior to the guidelines—is now an accepted part of the sentencing process.

The level of support for procedural aspects of the guidelines has been high. To cite one example, prosecutors and defense counsel attempted, briefly, to negotiate defendants' criminal history scores. The integrity of the guideline system rests on an objective measure of criminal history; commission members were thus incensed when they became aware of such negotiating efforts and immediately communicated their displeasure. There was little to fear, however, because probation officers who calculate criminal history scores in individual cases proved unwilling to accede. Because of the professionalism and status that accrue to probation officers in their roles as guideline experts, they resisted a weakening of the scoring procedures.

Another procedural matter around which the system has rallied is the dissemination of reports of departures from the guidelines. A judge is required to send a copy of the reasons for departure whenever he or she imposes a more lenient or harsher sentence than the guidelines permit. The applicable rule specifies that on such occasions sentencing reasons must be forwarded to the commission, but the rule does not specify a time limit within which they must be forwarded. Some judges were lax in sending departure reports, and considerable effort was spent in obtaining them. Once aware of the problem, the commission immediately took steps to correct the problem by initiating a change in the procedural rule and by publicizing the problem along with requests for greater judicial cooperation.

The vitality of the guideline procedures, and the success in coordinating sentencing policy with correctional resources, indicates that the guidelines have effectively become institutionalized. The problem, I have noted, has been in the implementation of the substantive policies of uniformity and proportionality. To reinforce these policies—especially, the policy of limiting imprisonment chiefly to offenses against the person—changes in the guidelines themselves will be called for. There is little doubt that the policy *could* be reinforced. Amendments could shift the use of imprisonment back to an emphasis on the more serious crimes, and that shift would in all probability be carried out in practice. The question is not the effectiveness of the guideline device in itself but the willingness of the commission to undertake these steps. To do so, the commission would have to undergo a change in composition or outlook that would permit recovery of the policy-making perspective it once had. The newly appointed chairman has a strong policy orientation, which may help. Whether such change will materialize remains to be seen, however. From all indications, it appears easier to institutionalize a program's procedures than its spirit and aims.

CHAPTER 9

Enforcing Sentencing Guidelines: Plea Bargaining and Review Mechanisms

Michael Tonry and John C. Coffee, Jr.

The recent debate over sentencing reform has led to a broad range of proposals and innovations, including plea-bargaining bans and rules, parole abolition and guidelines, mandatory sentence laws, and various forms of sentencing guidelines and presumptive sentencing statutes. Our aim here is to consider the problem of eliciting compliance with major changes in substantive sentencing policies, using presumptive sentencing guidelines for illustrative purposes. By presumptive guidelines we mean sentencing guidelines that were developed by a specialized rule-making agency and that have some degree of formal legal authority.

Presumptive sentencing guidelines can take a variety of forms. In this chapter we assume the existence of relatively detailed guidelines like Minnesota's, although the issues considered are general and—in attenuated form—will bedevil any presumptive guideline system.

A variety of interrelated questions arise concerning the impact of presumptive guidelines on sentencing outcomes and official behavior. Can such guidelines be enforced? How will guidelines affect plea bargaining? To what extent will they shift discretion from the sentencing judge to the prosecutor, and will this mean increased pressure on the defendant to plead guilty?

Once the issues of enforcement and compliance are candidly faced, complexity quickly arises. The design of any structure for dispositional decision making after conviction is necessarily confronted by a variety of ethically troubling trade-offs between civil libertarian values and pursuit of various sentencing-reform goals. In particular, three distinct clusters of problems confound any proposal for reform.

Substance and Illusion in Plea Bargaining   The goal of sentencing equity—provisionally defined as the treatment of "like cases alike"—is in direct conflict with every criminal defendant's desire to secure favorable treatment. Under the most prevalent form of plea bargaining—namely, "charge bargaining"—the defendant agrees to plead guilty to a lesser included charge, or to fewer than all of the charges against him. The effect of this plea concession is uncertain. Sometimes it is small because the court continues to sentence the defendant on the basis of the original or "real" offense. At other times the court may reward the defendant with leniency over and above that conferred by the prosecutor in his plea concession. Because of this inherent uncertainty, a problem arises: it seems unfair that the defendant should surrender constitutional rights (and, in some cases, the real possibility of acquittal) for illusory consideration. Yet if the benefits of the plea were made concrete and overt by means of a "discount" or "charge reduction guidelines," this would create a sentencing penalty for not pleading guilty and arguably chill the willingness of future defendants to go to trial.[1] A hard choice is thus inevitable, and any proposal for enforcing sentencing guidelines must be evaluated in light of this trade-off between possible unfairness and possible coercion.

Adaptive Responses and Enforcement   Sentencing reforms by definition are attempts to change sentencing outcomes from what they otherwise would have been. External interventions (whether by the legislature or by a sentencing commission) are likely to encounter serious organizational resistance. A major difference in perspective exists between those operating at the abstract level of sentencing-policy formulation and those participating at the adversarial level of individual sentencing hearings. Draftsmen, whatever their philosophical premises, are likely to give primary attention to the grading of offense severity and the achievement of reasonable proportionality between sentences for offenses of differing gravity. Yet this concern with proportionality and the overall coherence of sentencing outcomes is substantially lost once one shifts to the viewpoint of the individual participants. The attention of those in the courtroom is always focused on the individual case before them—the general goal of sentencing equity has no organizational champion to take up arms on its behalf. Aggressive counsel are likely to view sentencing standards as simply the going tariff off which they expect to receive a substantial discount. Pros-

143

ecutors do not have comparably strong interests in resisting discounts. Conventional wisdom suggests that prosecutors often define their professional success in terms of conviction rates, not sentence severity. Moreover, they often share the defense counsel's interest in the expeditious disposition of the cases and can sympathize with such counsel's need to win something for his client and thereby his fee.

A possibility more subversive for externally imposed reforms is that the participants may tacitly share a common set of sentencing criteria that guides their negotiations. Some social scientists view the sentencing decision as the product of a "work group" of regularly interacting professionals who accept common criteria for the determination of sentences.[2] In this view, the judge is neither the lone decision maker nor the powerless ratifier of plea agreements but an influential member of the group. Much in the work-group perspective can be questioned, but it again suggests that sentencing reforms—however well designed in principle—could produce little net change without some means of enforcement that can, when necessary, restrict the powers of the work group.

Early experience with legislative reform of sentencing in California and elsewhere, while uneven, suggests that reform has produced fewer changes than its proponents had expected. Even clearer is the experience with "voluntary" guidelines adopted by sentencing judges in Denver, Philadelphia, and Chicago and in Maryland and Florida; the reductions in sentencing variance appear to have been negligible.[3] This evidence need not be read to confirm the pessimistic hypothesis that nothing works and that reform is always futile.

Minnesota's and Washington's experiences with presumptive sentencing guidelines have been different; judges and lawyers appear in general to have cooperated with guidelines that significantly altered prior sentencing practices.[4] Still, the experience outside these states underscores the likelihood of adaptive responses by those participants who do not desire to have their behavior changed. Sentencing guidelines are particularly vulnerable to this problem because they necessarily use information which is manipulable. Manipulation can be most easily accomplished by plea bargaining for a charge reduction that reduces the likely sentence to one that the defendant will accept. Or, if this is formally prohibited, the parties can agree (tacitly or otherwise) to ignore factors that the guidelines deem significant (for example, whether the defendant was armed). To the extent that such practices can be attributed to the work group's willingness to reward the defendant for pleading guilty, the prosecutor has little incentive to contest sentencing decisions in which he has participated willingly. In short, the problem of enforcement dovetails with the problem of incentive, and for those whose objective is the reduction of unwarranted disparity, the critical issue becomes how to find or create a participant in the process who has as strong an interest in achieving sentencing equity as do the existing players in encouraging expeditious resolutions through pleas of guilty.

Judicial and Prosecutorial Discretion: the Trade-off   Most recent efforts at sentencing reform have been frankly designed to confine judicial discretion. In so doing, they risk reallocating discretion in ways that are unintended and possibly perversely counterproductive. If, as some have argued, the movement toward determinate sentencing shifts power from the judge and the parole board to the prosecutor, then sophisticated policy planning must predict the likely impact of the shift and, perhaps, find some means for offsetting the prosecutor's increased powers.[5]

To this point, we have sketched distinct scenarios for the frustration of sentencing reform. These are competing scenarios, because they involve inconsistent premises. The sentencing process cannot be simultaneously bureaucratic and adversarial. The judge cannot be both the neutral referee and the busy broker of mutually acceptable plea bargains. Similarly, if sentencing decisions result from collegial processes within work groups, then the danger that the prosecutor will use the enhanced discretion available in established sentencing standards to coerce guilty pleas seems less serious than if the prosecutor had a substantially different view of the appropriate sentence from that of the other participants. We need not resolve which of these scenarios most accurately characterizes sentencing. A diversity of legal cultures exists within the United States and within most states and must be anticipated by the intelligent policy planner.

We now turn to the possible options by which the guidelines' policy can be enforced. We focus on how presumptive guidelines affect the defendant's decision whether to plead guilty; consider proposals that are designed to regulate plea bargaining; and, finally, examine appellate review and internal administrative procedures

145

for securing greater compliance. In each case, our intent is not to present an optimal policy, prepackaged and ready for implementation, but to outline choices. The stance we have adopted—that of impartial policy analysts—is somewhat contrived. The present writers differ—in some cases vigorously—about the desirability and practicability of various of the policy choices discussed in this chapter. Many of these choices, however, are entrenched in the current reform agendas, and it is precisely because of their difficulty and controversy that we attempt to open them to view here.

The Effect of Sentencing Guidelines on Plea Bargaining: Who Wins? Who Loses? What Happens Next?

Other things being equal, sentencing guidelines can be expected to change the prevalent form of plea bargaining from charge bargaining to, in effect, sentence bargaining. Today, considerable uncertainty confronts the defendant offered a charge concession. Will the judge still sentence him on the basis of the real offense (say, armed robbery) instead of the offense of conviction (robbery)? Or, will the judge assign a sentence below even the median sentence for robbery to reward the plea of guilty? Presumptive guidelines, however, inherently reduce this uncertainty by specifying the range of sentences applicable to persons convicted of robbery and enhance the value of the charge concession offered by the prosecutor.

This analysis is, however, overly simple. Another possibility is that sentencing guidelines will reduce prosecutorial leverage by mitigating the potential penalty that he can threaten if the defendant goes to trial. In terms of the allocation of sentencing authority, the discretion gained by the prosecutor under a system of presumptive sentencing guidelines may be substantially less than that lost by the court. Thus, although discretion has been shifted from the judge to the prosecutor, it need not mean that the overall attempt to constrain sentencing behavior has not had substantial success. In principle, the maximum penalty that the court and the prosecutor together can bring to bear on the recalcitrant defendant who refuses to plead guilty may well be materially reduced under a guideline system, even though the prosecutor has gained increased control over the sentencing process. For example, before the Minnesota guidelines took effect, a robbery defendant who went to trial risked a sentence as long as twenty-five years. Under the present guidelines, however, these high statutory ceilings no longer have much relevance because the guidelines radically compress the defendant's real exposure to incarceration. But, as a necessary corollary, the effect of any charge reduction that the prosecutor can typically offer is thereby greatly reduced. Indeed, a charge reduction downward of one seriousness level will seldom reduce the applicable guideline range by more than a year, and often the reduction will be even less. Consequently, we face again an unsettling trade-off: although the prosecutor is a more biased decision maker than the judge, and sentencing guidelines do shift some power to him, the more important variable may be not the relative bias of the decision maker but rather the aggregate pressure on the defendant to plead guilty.

Better insight into this trade-off is gained by focusing on the psychology of the criminal defendant. Concern that plea bargaining under presumptive sentencing guidelines may unduly pressure defendants to plead guilty is implicitly based on the belief that the defendant compares the expected punishment cost of pleading guilty with that of going to trial and opts for the lesser expected cost. But this is not necessarily what the defendant does. At least two other possibilities exist: the defendant may be risk-averse and instead focus on the worst possible outcome (that is, the maximum sentence); or he may be a risk preferrer and focus on the best possible outcome (that is, the minimum sentence or acquittal). There are no compelling reasons to believe that defendants are risk-neutral and simply compare the two expected outcomes.

In fact, under conditions of uncertainty, few of us appear to be risk-neutral. Some of us are risk-averse: when faced with a risk of a substantial loss, we will avoid it even if this means accepting an alternative having a lower expected value. For example, although in theory the certainty of a one-year sentence and the 10 percent prospect of a ten-year sentence are equal (since they have the same discounted value of one year), the risk-averse defendant will opt for the certain one-year sentence (and possibly accept a two- or three-year sentence) before risking the ten-year sentence. For most of us, some risks—such as that of a death sentence or of losing at Russian roulette—are simply unacceptable even if the risk involved is remote; our minds have little capacity to discount them by their limited possibility of occurrence, and so their expected value becomes disproportionately large. Conversely, others may be risk preferrers; rather than focus on the worst possible outcome, such an individual gives disproportionate attention to the best possible outcome (here, acquittal). If so, this possibility may lead a defendant to go to trial, even though a purely neutral evaluation of the relative risks suggests that pleading guilty is the rational course. Either way, the discounting process is skewed by the defendant's subjective evaluation of the penalties.

Most economists who have studied deterrence have tended to assume that the defendant will behave in a risk-averse manner; that is, he will be more deterred by a high potential penalty coupled with a low probability of imposition than by a low penalty coupled with a high probability of imposition.[6] While criminologists have disagreed strongly, arguing that few individuals give much weight to severe sanctions that are only remotely possible and that therefore the probability of apprehension is the more critical variable,[7] the context of plea bargaining is very different from that of deterrence research in general; here, the criminal is already apprehended and the approaching trial date tends, in Dr. Johnson's phrase, "to concentrate the mind wonderfully." The risk of a severe sentence cannot be ignored or disdained in the same manner that the frequently remote possibility of apprehension can be disdained by the competent burglar. Nor does the defendant have the same control over his fate as does the resourceful criminal. His choices are limited: to bargain or not to bargain. Thus, the premise of risk aversion rests on a stronger foundation within this special context of plea bargaining, which leads to the conclusion that the prosecutor can obtain greater coercive pressure over the defendant by threatening the possibility of a severe sentence than by offering a virtually certain but more modest discount off the normal sentence for the crime.

Accordingly, because presumptive guidelines tend to prevent extreme sentences, they should logically be expected to reduce the pressure on the risk-averse defendant to surrender a substantial possibility of acquittal. The trade-off has two elements: presumptive sentencing guidelines may lead a defendant who has little prospect of acquittal to plead guilty (because they make a discount off the mean sentence more certain), but by the same token they protect the risk-averse defendant with a reasonable chance of acquittal from his inability to resist prosecutorial pressure in the form of a threatened lengthy sentence for failing to plead guilty. So viewed, the charge concession arguably becomes only a small bribe that society pays the clearly convictable defendant to surrender the nuisance value that his attorney can create on his behalf, but it is inadequate to compensate the defendant who has a serious chance of acquittal. Thus, it might be argued, guidelines only expedite results; they do not reverse outcomes from the state of affairs that would exist in a world without plea bargaining.

Attractive and benign as such a policy conclusion may seem, we are hesitant to endorse it without considerable qualification. Basically, our reservations stem from the ambiguity inherent in the concept of risk aversion. Much used as the concept is, it is simply not clear what it means. Does it mean only that some severe risks are disproportionately weighted by the defendant? Or, does it mean there is a boundary line beyond which any risk is wholly unacceptable, so that all the prosecutor has to do is credibly threaten a penalty in excess of this level in order to secure a guilty plea to a lesser charge? If the latter, much depends on where this boundary line is located. This idea comes into clearer focus if we suppose that for a hypothetical defendant the boundary line is at the in-out threshold between incarceration and probation; here, introduction of presumptive guidelines may mean that the defendant can escape what is for him the unacceptable risk of incarceration only by pleading guilty to a lesser charge for which probation is the presumptive disposition. Even if our hypothetical defendant had a probability of acquittal, it would be of little importance if we postulate that the defendant will do anything to avoid incarceration. In short, to the extent that the presumptive guideline ranges for the higher and lower offenses straddle the in-out watershed and this line looms disproportionately large to the defendant, concern for prosecutorial overreaching under presumptive guidelines seems to be on much stronger ground. Now the prosecutor has gained an ability to escalate the penalty so as to cross the critical threshold at which the defendant's resistance crumbles.

One other possible type of defendant must be considered: the risk preferrer. The risk preferrer is, in theory, the mirror image of the risk averter; he would prefer a 10 percent probability of $100 to the certainty of $10. Although the tendency in the economic literature is to see such a person as a rare phenomenon, a recurrent observation about plea bargaining is that some defendants who have virtually no chance of acquittal still steadfastly resist their own attorney's advice to plead guilty and insist that they will be acquitted. The impact of sentencing guidelines may often encourage such a defendant to go to trial. Why? Put simply, the introduction of sentencing guidelines is likely to reduce the court's ability (or willingness) to impose a nonincarcerative sentence. Although guidelines need not preclude such a possibility, they do reduce the variance in sentencing outcomes for any offense, at least marginally, and thus move the sentencing court in the direction of the mean sentence. Thus, by reducing the possibility of probation following a conviction for a number of offense categories, they lead the gambler to go to trial as the only means of obtaining the best possible outcome. This conclusion, however, is again subject to the rebuttal that if the guideline for the lesser-included charge is probation, the pure risk preferrer may see this as the best possible outcome and will not seek acquittal.

Who, then, loses under presumptive sentencing guidelines? One loser would seem to be the defendant with a substantial possibility of acquittal who, in the absence of such guidelines, could have negotiated a very substantial reduction in sentence because of the weakness of the prosecutor's case. The only hope for defendants who are so risk-averse that they will not go to trial (or cannot accept the public embarrassment incident thereto or cannot afford the costs of private counsel for a trial) is to negotiate the best possible bargain, and sentencing guidelines tend to reduce the maximum bargain obtainable. Where once prosecutors could have quietly indicated to the court their willingness to encourage a low sentence, the impact of such a signal is at least marginally diminished by the existence of presumptive guidelines that compress the sentencing scale. In short, guidelines encourage the defendant to go to trial where there is a real prospect of acquittal by denying the prosecution the ability to pay the price that the plea is worth in such a case; denied the fair value of the plea, the defendant is forced to make an all-or-nothing choice between trial or an "unfairly" low discount for a plea.

For the especially timid defendant for whom any prospect of imprisonment is unacceptable, guidelines may force a plea of guilty if the charge discount straddles the in-out watershed, even though the defendant would probably have been acquitted at trial. Whether such a defendant should, however, be classified as a loser is more questionable. Although a real prospect of acquittal has been sacrificed, the defendant has achieved his primary end. He has avoided the risk of imprisonment to which he would clearly be exposed in a legal system that did not tolerate plea bargaining. The clearest loser in such a case is once again the goal of sentencing equity, since like cases are not being treated alike.

The reduction in sentencing variance, which presumptive guidelines logically entail, thus poses an unavoidable trade-off: at the same time as it reduces pressure on risk-averse defendants who wish to go to trial but fear a sentence near the maximum, it deprives other defendants of the opportunity to plead guilty in return for a substantial discount.

Given the different impact of guidelines on these different classes of defendants, the next question is obvious: whose interests should the law seek to protect? On a normative level, these two classes *deserve* very different constitutional and jurisprudential protection. From a constitutional perspective, protection of the innocent defendant from the extortionate leverage that plea bargaining can produce deserves primacy among the multiple goals and values that have constitutional recognition. The defendant has a right to be convicted based only upon the level of certainty expressed by the constitutional standard of "proof beyond a reasonable doubt." The defendant has no similar right to trade doubt or nuisance value for a specific sentencing discount. To the extent that a conflict exists, the Constitution must be read to protect the risk-averse defendant, not the bargain hunter. Even if the introduction of presumptive guidelines did harm risk-neutral and risk-preferring defendants more than it aided risk-averse ones, we would argue that only the latter class has a constitutionally or jurisprudentially cognizable entitlement.

The skeptical reader may well have asked by now if there is any empirical corroboration for the hypotheses generated by the preceding analyses. At present, all we can say is that the relevant data are not inconsistent with our analyses.

Findings of the Minnesota self-evaluation seem corroborative of our earlier analyses.[8] Although the percentage of defendants going to trial declined somewhat after the introduction of guidelines, from 5 percent of cases in 1978 to 4 percent among the first 5,500 cases sentenced under the guidelines, these figures camouflage an interesting shift: trial rates fell by half for the five lowest offense-severity levels and nearly doubled for the five highest. These changes might suggest that persons charged with low-severity offenses that are presumptive "outs" became more likely under guidelines to plead guilty in order to receive a nearly certain nonincarcerative sentence rather than risk conviction for a more serious charge and be subject to greater judicial unpredictability. Persons charged with more serious crimes may have felt that the guidelines decreased the risk of an aberrantly long sentence; subject to a prison sentence under the guidelines in any event, they may have been prepared to risk a somewhat longer sentence than a charge bargain might have yielded.

A final lesson from Minnesota concerns the use that prosecutors may make of guidelines. Implicit in critiques of enhanced prosecutorial influence under guidelines is the thesis that the prosecutor will use the guidelines to maximize the pressure on each individual defendant to plead guilty. This may be an oversimplification, however. Other ends—including saving time and achieving better allocation of prosecutorial resources—are also pursued by the prosecutor and facilitated by the introduction of guidelines. Presumptive guidelines serve these goals by simplifying the negotiation process. In so doing, they enable the prosecutor to conserve his investment of resources in minor cases and thereby enable him to focus more intensively on major cases involving more serious crimes.

The Minnesota findings are interesting but preliminary and are based on aggregate data that can tell us little about the experience of defendants who are innocent or who have substantial possibilities of acquittal for other reasons. Much more needs to be learned about the effects of presumptive sentencing guidelines on plea negotiations. For now, it remains an open question exactly how presumptive guidelines will affect plea-negotiation practices and whether and when increased leverage afforded prosecutors will increase pressure on defendants who have a significant chance of acquittal.

To this point, we have assumed that sentencing reform is likely to elicit adaptive responses by the parties. Planners are not impotent, however, and measures are possible by which to curtail the more likely forms of evasion. Two possibilities stand out for dealing with circumvention of guidelines through plea bargaining. One is "real-offense" sentencing—under which the court makes use of the guideline applicable to the "actual offense behavior" determined by it to have occurred, rather than the guideline applicable to the offense of conviction. The other is express discounts for a guilty plea.[9]

Real-Offense Sentencing

The topic of real-offense sentencing tends to produce immediate, intense, and sweeping reactions. One side sees it as a blatant attempt to outflank the fundamental constitutional protections accorded to persons accused of crimes; the other sees it as the only realistic and feasible means to offset plea bargaining, reduce the differential between sentences following pleas and sentences following trial (and the pressure to plead guilty), and achieve equity based on real rather than artificial differences among offenders. The debate has recently been reinvigorated by inclusion of a proposal for "modified real-offence sentencing" in the preliminary draft of sentencing guidelines released by the U.S. Sentencing Commission in September 1986.

The term "real-offense sentencing" is new, but the practice is not. American judges have probably long given considerable weight to the offense behavior described by the prosecutor or by the presentence report, notwithstanding that such behavior was more serious than the charge to which the defendant pled guilty. What is new are proposals for the formalization of this practice. To date, real-offense sentencing has been adopted in some form by the U.S. Parole Commission's guidelines, several states' parole guidelines, the Model Sentencing and Corrections Act, and several local sentencing guideline systems.[10] Although rationales for real-offense sentencing differ in parole guidelines, voluntary sentencing guidelines, and presumptive sentencing guidelines, it is the last application with which we are concerned.[11]

Three criticisms of real-offense sentencing in a prescriptive sentencing system stand out. First, it downgrades the significance of the trial stage, where various constitutional safeguards protect the defendant, and instead postpones critical determinations to the informal and less reliable dispositional stages. Second, it produces illusory plea bargaining, under which the prosecutor implicitly promises the defendant a concession whose value is then diminished at a later stage by the court or parole agency. Third, it is unrealistic in that it permits no concession for a plea of guilty and hence attempts to erase plea bargaining in a single stroke. Each of these contentions has some undeniable force, but each is also misleading unless examined against the backdrop of existing and alternative practices.

The Effect of Real-Offense Sentencing on the Trial Stage

Real-offense sentencing pushes the determination of critical facts back to the dispositional stage where procedural informality prevails and errors adverse to the defendant are more likely. At trial the defendant can claim benefit of rules of evidence and constitutional procedures. He is entitled to be acquitted unless the finder of facts determines that every element of the offense charged has been proven beyond a reasonable doubt. He is entitled to confront his accuser and to have his attorney present evidence and cross-examine hostile witnesses. Yet, the defendant is entitled to few of these legal protections at sentencing. The rules of evidence do not apply, nor in general do the rules of constitutional criminal procedure. For example, the exclusionary rule which denies the state the ability to introduce illegally seized evidence at trial does not apply at sentencing. If the "real offense" is the determinant of sentence, the defendant may find that his bargain has bought less than nothing; not only is he subject to punishment for the dismissed offense with which he was originally charged, but he is subject to it on the basis of evidence less persuasive and less carefully sifted than if he had been convicted at trial.

From a different perspective the defendant's dilemma under real-offense sentencing is not entirely new but, instead, merely newly visible. Modern criminal codes define many crimes in broad generic terms and thereby spare the prosecutor the need to prove troublesome details. One robbery statute may cover the fifteen-year-old who takes a bicycle after threatening its owner and a masked gunman who robs a bank with a sawed-off shotgun. The crucial differences need be isolated only after conviction.

Various distinctions can be drawn to suggest a watershed between "trial facts" (those that if not proven at trial or admitted by a plea of guilty should not be taken into account at sentencing or parole) and true "sentencing facts" that are appropriate for the sentencing stage. To explore what such a distinction would involve, it is necessary to consider the different criminal court contexts in which real-offense sentencing issues arise.

▪ *The defendant is charged with larceny and convicted of larceny and yet sentenced under the guideline for robbery.*

Here the argument is that real-offense sentencing undermines the entire scheme of constitutional procedural protections. If it is allowed, in such a case one might argue, eventually the prosecutor would as a matter of course charge defendants with a relatively minor offense that is factually related to the "real offense" and avoid having to prove any material facts except under the relaxed rules of the sentencing hearing. At its reductionist extreme, such a practice would be little different from charging every defendant with a general offense of "antisocial conduct," the details to be proven later at sentencing. To the extent that the sentencing range legislatively authorized for a lesser crime (here, larceny) was broad (such as the zero-to-life range once authorized in California and Washington for many felonies), the defendant would not receive even the supposed value of a ceiling set by a lower-ranking crime. Such practices now obtain in the federal system, where the facts underlying a conviction for mail fraud may relate not to venial misuse of the mails but to government corruption or organized crime.

- *The defendant is charged with armed robbery but is convicted by a jury of simple robbery.*

Here the defendant can plausibly argue that he has been acquitted of armed robbery and that use of the real-offense guideline for armed robbery violates notions of double jeopardy as well as of due process. Still, juries must find facts "beyond a reasonable doubt," whereas evidentiary findings in sentencing hearings are subject to a much less exacting standard. Traditionally, a defendant may be held civilly liable for an offense of which he was earlier acquitted in a criminal proceeding. Thus, a sentencing finding based on "the preponderance of the evidence" is logically and constitutionally reconcilable with the jury's decision that the same facts were not proven beyond a reasonable doubt, but many may find it a discomfiting reconciliation. The use of the real-offense guideline is particularly disturbing where it follows an acquittal, because it is corrosive of the integrity of the trial stage. Indeed, the U.S. Parole Commission concedes this point by restricting use of the real-offense guideline where the defendant has been acquitted of the offense, unless new evidence is available.[12]

- *The defendant is charged with armed robbery but pleads guilty to simple robbery.*

This is the classic case that real-offense sentencing proposals were designed to address. To accord full deference to negotiated guilty pleas of this sort is to accept that sentencing guidelines will be systematically distorted by the pressures of plea bargaining. Still, even within this context, important distinctions can be drawn between information relating to the offense behavior generally and facts that are "legally recognized" in the sense that they are elements of substantive offense definitions and constitute the basis for hierarchical distinctions between offenses. Being armed, for example, distinguishes armed robbery from robbery and is therefore a legally recognized fact. On the other hand, the lethality of the weapon (that is, a gun versus a club), whether it was used against a person, the identity of the victim (that is, an elderly citizen), and whether injury was gratuitously inflicted are not distinctions typically drawn by robbery definitions, and thus, not being legally recognized "trial facts," these distinctions would be appropriate "sentencing facts." The robbery guilty plea to the armed robbery charge arguably requires the sentencing judge to blind himself to unproven and unadmitted "facts" that the legislature has determined are integral to the grading of offenses. Weapons use is what makes armed robbery "worse." To permit the state to rely in sentencing on facts that distinguish between the conviction offense and other more serious offenses can be said to trivialize the substantive law.

• *The defendant is charged with robbery, under a broadly formulated statute that does not distinguish armed robbery and simple robbery, and pleads guilty.*

Here, because the use of a firearm is not "legally recognized," weapon use may be freely taken into account at sentencing. It should be noted, however, that if this distinction is accepted, an incentive may arise for the legislature to define criminal charges broadly, using a minimum of elements that the prosecution must prove beyond a reasonable doubt and thereby pushing the determination of even more critical issues back to the sentencing stage. Still, the legislature is arguably a more appropriate institution to make such a policy choice than is a sentencing commission. Systematic trade-offs between individual liberty interests and governmental interests in administrative or economic efficiency raise fundamental political issues that, arguably, are best addressed by the most directly representative agencies of government. It may be that—in light of public attention—legislatures would be less likely than less-visible administrative agencies to adopt policies that are practical but unprincipled.

An Excursus in the Case Law   We are purposely not stressing legal analysis here. Two lines of constitutional case law that may be relevant to consideration of the constitutionality of some forms of real-offense sentencing are discussed in an earlier, longer version of this chapter.[13] A recent Supreme Court decision, however, suggests that constitutional considerations will offer few impediments to implementation of real offense schemes. In *McMillan v. Pennsylvania*, 39 CR.L. 3161 (June 18, 1986), the Court by a 5–4 vote upheld a Pennsylvania mandatory sentencing law that was tantamount to real-offense sentencing. Pennsylvania's disputed law provided that anyone convicted of certain felonies be sentenced to a mandatory minimum sentence of five years' imprisonment if the sentencing judge found, by a preponderance of the evidence, that the person "visibly possessed a firearm" during the commission of the offense. Many states have enacted mandatory firearms sentencing laws but make the use of a firearm an element of the conviction offense, which means that the firearm's role must be proven "beyond a reasonable doubt." Under the Pennsylvania law, the prosecutor need only introduce evidence of firearm possession after conviction, at sentencing, to trigger the mandatory sentence. In explaining its decision, the majority created a new concept of "sentencing factors" and held that the courts should generally accord great deference to legislative decisions to define offense circumstances as elements of a crime or as "sentencing factors." The opinion, of course, contains close analysis of competing legal doctrines and seemingly inconsistent prior decisions. Exegesis of those analyses is better placed in a law review than here (and no doubt soon will be). The broad thrust of *McMillan,* however, can give very little solace to those who look to the courts for constraints on real-offense sentencing.

The constitutional debate in this area seems likely to continue for some time. Still, this is not the relevant issue. Legislatively, a higher standard of proof could be established for factual findings at sentencing that result in a determination that the real offense has a higher severity level than the offense of conviction. In addition, procedural safeguards—such as cross-examination and the use of witnesses—could be required where the defendant raises a credible challenge to the presentence report's description of the offense behavior. One practical means to achieve this would be to treat real-offense determinations as departures from the guidelines and to require a more formalized hearing for factual findings used to justify sentences in excess of the guideline range. The American Bar Association Standards recommend such a requirement, in contrast to the Model Sentencing and Corrections Act, which specifies only that there be "substantial evidence" in the record to support the probation officer's determination.[14] The ABA approach, which in effect "exceptionalizes" decisions above the guidelines, thereby places a procedural burden on their imposition and also desirably focuses appellate review on these cases, since presumably departures from the guidelines would be subject to closer scrutiny.

Establishment of such evidentiary and procedural requirements could to a substantial extent address the first objection to real-offense sentencing—that critical facts are pushed back to sentencing, where the determination will always remain relatively less formal and reliable. Although the determination of offense severity would still be delayed until this later stage, it would be made with a degree of procedural formality only marginally less accurate than at trial. In principle the difference between the standard of "clear and convincing evidence" and "proof beyond a reasonable doubt" is not great and probably can be defined only by the theologians of the law of evidence. In any event there is reason to believe that juries have great difficulty understanding that difference. Nonetheless, there would still be a cost in terms of other due-process values. First, the defendant would lose the right to a jury determination of offense severity, the area where juries have classically compromised by refusing to convict on the more serious offense. Second, given the long history of procedural informality at sentencing, there is no assurance that courts would rigorously apply whatever evidentiary and procedural requirements were transposed to this setting.

Ultimately the hard choice posed here involves two distinct questions. First is the question of which danger is worse: will prosecutors distort guidelines through charging concessions or will defendants be prejudiced by the delay of factual determinations to a forum more favorable to the state? Second is the symbolic question of the importance to be attached to the appearance of fairness and regularity in the criminal court.

The Problem of Illusory Plea Bargaining

A second general problem with real-offense sentencing is that it appears to involve the state's reneging on its own deal. If the plea bargain involves a dismissal of a more serious charge, the defendant's gain under a real-offense scheme is arguably illusory, in that the dismissed, more serious charge actually determines the sentence. Here we should digress to distinguish between charge and sentence bargaining. The problem of illusory plea bargains affects charge bargains. Guilty pleas involving a sentence bargain are a different story. A real-offense system can easily be circumvented if the prosecutor is willing to bargain over a sentence and the judge is willing to approve such a negotiated sentence below what the guidelines specify. As a practical matter, sentence bargaining is a nearly perfect circumvention. Constitutional principles preclude the prosecutor from appealing a sentence he has accepted in a plea bargain, and he has little interest in doing so. If the judge also has agreed to go along, the excessively lenient sentence will pass unnoticed in a busy urban court, and the judge need do no more than accept the plea, whatever the guidelines say. If necessary or politic, the judge can easily obscure the transaction by stating for the record some plausible pretext (the defendant's contrition; the plight of his dependents; emotional stress that precipitated his conduct) to justify a lenient departure from the guidelines. Thus, even if parole is retained as the medium for determining the real offense, its jurisdiction can be nullified if the parties can agree on a sentence having a maximum term equal to or below the guidelines for the offense of conviction.

Still, sentence bargaining is rare in many jurisdictions. It is in those jurisdictions where charge bargaining is common that the problem of the illusory bargain is most acute. Yet, although critics contend that real-offense guidelines inherently permit the state to renege on its bargain, this contention is highly debatable. First, the charge dismissals may often protect the defendant from a long sentence. Consider again, the crimes of simple robbery and armed robbery; and, suppose that the statutory maximums for these crimes are five years and ten years, respectively, and their normal guideline ranges are one to two years and three to four years, respectively. Stephen Schulhofer has argued that the prosecutor is stealing the advantage of the bargain if he seeks to prove armed robbery at sentencing after accepting a plea bargain to robbery.[15] The counterargument, made by Louis Schwartz, is that the bargain is supported by valid consideration because the statutory ceiling is reduced from ten years to five.[16] Schwartz's position may sound formalistic on these facts, but the hypothetical case is overly simple. Suppose the guideline range for either offense could go to six years (or more) given particular offender characteristics (for example, two prior convictions). Now, our defendant is protecting himself from a six-year sentence by pleading guilty, because the maximum lawful sentence for simple robbery, no matter what the number of prior convictions, is five years. In this light, the Schulhofer/Schwartz debate is the mirror image of our discussion in the preceding section as to whether the defendant behaves in a risk-neutral, risk-averse, or risk-preferring manner.

The claim that the bargain is inherently deceptive—because the defendant does not know that the prosecutor plans to allege at sentencing that the actual offense was more serious than that pleaded to—is also open to rebuttal. Competent defense counsel should know how sentencing guidelines are applied. This response, however, is not by itself fully adequate. Defense counsel may ignore the sentencing stage, either because trial lawyers are socialized to focus on the trial stage or because economic considerations make it expedient for counsel to gain his client's consent to the plea. A prosecutor could convey the impression that he will not contest the "offense of conviction" or appeal the sentence and later renege (particularly where a lenient sentence elicited public attention and disapproval); alternatively, defense counsel could misrepresent the prosecutor's position in order to induce the client to accept it.

Such possibilities raise two distinct questions: Should a court enforce such understandings that are in derogation of guidelines or should it, instead, declare agreements not to appeal to be against public policy (much like gambling contracts) and hence unenforceable? If and to the extent one does wish to grant a remedy (possibly on the theory that the prosecutor is the true culprit and the defendant only the victim), what remedy is appropriate?

Since *Santobello v. New York*, 404 U.S. 257 (1971), it is established principle that due process requires the prosecutor to honor his plea commitments. Thus, it seems more likely than not that some remedy will be provided when the prosecutor reneges overtly or with obvious duplicity, even though the failure to enforce such agreements might in the long run be the surest way to ensure that they would not be made (since defense counsel eventually would learn not to rely on them). The need for a remedy, however, does not mean that the remedy should be to honor the defendant's expectations. Rather, recent cases suggest that the appropriate remedy is to permit the defendant to withdraw the plea (*United States ex rel Goldberg v. Warden, Allenwood*, 622 F.2d 60 [3d Cir. 1980]; *United States v. Cook*, 668 F.2d 317 [7th Cir. 1982]). Such a remedy—voiding the bargain but not granting specific enforcement— may well be optimal: it deters the prosecutor but does not necessarily amount to a windfall for the defendant. Each party is brought back to the same starting point—a position probably neither of them wants to be in or they would not initially have negotiated a plea. The upshot of such a remedy would be to discourage the making of implicit deals not to appeal, but not at the price of leaving the defendant victimized by prosecutorial bad faith.

Procedurally, the problem of illusory plea bargaining can also be dealt with through disclosure. The unfair surprise that results when the defendant suddenly learns that real-offense guidelines will cancel out the advantage he saw in the original bargain can be most simply prevented if the court makes certain that the defendant understands this possibility before the guilty plea is accepted. A clear and simple illustration could be explained to the defendant so that he understands what a charging concession does and does not entail. Of course, this sort of reform sounds formalistic: the inexperienced or anxious defendant will not be listening during the pressure-laden context of sentencing, or will in reality be listening to his counsel (who wants to strike a quick plea-bargain). But this is the dilemma of most consumer reform efforts; that the consumer does not or cannot comprehend the disclosure as much confounds truth-in-lending legislation as it would such truth-in-plea-bargaining reforms.

The Practicality of Real-Offense Sentencing
Even if real-offense sentencing were constitutional and were thought to be desirable, there remain very serious questions about whether it could be effectively implemented at sentencing. It is a reform without any organizational champion among the current sentencing participants. Two questions therefore stand out. How would it be reconciled with plea bargaining? Who would enforce it, given that the incentive for the prosecutor is to secure a conviction, not to achieve sentencing equity?

The first of these problems is examined in the next section, "Guilty-Plea Concessions," but a brief word is here appropriate about the second—the problem of prosecutorial appeals. Prosecutors who need to strike plea bargains are in an awkward position with respect to real-offense guidelines: if they appear to be undercutting their own agreement, their credibility is injured. No merchant can long do business in the same marketplace if he is perceived to be a "welsher." Thus, given this constraint on prosecutors, others may have to be relied upon to enforce the real-offense determination. Since the initial determination of the real offense will probably be made by the probation department at the time it prepares its presentence report, one approach to this problem might be to give the probation department the ultimate responsibility for contesting and proving the real offense. If the defendant challenges the accuracy of that report, some form of hearing will obviously be necessary. Such a hearing seems a mismatch if the lay probation officer must represent himself against counsel. The probation officer would be in the position of being both witness and advocate as he tried to

161

explain his conclusion that the real-offense behavior was more serious than the crime of conviction. Yet, unless the burden is placed
on the state to prove its contention, the civil libertarian's objection
to real-offense sentencing seems compelling: it would be profoundly
unfair to ask the defendant to disprove the presentence report (which
too often is based on little more than the prosecutor's original case
file). Some decisions have indeed held that the defendant may not
be so required to "prove a negative" at sentencing (see, for example,
Weston v. United States, 448 F.2d 626 [9th Cir. 1971]; *United States
v. Fatico,* 603 F.2d 1053 [2d Cir. 1979]). But who then is going to
represent the probation officer in any such hearing? If we say the
prosecutor, we have only come back full circle to the problem of
inadequate incentive, because the prosecutor has only to announce
that in the exercise of its discretion it will not seek to prove a higher
real offense and the proceeding is at an end. To force the state to
seek to prove a weak case is a dubious use of prosecutorial and
judicial time.

One logical answer to this problem would be to give the probation
department its own counsel, who, being independent of the prosecutor, would have no interest in upholding implicit commitments
made by the prosecutor. Such a counsel to the probation department
could conduct the formalized sentencing hearing that would be required when the probation department sought to prove the case for
a real-offense guideline. This approach would achieve the same independence that a parole agency now has from the exigencies of
plea bargaining but without sacrificing the due-process values that
are irretrievably lost when a parole hearing is based on a cold written
record rather than live witnesses.

A final objection is, however, more serious, because it goes again
to the organizational processes and incentive structure of the criminal justice system. The probation department in most jurisdictions
is under the administration of the courts and often is directly controlled by the chief judge. To the extent that the sentencing judge
is a willing co-conspirator in the toleration of plea bargains, it seems
unlikely that his agents—even if they are neutral and zealous—could
long remain uncompromised by the process in which their superiors
are deeply enmeshed. Thus neither the probation officer nor his
counsel is a likely candidate to exercise an independent appeal power
in cases of excessive leniency.

There is some limited experience in Minnesota that suggests that
the probation officer may have more influence, and may offer a

better prospect of protecting the integrity of the guidelines, than the preceding analysis suggests. When, in Minnesota, counsel attempted to manipulate the guidelines by agreeing not to "count" prior convictions in the criminal history score calculations, probation officers protested loudly and effectively and Minnesota appellate courts emphatically denounced the practice.[17] The probation officer compiles the information on which guidelines are based and is likely in most places to calculate the presumptive guidelines sentence. This role as the central guidelines administrator may cause probation officers to link their own sense of professional status with their responsibility for the guideline system's integrity. This Minnesota experience, however, concerns a question of general policy and not an independent adversary probation officer role in individual proceedings.

We end, then, on an inconclusive and skeptical note. Although it may be constitutionally permissible to design a sentencing structure that assigns punishment based on the real offense, rather than on an artifact created by the plea-bargaining process, both the constitutional uncertainties and the organizational obstacles suggest that such an attempt is feasible only through the vehicle of a parole agency.

Guilty-Plea Concessions

Sentencing guidelines highlight the impact of the guilty plea and thus expose one of the secrets of our criminal justice system. A study by Hans Zeisel compares sentence bargains offered to New York City defendants who turned them down with the sentences imposed on those same defendants after trial. The average penalty imposed was 136 percent of the sentence initially offered.[18] The evaluation of Alaska's ban on plea bargaining concluded that conviction at trial rather than by guilty plea increased sentences for violent offenses substantially both before and after the plea-bargaining ban took effect.[19]

Accordingly, there would seem to be two possible immediate reactions if Minnesota-type sentencing guidelines are introduced in a jurisdiction. First, the incentive to plead guilty will be lessened substantially, with resulting dislocation to the criminal justice system (but also with arguably more than compensating gain to the constitutional values underlying the system); or, second, guidelines in the long run will be subverted, as courts and prosecutors find covert methods to reward guilty pleas. The reaction in most jurisdictions would probably fall somewhere between these two poles, but nonetheless it is understandable that various commentators have recommended that an explicit guilty-plea discount be recognized. One proposal specifies that every cell in the guideline grid contain two different guideline sentences or ranges; the first for defendants convicted at trial, the second for those who plead guilty.[20] A second proposal would make the discount somewhat less stark. Schulhofer has recommended that discounts be awarded by shifting the applicable guideline cell by one row so that, for example, a defendant charged with an offense of severity-level six would be given the opportunity to plead guilty and be sentenced under the guidelines applicable to an offense of severity-level five.[21] A third proposal for guilty-plea discounts, one that predates sentencing guidelines, suggests that guilty pleas be rewarded with a standard percentage discount—say 10 percent—from the other applicable sentence. Other possibilities are discussed below.

We do not devote substantial attention here to the mechanics of any guilty-plea discount system. It suffices to say that any such proposal presents significant policy and operational problems. To be palatable even to those not much troubled by the constitutional implications, any such proposal must strike a difficult balance that encourages pleas from the genuinely guilty but does not coerce them from the innocent. For example, an across-the-board two-year discount for guilty pleas might represent too small a concession to induce a guilty plea from a defendant otherwise subject to a ten-year sentence, while it might exert too much influence over a defendant who otherwise would receive a two- to three-year sentence. Whether such a balance can be struck is open to serious question, once one looks closely at existing systems. The critical problem is that the architecture of existing guideline systems seems to place many defendants in a guideline cell that immediately adjoins the in-out line on either side. This means simply that plea bargains that straddle the in-out line are frequently possible, and as noted earlier such bargains are difficult to resist. Minnesota's experience was that roughly three-quarters of the "imprisonable" cases in their construction sample (on which Minnesota's guidelines were based) fell in cells abutting this in-out line. To offer such defendants a discount that means the difference between the probability of imprisonment and the near certainty of freedom may or may not constitute excessive pressure, but it is highly unlikely that the goal of sentencing equity can be realized under such a structure.

A sentencing guideline system that awards an explicit guilty-plea discount can be seen in three very different lights. First, it is an incentive to plead guilty and so disfavors those defendants who go to trial. Second, it is a limitation on the amount of credit that can be given for such a plea; that is, it is as much a ceiling on the permissible reward as a disincentive to profess innocence. Third, it is a form of consumer protection for offenders. Offenders sometimes plead guilty in return for a valueless consideration: as discussed earlier, the difference between the statutory ceilings for most offenses and for their lesser included offenses may be irrelevant, because the likely sentence for either crime is below the lower ceiling; similarly, when collateral counts are dropped, they may not have much impact on the sentence (as when ninety-nine counts of mail fraud, each based on a different use of the mails, are reduced to fifteen). Underlying such one-sided negotiations may be either a conflict of interest between defense counsel and the client (so that the attorney does not explain to the client the limited value of the benefit) or simply self-deception on the part of a clearly guilty defendant, which requires that he be able to tell himself that he got something in return for his admission of guilt.

In contrast to such illusory consideration, a specific sentence discount off the guideline range (whether stated in terms of months, percentages, or a shift in applicable cells) would ensure that the defendant gets something in return. From the common perspective that sees the private criminal-law practitioner as forced to engage in a high-volume operation which prevents him from representing his clients' interests adequately, such a "reform" arguably represents not pressure on the defendant but a truth-in-plea-bargaining act.

Nonetheless, the civil libertarian will see matters differently, and any attempt to grant explicit concessions for a plea of guilty will provoke a constitutional challenge. At present, all that can be said with respect to such a challenge is that such an explicit credit may be constitutional, at least if done with appropriate artfulness. The key case is a 1978 decision, *Corbitt v. New Jersey*, 439 U.S. 212 (1978), in which the Supreme Court upheld a statutory structure that permitted substantially more lenient sentences for defendants who pled guilty than for those who went to trial. Under New Jersey law, a defendant found guilty of first-degree homicide received a life sentence. But, a defendant who pled *non vult* (no contest) was eligible for a substantially lesser sentence. Stephen Schulhofer has argued that the decision means that the Court "would uphold a guideline system providing separate sentencing ranges for contested and uncontested cases, at least if the two ranges overlapped."[22]

Assuming that explicit discounts may survive judicial scrutiny, the next question becomes, How should the credit be awarded if the decision is made to award one? One unexplored approach would be to rely on the principle of the least restrictive alternative: such a discount should be granted only to the extent that the state received a corresponding benefit. Thus, it can be argued that jury trials should be distinguished from bench trials because the former place a considerably higher burden on the state than do the latter. Schulhofer has indeed proposed separate and additive "guilty-plea discounts" and "jury-trial waiver discounts" to reflect this distinction.[23] The arguments for such a division of the discount are clear. Particularly in jurisdictions where the attorneys choose the jury, a jury trial may involve weeks of skirmishing over collateral issues (chiefly, jury selection), while the same trial before a judge could be accomplished in a day or two. Jury trials also impose financial costs on the judicial system, and in many courthouses the number of courtrooms that can accommodate jury trials is limited, thereby causing logistical problems and further delays. Thus, from the standpoint of the benefit to the state, it seems unjustifiable to place the same pressure on the defendant to waive a bench trial as a jury trial. To illustrate, it would be consistent with such a premise to sentence the same offender to thirty-six months if he went to trial before a jury, eighteen months if he pled guilty, and twenty-four months if he were convicted after a bench trial. Of course, such an à la carte shopping list simultaneously increases both the candor of the system and the dismay of those concerned about the appearance of justice.

In a more recent article (1984), Schulhofer has argued that Philadelphia, in practice, has a system that resembles his proposals. Only a minority of convictions result from guilty pleas. The rest are divided between "list" courts having bench trials, which on average consume an hour of court time, and "calendar" (jury) courts, where trials take much longer. The more severe judges work in the calendar courts, and offenders are generally believed to receive much severer sanctions after jury trial convictions than they would have received after a bench trial conviction. The effect is a system that gives a discount for waiving a jury trial but gives no discount for a guilty plea; by funneling a preponderance of cases into efficient adversary trials, argues Schulhofer, such a system offers a meaningful alternative to plea bargaining.[24]

The greatest practical difficulty with discounts involves the predictable attempt by defense counsel to win something extra for his client. In an adversarial system of justice, defendants can be expected to bargain off the lower guideline range. If every defendant is entitled to a guilty-plea discount, a determined defense lawyer will insist also on a charge reduction. The result is double counting. Instead of reducing the pressure to plead guilty by limiting the concession to a modest amount, the original evil is compounded. Various techniques must therefore be considered to prevent such a distortion of the intent of the guideline discount system.

One obvious technique for preventing such double discounts takes us back full circle to our earlier focus on real-offense sentencing. Real-offense sentencing systems could potentially cancel the prosecutor's charge concession and thereby prevent double discounts (unless, of course, the prosecutorial concession interposed a statutory ceiling between the offense of conviction and the guideline range for the real offense). At bottom the proper intent of a real-offense system is to transfer discretion over the sentence back to the court from the prosecutor. This problem of double discounts suggests that guilty-plea discounts are highly unsafe at the sentencing stage unless combined with real-offense sentencing. Yet, as noted in the preceding section, the feasibility of real-offense sentencing remains open to very serious question at the sentencing stage.

Thus far, we have considered methods of structuring guideline systems to anticipate and counter adaptive responses. It is difficult to place much confidence in either real-offense sentencing or guilty-plea discounts as a means for achieving greater sentencing equity at the sentencing stage. Perhaps workable variations of each can be imagined, but a combination of public opposition and legislative indifference seems likely to interfere with their effective implementation. To work, real-offense sentencing requires some enforcement mechanism that must be independent of the sentencing work group if it is to overcome the natural impulse of the parties to use guidelines as only the opening position for further bargaining. Guilty-plea discounts are on even less firm constitutional ground and predictably face even stronger civil libertarian opposition.

Michael Tonry and John C. Coffee, Jr.

Sentencing Appeals and Internal Controls

Early experience with "voluntary" judicially adopted sentencing guidelines casts doubt on whether guidelines, without adequate enforcement mechanisms, will result in a significant reduction in sentencing variance.[25] Plea bargaining is not the only cause of this observed persistence of sentencing disparities after the introduction of guidelines. Other explanations include judicial individualism and confusion as to the meaning or applicability of the guidelines. In this section we appraise "external" mechanisms for monitoring compliance with presumptive sentencing guidelines.

Prosecutorial Appeals

From the standpoint of the defendant, the answer to the intransigent judge who flouts the guidelines seems obvious: permit the defendant to appeal and instruct the appellate court to shift the burden to the state to justify a sentence outside the appropriate guideline by explaining what special factors merit a departure. Such an answer seems basically satisfactory, since the defendant can be counted upon to pursue his own interests. The only major drawback is the possibility that judicial or prosecutorial pressure may chill the defendant's willingness to appeal. For example, if the prosecutor were to threaten a cross-appeal if the defendant appealed, a risk-averse defendant might be deterred from appealing even an excessive sentence. The defendant may also have reason to fear the consequences of his own decision to appeal: if his appeal prevails and the appellate court remands the case to the original judge, that judge might be able to justify an even higher sentence by manipulating the guideline categories. Zeisel and Diamond found that a small number of defendants' appeals in Massachusetts did result in sentence increases and speculated that this risk of an increased sentence deterred some defendants from appealing.[26]

Two simple techniques could be used, however, to discourage retaliatory cross-appeals by the prosecutor. First, they could be prevented altogether by limiting prosecutorial appeals to cases in which the judge imposed a sentence more lenient than the minimum guideline sentence (and limiting defense appeals to sentences more severe than the guidelines prescribe). Second, if the defendant were given additional time to appeal the sentence after the prosecutor's time for appeal had expired, the defendant could exercise his right to appeal undeterred by the latent threat of retaliation. To be sure, the prosecutor could anticipate such an appeal and file his own appeal first in hopes of later agreeing to a mutual dismissal, but such preemptive strikes appear unrealistic: the prosecutor would have to file an appeal in virtually every case, which could mean substantial wasted effort; and such a policy would encounter judicial resistance if it consumed judicial time. These factors, plus the prosecutor's own sense of professional ethics, make a policy of uniform appeals by the prosecutor with respect to sentencing appeals seem an imaginary horror.

Similarly, to allay the fear that the appellate court would remand to the same court for resentencing requires only that appellate courts adopt a policy of systematically remanding to a different judge on resentencings. Some decisions have already gone part way down this road. If the objection is raised that such a rule wastes the judicial time needed to acquaint a new judge with the facts, another alternative is to preclude by statute higher sentences following an appeal, unless based on verifiable new evidence.

Should the prosecutor have the right to appeal the sentence? Historically the perceived obstacle to a prosecutorial power to appeal was the federal Constitution's double jeopardy clause, which forbids not only multiple prosecutions for the same offense but also multiple punishment for the same crime. This restraint has long been (and continues to be) interpreted to preclude the sentencing judge from increasing the sentence once service of it has begun.

But does the double-jeopardy clause therefore preclude a prompt appeal by the prosecutor to an appellate court where the sentence is below the guideline range? It does not appear so. Late in 1980 the Supreme Court resolved a closely comparable issue in *United States v. DiFrancesco,* 449 U.S. 117 (1980), holding in a five-to-four decision that governmental appeals do not offend the double-jeopardy clause simply because they deprive the offender of a more lenient sentence. The Supreme Court has recently decided a considerable number of cases presenting double-jeopardy questions. In general the Court appears to be narrowing the reach of the double-jeopardy clause, and although legitimate doubt still exists as to whether there could be a new hearing after a remand at which the sentence is increased, the appellate court seems clearly to possess the authority to reverse the sentencing court's decision to impose a sentence below the guidelines.

Resolution of the constitutional issues will not resolve the policy

Michael Tonry and John C. Coffee, Jr.

issues. If we set aside the constitutional questions, a number of
practical implementation issues warrant consideration. How are
governmental appeals to be reconciled with bargained-for guilty
pleas? That is, is the prosecutor reneging on the implicit bargain
when he agrees to drop charges in return for a plea? Are governmental appeals feasible? That is, will the prosecutor have so weak
an incentive to appeal lenient sentences as to make such appeals
rare events? If the prosecutor is likely to waive an appeal where it
is justified, what alternatives are available by which to review un-
justified judicial leniency?

This brings us to the problem of governmental appeals in a world
of charge bargaining. Is the prosecutor reneging on his bargain?
Has the defendant been cheated out of his right to a trial by the
payment of no more than an illusory consideration? These pejorative
questions may assume what is to be proved. What should the prosecutor's agreement to dismiss some charges in the indictment be
interpreted to mean? Constitutionally, it is settled law that the prosecutor must honor his bargain. But what bargain has he made?
Here, distinctions can be drawn between various types of bargains.
First, there is the classic "horizontal" charge bargain, in which multiple counts of the same or a lesser-level offense are dropped; such
a bargain protects the defendant only against the limited possibility
that the court might cumulate the penalty through consecutive sentences. Conversely, there is the "vertical" plea bargain in which a
plea is accepted to a lesser included offense and the more serious
charge is dropped. This bargain protects the defendant against the
higher statutory ceiling, but will also probably result in a somewhat
lesser actual sentence (although not necessarily, because the court
may still sentence on the basis of its notion of the real offense).
Next, there are various forms of bargains that involve a prosecutorial
recommendation of a sentence (or a recommendation that the sentence not exceed a specified length). This format comes closer to a
prosecutorial agreement to use its best efforts to obtain a given sentence. Here, although the prosecutor cannot guarantee the sentence,
there is a good-faith undertaking to attempt to achieve it, which
undertaking is violated by a subsequent appeal. Finally, there are
the express sentence bargains, in which counsel, with judicial approval, settle on the precise sentence to be imposed. In this situation
no one has an interest in changing the sentence, and it will clearly
be immune from review unless a third party is given standing to
intervene. Probably only in these latter two cases is the prosecutor

170

clearly expressing his approval of the sentence which the defendant anticipates, but in all these cases there is a possibility of misunderstanding by the defendant.

Accordingly, if a plea agreement not involving a sentence bargain is formalized and contains an express reservation by the prosecutor of a right to appeal the sentence (possibly limited to an appeal of any sentence below defined criteria), it would seem implausible to claim that the prosecutor had deceived the defendant. Indeed, it may be desirable in all cases to require the prosecutor to reserve such a right so that the defendant will fully understand the limited scope of the agreement. In consequence, if the objection to governmental appeals is based on arguments about deception or reneging, the result is likely to be only that prosecutors will learn to be more careful in contracting and will "put it in writing." Of course, the defendant might in theory reject such a limited deal, and the outcome might depend on the relative bargaining advantage of the parties— a result that would seem likely to enhance the possibility of disparities. Yet, the basic point is that if the grievance is phrased in terms of deception, the logical remedy should be disclosure rather than a prophylactic ban on prosecutorial appeals. In all candor, however, we are not optimistic about the efficacy of such disclosures. The defendant is seldom the equivalent of the intelligent middle-class shopper; rather he must rely on counsel, who frequently has a strong interest in the bargain's being accepted.

Appeals by Other Participants
If prosecutorial appeals raise fairness issues and are likely to be ineffective in a world dominated by plea bargaining, who else is available to enforce sentencing guidelines? Three candidates are available, and none need be exclusive of the others.

Strong arguments support giving the victim the right to appeal. Not only would the victim have an incentive to appeal, but the potential for such appeals might supply a check on gross prosecutorial discounting of serious crimes. There are, however, serious problems of feasibility with such a proposal. First, who are the victims? In many crime categories, the "victim" is only a broad class of citizens: consumers, the public generally, or the government itself (in tax-fraud cases). By analogy with the law on criminal restitution, the class of eligible victims entitled to appeal might be sensibly limited to those identified in the indictment. Alternatively, the presentence report could determine their identity. Still, few eligible victims are likely to be found for a broad range of white-collar offenses. Second, and even more important, although crime victims may have the incentive, they generally lack the financial ability, time, and legal sophistication required for an effective appeal. Public legal-services offices are hardly in a position today to take on this added responsibility.

Thus, a more realistic alternative might be to give the appeal decision to an independent body. One candidate might be an arm of the sentencing commission. Precedent for such a legislative step is largely lacking. Minnesota permits its sentencing commission staff to monitor and correspond with sentencing judges, and in California the Board of Prison Terms may request a reconsideration by the original court; but both these steps fall considerably short of appeal. Such a mechanism would, however, respond to a variety of problems. The commission would have little reason to use the appeal mechanism to chill defendants' appeals, since its real loyalty would be to the integrity of its guidelines. The "reneging" problem would disappear, since defendants would be forced to recognize that the right to appeal, because it belonged to others as well, could not be bargained away by the prosecutor. The staff could prepare the factual support for a sentencing hearing in those cases where a remand was necessary. Sentencing judges would find it far harder to intimidate the commission's staff from appealing than a prosecutor or probation officer who depended on the judge's favorable disposition.

Of course, other variations are possible, such as removing sentencing from the courts and placing it in the hands of an administrative agency like the parole board. We doubt, however, that it is realistic to seek to take the in-out decision from the trial court. Such an invasion of the traditional zone of judicial autonomy will predictably be resisted fiercely, and it is doubtful that any alternative mechanism could expeditiously screen out cases for probation.

The concept of governmental appeals needs to be distinguished from that of prosecutorial appeals. Many of the problems with the latter dissipate once an independent body—such as the sentencing commission—is given the authority to take the appeal. By a variety of restraints prosecutorial appeals can also be substantially tamed. Indeed, their greatest problem is apt to be their infrequency.

Internal Controls: The Cooptation of the Sentencing Bureaucracy

As do other professionals, lawyers tend to have tunnel vision, which emphasizes the centrality of their own procedures and processes and ignores the contributions of others. Thus, lawyers automatically focus on the appeal as the basic means for reducing sentencing variance. But from an organizational perspective, there is considerable basis for believing that a more important technique for increasing compliance may lie in focusing not on the judge but on the probation officer, and less on the appeal than on the process prior to the court's determination. It has long been known that judges tend to rely heavily on the probation officer's sentencing recommendation, and in some court systems it has been observed that the probation officer is in fact the real sentencer, since his recommendations are generally followed. Thus, the probation officer represents an underused leverage point which can be exploited to increase sentencing conformity.

To do so, the sentencing commission's staff would review the presentence report, which would include a mandatory section tabulating the presumptive sentence under the guidelines, *before* it is submitted to the court. Review at this point will likely have greater impact, since it can affect the basic information the court will receive and thus can influence the court before it forms its tentative conclusions. In contrast, the lawyers' oral arguments on the day of sentencing usually come after the court has formed a tentative judgment. The tyranny of first impressions is well known, and it applies to sentencing as to other decisions.

The feasibility of prior review of the probation officer's report by the sentencing commission's staff sounds questionable. Yet, this is precisely what Minnesota has done: copies of a guideline tabulation sheet are reviewed for compliance by the technical staff of the Minnesota Sentencing Guidelines Commission, and the probation officer is instructed to correct any erroneous interpretation of the guidelines before the presentence report is submitted to the court (see chapter 7). Such a procedure delays sentencing somewhat and is not without cost, but early data from Minnesota showed a high rate of compliance with its guidelines (see chapters 2 and 8). One cannot know that the use of prior review procedures significantly affected these high rates of compliance, but the uniqueness of the Minnesota experience suggests the desirability of giving closer attention to such procedures, which ultimately involve neither the cost, the delay, nor the formality of litigation remedies (such as the appeal).

A focus on the probation officer seems desirable on a more generalized level as well. Special training programs, workshops, and sophisticated proselytizing of the probation bureaucracy may pay higher returns than any formal legal remedy. Social scientists have increasingly placed less emphasis on judicial or administrative review than on broader "quality assurance programs," which use a variety of socializing techniques, to reduce variance in decision making. Such attempts may have particular success with probation departments, whose very reason for being has been challenged by the gradual discrediting of a rehabilitative model for corrections. Put simply, the probation officer's claim to professional status (an all-important consideration in any occupation) must rest on some basic set of shared values—a professional ideology. In the past, the probation officer could conceive of himself as an expert in rehabilitation. With the decline of the rehabilitative model, the professional status of the probation officer has been exposed to doubt. Yet, the goal of sentencing equity and the inevitable complexity of guidelines permit the probation bureaucracy to reassert its claims to professional status. Its mission could now become the achievement of equity—a different but no less heroic task than the diagnosis of social illness or rehabilitative potential.

This point is not a cynical one. No reform can work without acceptance by those who must implement it. Yet, no interest group of professional participants is more directly affected by sentencing reform than the probation staff, whose tasks are complicated by guidelines but whose professional status is thereby potentially elevated. To fail to seize upon this opportunity and to encourage the professional bureaucracy to identify with the goals of the guideline model would be to show the self-preoccupied shortsightedness which, as often as not, characterizes the lawyer as reformer.

Adverse Publicity

Still another technique for encouraging compliance is the use of adverse publicity. Such publicity could be internal or external (that is, the names of those judges who deviated from the guidelines most frequently could be publicized, either within the judiciary or more generally to the public). Internal publicity is an already popular tactic by which to encourage compliance; in many court systems the names of judges who have failed to dispose of cases or finish opinions within prescribed time limits are internally circulated. Anecdotal wisdom suggests that such tactics are frequently effective.

External publicity is a two-edged sword. Particularly where judges are elected, some judges may desire to be known as "tough" judges who defy the guidelines and sentence in excess of them. Thus, we would counsel caution and place primary emphasis on internal publicity, to be followed by judicial conferences at which the problem would be discussed and collegial pressure brought to bear on the intransigent. Such conferences obviously are also necessary to discuss the impact of the guidelines and the probable need for fine-tuning adjustments. The basic point, however, is simply that social pressure is one means of "enforcing" guidelines, and it can be harnessed in the same manner as is done to secure compliance with other actions undertaken by the judiciary collectively.

We have not sought in this chapter to present any package of reforms for immediate adoption. Several reasons underlie our reluctance to do so. First, it would be highly desirable to know more about recent experience before any option is chosen. For example, to what extent has real-offense sentencing by the U.S. Parole Commission already led defense counsel in federal cases to insist upon a plea bargain under which the maximum sentence is below the applicable guideline? Similarly, to what extent is "fact bargaining" over sentencing enhancements in California and other jurisdictions nullifying the intent of determinate sentencing? What effect have Minnesota's guidelines had on the defendant who has a significant possibility of acquittal? To what extent is our hypothesis that sentencing guidelines reduce the pressure to plead guilty on a defendant charged with a serious felony but increase it on the defendant charged with a lesser crime (where the guidelines straddle the in-out line) borne out in jurisdictions other than Minnesota? Answers to these questions do not lie in the observation that plea bargaining has persisted more or less as before in each of these jurisdictions; more intensive empirical scrutiny is needed. Second, the variable of legal culture also leads us to doubt that there is any magic formula that will work in all jurisdictions under all circumstances.

We cannot point in these pages to compelling answers to the questions raised by plea-bargaining manipulations of guidelines specifically, or adaptive responses, generally. Ten years ago, however, no one had heard or thought of real-offense sentencing or guilty-plea discounts or the refinements of those proposals that are discussed here. That advance in itself may seem a small—even a questionable—accomplishment. It is, however, only in an era when the achievement of consistency and principle in sentencing has come to be seen as an important public policy goal that the problem of implementation has become sufficiently real to invite solutions. Reform is usually piecemeal and incremental. That proposals such as those discussed here have been made suggests that people are working to devise ways to improve the quality of justice, and that is progress.

A Summary of the Minnesota, Washington, and Pennsylvania Guidelines

This appendix briefly summarizes the Minnesota, Washington and Pennsylvania sentencing guidelines. Readers interested in further details should consult the full texts, cited in the bibliography.

Minnesota

The Minnesota guidelines took effect May 1, 1981, and were most recently revised (as of this writing) on August 1, 1986. The guidelines' most significant features are (1) the scoring system for crime seriousness, (2) the criminal history scoring system, (3) the sentencing grid, and (4) the rules governing departures.

Crime Seriousness

The offender's current offense is graded according to the offense of conviction. The guidelines assign scores from 1 (lowest) to 10 (highest) to the various statutory offense categories or subcategories. Examples of the crimes assigned to the various grades are as follows:

Offense score	Crime category
10	Murder—intentional but not premeditated
9	Felony murder
8	Assault—great bodily harm
7	Armed robbery
	Burglary—with weapon or assault
6	Burglary—of occupied dwelling
5	Burglary—of unoccupied dwelling
4	Nonresidential burglary
	Theft over $2500

Offense score	Crime category
3	Theft ($250–$2500)
	Possession of heroin
2	Various lesser theft-related felonies
1	Unauthorized use of vehicle
	Marijuana possession

Criminal History

The criminal history score is based upon the offender's prior *convictions*. Prior arrests not leading to conviction are not counted. Each prior felony conviction counts *one* point. Each prior gross misdemeanor conviction counts *one-half* point, and each prior misdemeanor conviction counts *one-quarter* point. There are special rules for: (1) crimes committed while on probation or parole, and (2) prior crimes as a juvenile.

The Sentencing Grid

The sentencing grid (Table A-1) sets forth (1) when imprisonment presumptively is appropriate, and (2) the presumptive duration of prison sentences. Unless the offender loses "good time" for infractions committed in prison, he will serve two-thirds of any prison sentence in confinement, and the remaining one-third under supervision in the community.

On the grid, set forth below, cells with recommended prison terms are below the heavy black line (known as the dispositional line). In each such cell, the single number is the recommended duration of sentence. The italicized range below that number is the range within which the judge may sentence without supplying reasons. Any sentence outside that range constitutes a departure from the guidelines.

Above the dispositional line, the cells prescribe a presumption of a sentence other than imprisonment, designated as "N." This nonimprisonment sentence may, within the judge's discretion and statutory limits, include a jail term of up to one year, or else probation, fine, or other community disposition. The guidelines, in other words, limit the use and duration of imprisonment—but leave discretion in the choice among nonprison sanctions. (The actual guidelines provide, in each cell above the line, a number representing the duration of reconfinement upon revocation of probation or other stayed prison sentence—but these numbers are not reproduced here.)

Minnesota sentencing grid

Seriousness Levels of Conviction Offense	Criminal History Score						
	0	1	2	3	4	5	6 or more
1 Unauthorized use of motor vehicle Possession of marijuana	N	N	N	N	N	N	19 18–20
2 Theft-related crimes ($250–$2500) Aggravated forgery ($250–$2500)	N	N	N	N	N	N	21 20–22
3 Theft crimes ($250–$2500)	N	N	N	N	19 18–20	22 21–23	25 24–26
4 Nonresidential burglary Theft crimes (over $2500)	N	N	N	N	25 24–26	32 30–34	41 37–45
5 Residential burglary Simple robbery	N	N	N	30 29–31	38 36–40	46 43–49	54 50–58
6 Criminal sexual conduct, 2nd degree	N	N	N	34 33–35	44 42–46	54 50–58	65 60–70
7 Aggravated robbery	24 23–25	32 30–34	41 38–44	49 45–53	65 60–70	81 75–87	97 90–104
8 Criminal sexual conduct, 1st degree Assault, 1st degree	43 41–45	54 50–58	65 60–70	76 71–81	95 89–101	113 106–120	132 124–140
9 Murder, 3rd degree Murder, 2nd degree (felony murder)	105 102–108	119 116–122	127 124–130	149 143–155	176 168–184	205 195–215	230 218–242
10 Murder, 2nd degree (with intent)	120 116–124	140 133–147	162 153–171	203 192–214	243 231–255	284 270–298	324 309–339

Note: "N" denotes a presumption of a nonimprisonment sentence.

Departures

The guidelines provide that the court may depart from the grid's presumptive sentences, only in "substantial and compelling circumstances."

Certain circumstances may *not* be considered as grounds of departure. These are:

- Race
- Sex
- Employment factors, including:
    1. occupation or impact of sentence on profession or occupation
    2. employment history
    3. employment at time of offense
    4. employment at time of sentencing
- Social factors, including:
    1. educational attainment
    2. living arrangements at time of offense or sentencing
    3. length of residence
    4. marital status
- The exercise of constitutional rights by the defendant during the adjudication process.

A *nonexclusive* list of mitigating factors is provided. The court may impose a sentence less severe than the indicated range if the court makes the appropriate substantial-and-compelling finding. The list consists of the following four items:

1. The victim was an aggressor in the incident.
2. The offender played a minor or passive role in the crime or participated under circumstances of coercion or duress.
3. The offender, because of physical or mental impairment, lacked substantial capacity for judgment when the offense was committed. The voluntary use of intoxicants (drugs or alcohol) is not included.
4. Other substantial grounds exist which tend to excuse or mitigate the offender's culpability, although not amounting to a defense.

A nonexclusive list of aggravating factors is likewise provided, consisting of the following seven items:

1. The victim was particularly vulnerable owing to age, infirmity, or reduced physical or mental capacity, which was known or should have been known to the offender.

2. The victim was treated with particular cruelty for which the individual offender should be held responsible.

3. The current conviction is for an offense in which the victim was injured and there is a prior felony conviction for an offense in which the victim was injured.

4. The offense was a major economic offense, identified as an illegal act or series of illegal acts committed by other than physical means and by concealment or guile to obtain money or property, to avoid payment or loss of money or property, or to obtain business or professional advantage. Two or more of the circumstances listed below combine to form an aggravating factor with respect to the offense:
   a. the offense involved multiple victims or multiple incidents per victim;
   b. the offense involved an attempted or actual monetary loss substantially greater than the usual offense or substantially greater than the minimum loss specified in the statutes;
   c. the offense involved a high degree of sophistication or planning or occurred over a lengthy period of time;
   d. the defendant used his or her position or status to facilitate the commission of the offense, including a position of trust, confidence, or fiduciary relationship;
   e. the defendant has been involved in other conduct similar to the current offense as evidenced by the findings of civil or administrative law proceedings or the imposition of professional sanctions.

5. The offense was a major controlled-substance offense, identified as an offense or series of offenses related to trafficking in controlled substances under circumstances more onerous than the usual offense. (Specific factors that are aggravating with respect to such major drug offenses are then listed.)

6. The offender committed, for hire, a crime against the person.

7. The offender committed a crime against the person in furtherance of criminal activity by an organized gang. An "organized gang" is defined as an association of five or

more persons, with an established hierarchy, formed to
encourage gang members to perpetrate crimes or to provide
support to gang members who do commit crimes.

Washington

The Washington guidelines initially took effect July 1, 1984, and
were (as of this writing) most recently revised in 1986.

Crime Seriousness
The offender's current conviction offense is graded on a 14-point
rating scale. The scale, which grades only felonies, is based on statutory offense classifications, and runs from 1 (least serious) to 14
(most serious). Sample classifications are:

Rating	Crime
13	Felony murder
11	Assault—great bodily harm
9	Armed robbery
7	Burglary—occupied dwelling
4	Strongarm robbery
2	Burglary—unoccupied dwelling Theft (over $1500)
1	Lesser theft

Criminal History
The criminal history score, as in Minnesota, is based on prior *convictions*. However, the scoring system is more complex, and depends
both on the gravity of the current crime and the gravity of the prior
convictions. An offender currently convicted of a serious violent
crime (e.g., murder or rape) will receive 3 points for each prior
serious violent crime, 2 points for each prior violent crime, and 1
point for each other prior conviction. If, however, the current crime
is less serious, then the point scores for any priors are lower.

The Sentencing Grid
The sentencing grid (Table A-2) sets forth (1) when imprisonment
or jail is appropriate, and (2) the presumptive duration of confinement. The offender is to serve the prescribed time, less one-third
for good behavior. There is no community supervision upon release

Washington Sentencing Grid

Seriousness Score	Offender Score									
	0	1	2	3	4	5	6	7	8	9 or more
14	Life Sentence without Parole/Death Penalty									
13	23y 4m 240–320	24y 4m 250–333	25y 4m 261–347	26y 4m 271–361	27y 4m 281–374	28y 4m 291–388	30y 4m 312–416	32y 10m 338–450	36y 370–493	40y 411–548
12	12y 123–164	13y 134–178	14y 144–192	15y 154–205	16y 165–219	17y 175–233	19y 195–260	21y 216–288	25y 257–342	29y 298–397
11	6y 62–82	6y 9m 69–92	7y 6m 77–102	8y 3m 85–113	9y 93–123	9y 9m 100–133	12y 6m 129–171	13y 6m 139–185	15y 6m 159–212	17y 6m 180–240
10	5y 51–68	5y 6m 57–75	6y 62–82	6y 6m 67–89	7y 72–96	7y 6m 77–102	9y 6m 98–130	10y 6m 108–144	12y 6m 129–171	14y 6m 149–198
9	3y 31–41	3y 6m 36–48	4y 41–54	4y 6m 46–61	5y 51–68	5y 6m 57–75	7y 6m 77–102	8y 6m 87–116	10y 6m 108–144	12y 6m 129–171
8	2y 21–27	2y 6m 26–34	3y 31–41	3y 6m 36–48	4y 41–54	4y 6m 46–61	6y 6m 67–89	7y 6m 77–102	8y 6m 87–116	10y 6m 108–144
7	18m 15–20	2y 21–27	2y 6m 26–34	3y 31–41	3y 6m 36–48	4y 41–54	5y 6m 57–75	6y 6m 67–89	7y 6m 77–102	8y 6m 87–116
6	13m 12+–14	18m 15–20	2y 21–27	2y 6m 26–34	3y 31–41	3y 6m 36–48	4y 6m 46–61	5y 6m 57–75	6y 6m 67–89	7y 6m 77–102
5	9m 6–12	13m 12+–14	15m 13–17	18m 15–20	2y 2m 22–29	3y 2m 33–43	4y 41–54	5y 51–68	6y 62–82	7y 72–96
4	6m 3–9	9m 6–12	13m 12+–14	15m 13–17	18m 15–20	2y 2m 22–29	3y 2m 33–43	4y 2m 43–57	5y 2m 53–70	6y 2m 63–84
3	2m 1–3	5m 3–8	8m 4–12	11m 9–12	14m 12+–16	20m 17–20	2y 2m 22–29	3y 2m 33–43	4y 2m 43–57	5y 51–68
2	0–90 Days	4m 2–6	6m 3–9	8m 4–12	13m 12+–14	16m 14–18	20m 17–22	2y 2m 22–29	3y 2m 33–43	4y 2m 43–57
1	0–60 Days	0–90 Days	3m 2–5	4m 2–6	5m 3–8	8m 4–12	13m 12+–14	16m 14–18	20m 17–22	2y 2m 22–29

from imprisonment. As in Minnesota, the single number in each cell represents the midpoint, and the range below it represents the permissible bounds the judge may utilize without having to give reasons.

The grid ranges are subject to the following adjustments:

1. Enhancement for being armed. If the offender was armed with a deadly weapon, then between 12 and 24 months are added to the grid sentence, depending on the nature of the current conviction.

2. Waiver for first-time offender. For a first-time offender whose crime is not violent, the court has discretion to waive the grid sentence and impose a sentence of community supervision, with the option of up to 90 days in jail.

3. Conversion for sentences below 12 months. For grid sentences of less than 12 months, the court may impose, instead, a noncustodial sentence, including partial confinement, community service, or fines.

Departure Rules

The court may depart from the grid ranges only for "substantial and compelling" circumstances. The guidelines provide a nonexclusive list of "illustrative" factors of aggravation and mitigation. The listed mitigating factors are as follows:

1. To a significant degree, the victim was an initiator, willing participant, aggressor, or provoker of the incident.

2. Before detection, the defendant compensated, or made a good faith effort to compensate, the victim of the criminal conduct for any damage or injury sustained.

3. The defendant committed the crime under duress, coercion, threat, or compulsion insufficient to constitute a complete defense but which significantly affected his or her conduct.

4. The defendant, with no apparent predisposition to do so, was induced by others to participate in the crime.

5. The defendant's capacity to appreciate the wrongfulness of his conduct or to conform his conduct to the requirements of the law, was significantly impaired (voluntary use of drugs or alcohol excluded).

6. The offense was principally accomplished by another

person and the defendant manifested extreme caution or sincere concern for the safety or well-being of the victim.

The listed aggravating factors are as follows:

1. The defendant's conduct during the commission of the offense manifested deliberate cruelty to the victim.
2. The defendant knew or should have known that the victim of the offense was particularly vulnerable or incapable of resistance due to extreme youth, advanced age, disability, or ill health.
3. The offense was a major economic offense or series of offenses, so identified by a consideration of any of the following factors:
   a. the offense involved multiple victims or multiple incidents per victim;
   b. the offense involved attempted or actual monetary loss substantially greater than typical for the offense;
   c. the offense involved a high degree of sophistication or planning or occurred over a lengthy period of time;
   d. the defendant used his or her position of trust, confidence, or fiduciary responsibility to facilitate the commission of the offense.
4. The offense was a major violation related to trafficking in controlled substances, which was more onerous than the typical offense of its statutory definition.

Unlike Minnesota's, the guidelines do *not* list factors which are barred from consideration, such as age, sex, economic status, etc.

Pennsylvania

The Pennsylvania guidelines apply only to the minimum sentence imposed by the judge, which determines the defendant's eligibility to be considered for parole release. Actual duration of confinement is, in the case of prison sentences, then determined by the parole board—subject to a maximum sentence also imposed by the judge, which the guidelines do not govern.

The guidelines classify the seriousness of current conviction offenses. They also have a prior-record score that depends upon the seriousness as well as number of prior convictions. The grid then sets forth a normal range, an aggravated range, and a mitigated range. There are, however, no standards governing the definition of aggravating and mitigating circumstances. If a deadly weapon was used, from twelve to twenty-four months must be added to the grid ranges.

Table A–3
Pennsylvania sentencing grid

Offense Gravity Score	Prior Record Score	Minimum Range	Aggravated Minimum Range	Mitigated Minimum Range
10	0	48–120	statutory limit	36–48
Third degree murder	1	54–120	statutory limit	40–54
	2	60–120	statutory limit	45–60
	3	72–120	statutory limit	54–72
	4	84–120	statutory limit	63–84
	5	96–120	statutory limit	72–96
	6	102–120	statutory limit	76–102
9	0	36–60	60–75	27–36
e.g.: rape;	1	42–66	66–82	31–42
robbery inflicting	2	48–72	72–90	36–48
serious bodily injury	3	54–78	78–97	40–54
	4	66–84	84–105	49–66
	5	72–90	90–112	54–72
	6	78–102	102–120	58–78
8	0	24–48	48–60	18–24
e.g.: kidnapping;	1	30–54	54–68	22–30
arson (Felony 1)	2	36–60	60–75	27–36
voluntary	3	42–66	66–82	32–42
manslaughter	4	54–72	72–90	40–54
	5	60–78	78–98	45–60
	6	66–90	90–112	50–66

Table A–3 (*continued*)

Offense Gravity Score	Prior Record Score	Minimum Range	Aggravated Minimum Range	Mitigated Minimum Range
7	0	8–12	12–18	4–8
e.g.: aggravated	1	12–29	29–36	9–12
assault causing serious	2	17–34	34–42	12–17
bodily injury; robbery	3	22–39	39–49	16–22
threatening serious	4	33–49	49–61	25–33
bodily injury	5	38–54	54–68	28–38
	6	43–64	64–80	32–43
6	0	4–12	12–18	2–4
e.g.: robbery	1	6–12	12–18	3–6
inflicting bodily	2	8–12	12–18	4–8
injury; theft by	3	12–29	29–36	9–12
extortion (Felony 3)	4	23–34	34–42	17–23
	5	28–44	44–55	21–28
	6	33–49	49–61	25–33
5	0	0–12	12–18	non-confinement
e.g.: criminal mischief	1	3–12	12–18	$1\frac{1}{2}$–3
(Felony 3); theft	2	5–12	12–18	$2\frac{1}{2}$–5
by unlawful taking	3	8–12	12–18	4–8
(Felony 3); theft	4	18–27	27–34	14–18
by receiving stolen	5	21–30	30–38	16–21
property (Felony 3)	6	24–36	36–45	18–24
bribery				
4	0	0–12	12–18	non-confinement
e.g.: theft by receiving	1	0–12	12–18	non-confinement
stolen property, less	2	0–12	12–18	non-confinement
than $2,000, by force	3	5–12	12–18	$2\frac{1}{2}$–5
or threat of force, or	4	8–12	12–18	4–8
in breach of fiduciary	5	18–27	27–34	14–18
obligation	6	21–30	30–38	16–21
3	0	0–12	12–18	non-confinement
Most misdemeanor 1's	1	0–12	12–18	non-confinement
	2	0–12	12–18	non-confinement
	3	0–12	12–18	non-confinement
	4	3–12	12–18	$1\frac{1}{2}$–3
	5	5–12	12–18	$2\frac{1}{2}$–5
	6	8–12	12–18	4–8

Table A–3 (*continued*)

Offense Gravity Score	Prior Record Score	Minimum Range	Aggravated Minimum Range	Mitigated Minimum Range
2 Most misdemeanor 2's	0	0–12	statutory limit	non-confinement
	1	0–12	statutory limit	non-confinement
	2	0–12	statutory limit	non-confinement
	3	0–12	statutory limit	non-confinement
	4	0–12	statutory limit	non-confinement
	5	2–12	statutory limit	1–2
	6	5–12	statutory limit	$2\frac{1}{2}$–5
1 Most misdemeanor 3's	0	0–6	statutory limit	non-confinement
	1	0–6	statutory limit	non-confinement
	2	0–6	statutory limit	non-confinement
	3	0–6	statutory limit	non-confinement
	4	0–6	statutory limit	non-confinement
	5	0–6	statutory limit	non-confinement
	6	0–6	statutory limit	non-confinement

Notes

Chapter 1

1. See, e.g., Allen, *The Decline of the Rehabilitative Ideal.*

2. See, e.g., the 1979 report of the National Academy of Science's Panel on Research on Rehabilitative Techniques. The report is set forth in Sechrest, White, and Brown, *The Rehabilitation of Criminal Offenders,* 3–118.

3. Allen, *The Decline of the Rehabilitative Ideal,* 11–20.

4. See von Hirsch, *Doing Justice,* chaps. 2, 14.

5. Ibid.; von Hirsch, *Past or Future Crimes,* chaps. 3–8; Kleinig, *Punishment and Desert;* Singer, *Just Deserts.*

6. von Hirsch, *Past or Future Crimes,* chaps. 9–12; Wilson, *Thinking About Crime,* chap. 8; Greenwood, *Selective Incapacitation.*

7. Chapter 5 of this volume; von Hirsch, *Past or Future Crimes.*

8. See von Hirsch, *Past or Future Crimes,* chap. 3.

9. Frankel, *Criminal Sentences;* Gottfredson, "Sentencing Guidelines."

10. Frankel, *Criminal Sentences;* von Hirsch, *Doing Justice,* chap. 4.

11. For an analysis of the California law, see von Hirsch and Mueller, "California's Determinate Sentencing Law." For an analysis of the Indiana law, see von Hirsch, "The New Indiana Sentencing Code." For a survey of such legislation in the other states, see von Hirsch and Hanrahan, "Determinate Penalty Systems in America," 299–303.

12. von Hirsch and Mueller, "California's Determinate Sentencing Law," 264–65, 284–86.

13. von Hirsch, "The New Indiana Sentencing Code."

14. See von Hirsch and Hanrahan, *The Question of Parole,* 83–86.

15. States that have eliminated discretionary parole release include California, Illinois, Indiana, Minnesota, and Washington.

16. von Hirsch and Hanrahan, "Determinate Penalty Systems."

17. Ibid.

18. Stone-Meierhoefer and Hoffman, "Presumptive Parole Dates."

19. There remains, however, the question whether the parole board's discretionary releasing authority should be abrogated when a sentencing

commission is established. Minnesota did eliminate that authority: offenders are released automatically after two-thirds of their sentence and then serve the remainder of that sentence under supervision in the community. (An offender who loses good-time credit by committing infractions in the prison, however, can be held beyond the two-thirds of his sentence.) Pennsylvania, on the other hand, retained parole release after the sentencing guidelines took effect. For discussion of this issue, see chapter 4. See also von Hirsch and Hanrahan, *The Question of Parole,* chap. 9.

20. Frankel, *Criminal Sentences,* 118–23. For his more recent thoughts on the sentencing-commission device, see Frankel and Orland, "Sentencing Commissions and Guidelines."

21. Frankel proposed that the guidelines take effect after their publication by the commission, in the absence of disapproval by the legislature. Minnesota used this technique. The Washington guidelines, however, required actual legislative approval of the guidelines before they take effect. See chapter 4 of this volume.

22. The Minnesota, Washington, and Pennsylvania guidelines are summarized in the appendix and cited in the bibliography. The proposed New York guidelines are set forth in New York State, *Determinate Sentencing.* The U.S. Sentencing Commission was created by legislation approved by Congress in the fall of 1984 (Public Law 98–473 [1984]).

23. For further discussion, see chapters 4 and 5 of this volume.

24. See, e.g., Greenwood, *Selective Incapacitation,* 50.

25. See chapter 5 of this volume. For fuller analysis, see von Hirsch, *Past or Future Crimes,* chap. 7.

26. See chapter 5 of this volume; see also, von Hirsch, *Past or Future Crimes,* chaps. 11 and 14.

27. See von Hirsch, *Past or Future Crimes,* chaps. 9–11 and 3–8.

28. Ibid., chap. 11.

29. For fuller analysis, see chapter 5 of this volume.

30. Ibid.

31. Methods for making these population projections are discussed in chapter 6.

32. See Martin, "Interests and Politics in Sentencing Reform," 101, 104–6.

33. von Hirsch, *Past or Future Crimes,* chaps. 4 and 8.

34. See, e.g., Posner, *Economic Analysis of Law,* 163–73, for a general statement of this view. Posner relies on deterrent effects in his argument, but the same essential view undergirds sentencing philosophies giving primacy to incapacitation or rehabilitation.

Chapter 2

1. O'Donnell, Curtis, and Churgin, *Toward a Just and Effective Sentencing System.*

2. Minnesota Sentencing Guidelines Commission, *The Impact of the Minnesota Sentencing Guidelines.* See also Knapp, *Minnesota Sentencing Guidelines and Commentary Annotated.*

3. Phillips, *Final Report of the Maine Sentencing Commission.*

4. Shane-DuBow, Brown, and Olsen, *Sentencing Reform in the United States,* 48.

5. Keeler, "The Debate Over Sentencing."

6. The guideline development process in Pennsylvania is described in Martin, "Interests and Politics in Sentencing Reform."

7. McCloskey, "The Effectiveness of Independent Sentencing Commission Guidelines."

8. Pennsylvania Commission on Sentencing, *Proposed Sentencing Guidelines.*

9. This summary relies heavily on Martin, "Interests and Politics in Sentencing Reform."

10. For a recent description of Washington's guideline system, see Boerner, *Sentencing in Washington.*

11. Minnesota Sentencing Guidelines Commission, *The Impact of the Minnesota Sentencing Guidelines.* Miethe and Moore, "Socioeconomic Disparities under Determinate Sentencing Systems." Pennsylvania Commission on Sentencing, *1983 Report* and *1984 Report;* see also Kramer and Lubitz, "Pennsylvania's Sentencing Reform." See Kramer, Lubitz, and Kempinen, "Sentencing Guidelines," and Kramer and Scirica, "Complex Policy Choices." Washington Sentencing Commission, *Sentencing Practices under the Sentencing Reform Act* and *Report to the Legislature.*

12. Kramer and Lubitz, "Pennsylvania's Sentencing Reform."

13. For evidence that something comparable has happened in California, see Casper, Brereton, and Neal, "The California Determinate Sentence Law," 412.

14. Washington Sentencing Commission, *Report to the Legislature.*

15. Minnesota Sentencing Guidelines Commission, *The Impact of the Minnesota Sentencing Guidelines,"* 31.

16. Pennsylvania Commission on Sentencing, *1983 Report,* and *1984 Report.*

17. Minnesota Sentencing Guidelines Commission, *The Impact of the Minnesota Sentencing Guidelines,* 30.

18. Ibid., v–vi.

19. Miethe and Moore, "Socioeconomic Disparities under Determinate Sentencing Systems."

20. Minnesota Sentencing Guidelines Commission, *The Impact of the Minnesota Sentencing Guidelines,* 48.

21. Pennsylvania Commission on Sentencing, *1983 Report,* and *1984 Report.*

22. Kramer and Lubitz, "Pennsylvania's Sentencing Reform," table 4.

23. Rathke, "Plea Negotiating under the Sentencing Guidelines," 271.

24. Minnesota Sentencing Guidelines Commission, *The Impact of the Minnesota Sentencing Guidelines*, vi.

25. Ibid., 78.

26. Ibid., 31, 71–86.

27. Washington Sentencing Commission, *Sentencing Practices under the Sentencing Reform Act*, 3.

28. Minnesota Sentencing Guidelines Commission, *The Impact of the Minnesota Sentencing Guidelines*, 72.

29. Knapp, *Minnesota Sentencing Guidelines and Commentary Annotated*.

Chapter 3

1. See, e.g., Cullen and Gilbert, *Reaffirming Rehabilitation*.

2. For the limited role of prior convictions on a desert rationale, see von Hirsch, *Past or Future Crimes*, chaps. 7, 8, 14.

3. Note, "Appellate Review of Primary Sentencing Decisions: A Connecticut Case Study." See also chapter 2 of this volume.

4. Thomas, "Sentencing Guidance." For an example of such a "guideline" sentence, see R. v. Billiam, [1986], 1 All ER 985, prescribing five years' imprisonment as the "starting point" in contested cases of forcible rape.

5. Some of the issues include: a one-sided appeal (by defendant only) means that unwarrantedly lenient sentences cannot be appealed, impeding development of a case-law jurisprudence; and it also is not certain to what extent trial courts and magistrates actually follow the Court of Appeals' opinions in unappealed cases, and the extent of such compliance or noncompliance has not systematically been measured. For a useful discussion, see Ashworth, "Techniques of Guidance on Sentencing."

6. Wasik, "Guidance and Guidelines in Sentencing."

7. See National Academy of Science report on deterrence research, in Blumstein, Cohen, and Nagin, *Deterrence and Incapacitation*, 19–63.

8. Thomas, *Principles of Sentencing*, 14–15.

9. German Penal Code (Strafgesetzbuch) sec. 46. Translation by this author.

10. For current German sentencing doctrine, see Bruns, *Das Recht der Strafzumessung*. Bruns attempts to resolve this conflict of aims by asserting that desert creates upper and lower limits on the sentence, within which there exists a "Spielraum" (latitude) for invoking preventive measures (ibid., 105–9). However, he concedes there is no doctrine on deciding the breadth of this latitude, or on determining the location of the desert limits (ibid., 107–8). There exists a comparable American theory of desert as providing only limits, which I criticize in von Hirsch, *Past or Future Crimes*, chaps. 4, 12.

11. Penal Code of Finland, art. 6, sec. 1. Translation by Matti Joutsen.

12. For a discussion of the rationale underlying the Finnish statute, see Jareborg and von Hirsch, " 'Neoklassizismus' in der Skandinavischen Kriminalpolitik."

13. The listed mitigating factors in the Finnish Penal Code (art. 6, sec. 3) include partial duress or pressure when committing offense, reduced mental capacity or "exceptional temptation" or "strong human sympathy leading to the offense," and voluntary attempts to alleviate the effect of the offense.

14. Penal Code of Finland, art. 6, sec. 2(4).

15. von Hirsch, *Past or Future Crimes,* chap. 7.

16. A study is now under way by a doctoral student at the law faculty of Helsinki University, Tapio Lappi-Seppälä.

17. Swedish Ministry of Justice, *Påföljd för Brott.*

18. For an analysis and English translation of these proposed chapters, see von Hirsch, "Principles for Choosing Sanctions," which also sketches the background of the proposals; *New England Journal on Criminal and Civil Confinement* 13, no. 2 (1987).

19. The working group consisted of Erland Aspelin, Carl-Johan Cosmo, Sten Heckscher, Nils Jareborg, Eckart Kühlhorn, Axel Lundqvist, Axel Morath, Knut Sveri, and Dag Victor.

20. Proposed chap. 33, sec. 5.

21. This is a somewhat simplified account of the Swedish proposals. The rationale is embodied in a proposed chapter 33 of the Swedish Penal Code and governs the choice between Sweden's two traditional sentences, imprisonment and fines. The tripartite scheme of penalties described in the text is set forth in a proposed chapter 34, dealing with the circumstances under which conditional sentences or probation may be substituted for imprisonment (Swedish Ministry of Justice, *Påföljd för Brott* 1:76–80).

22. The draft explicitly permits the offender's likelihood of recidivism to be considered in choosing between sanctions of comparable severity— viz., conditional sentence and probation (proposed chap. 34, sec. 10). However, this provision does not authorize the use of predictive factors in choosing sanctions of such substantially different severity as probation and imprisonment.

23. Unlike England, Sweden permits prosecutorial appeals.

24. The drafting body could use a grid for heuristic purposes in the course of developing the rationale. The grid would not be part of the final product, however. See von Hirsch, *Past or Future Crimes,* chap. 2.

25. See chapter 5 of this volume.

26. See, e.g., State v. Hagen, 317 N.W.2d 701 (Minn. 1982); State v. King, 337 N.W.2d 674 (Minn. 1983).

27. Jareborg and von Hirsch, " 'Neoklassimus' in der Skandinavischen Kriminalpolik." Swedish appellate courts tend to give considerable weight

to the explanatory reports, such as the report of the Committee on Prison Sanctions (cited in note 17) accompanying this proposed legislation.

Chapter 4

1. See Minnesota Sentencing Commission Act; Washington Sentencing Reform Act of 1981; Pennsylvania Sentencing Commission Act; and New York Sentencing Commission Act. See also, the 1984 legislation creating the U.S. Sentencing Commission (Public Law 98–473); that body's powers are set forth in 18 *United States Code (USC)* 991–98.

2. See von Hirsch, "Constructing Guidelines for Sentencing," 171–76.

3. Minnesota Sentencing Commission Act, sec. 9(5).

4. Minnesota Sentencing Guidelines Commission, *The Impact of the Minnesota Sentencing Guidelines,* 129–31.

5. Washington Sentencing Reform Act of 1981, sec. 4(3). The guidelines themselves offer considerable discretion, however, with respect to nonviolent first offenders. See chapter 2 of this volume, and the summary of the Washington guidelines set forth in the appendix.

6. Martin, "Interests and Politics in Sentencing Reform," 73–74.

7. The Pennsylvania statute directs that sentencing judges "shall consider" the guidelines. But it also states that judges shall impose an amount of confinement "that is consistent with the protection of the public, the gravity of the offense as it relates to the impact on the life of the victim and on the community, and the rehabilitative needs of the defendant." The comparative priority of those directives is not explained (18 *Pennsylvania Consolidated Statutes,* sec. 1321[b]). For the Pennsylvania courts' interpretations, see McCloskey, "The Effectiveness of Independent Sentencing Commission Guidelines."

8. The Minnesota enabling statute states that the grid's prescribed durations are "presumptive" (Minnesota Sentencing Commission Act, sec. 9[5]).

9. *Minnesota Sentencing Guidelines,* sec. II.D. For discussion of this standard, see chapter 5. Washington has also adopted the "substantial and compelling" formulation by statute (Washington Sentencing Reform Act, sec. 12[2]). A variety of alternative formulations is possible, however, e.g., that departures are permissible only in "exceptional" circumstances.

10. It should be up to the commission to decide the relative merits of definite presumptive sentences, presumptive ranges, and hybrids such as Minnesota's, where, although a definite term is the suggested sentence, judges may use a range around that term without departing from the guidelines or having to explain their reasons. See *Minnesota Sentencing Guidelines,* sec. V.

11. The 15% limit is set forth in Minnesota Sentencing Commission Act, sec. 9(5). The federal statute, 18 *USC* 994(b), provides that the top

of any standard range specifying imprisonment shall not exceed the bottom of the range by more than 25 percent. The enormous 48–120 month range in Pennsylvania is provided for conviction of third-degree murder without a prior record (*Pennsylvania Sentencing Guidelines,* sec. 303.9); New York's wide proposed ranges are set forth in New York State, *Determinate Sentencing,* 56.

12. The Washington Sentencing Reform Act's statement of purposes (sec. 1 of the act) provides that the guidelines are to:

1. Ensure that punishment for a criminal offense is proportionate to the seriousness of the offense and the offender's criminal history;
2. Promote respect for law by providing punishment which is just;
3. Be commensurate with the punishment imposed on others committing similar offenses;
4. Protect the public;
5. Offer the offender an opportunity to improve himself or herself; and
6. Make frugal use of the state's resources.

Subdivisions 1–3 emphasize desert; only subdivision 4 is explicitly crime-preventative.

13. Minnesota Sentencing Commission Act, sec. 9(5)(2).

14. von Hirsch, *Past or Future Crimes.*

15. New York Sentencing Commission Act, secs. 2(1), 2(3).

16. See Morris, *Madness and the Criminal Law,* chap. 5.

17. von Hirsch, *Past or Future Crimes,* chaps. 4, 12.

18. For a description of Pennsylvania's guidelines, see chapter 2 of this volume and Martin, "Interests and Politics in Sentencing Reform," 78–99. The guidelines place quite a heavy emphasis on the offender's criminal record—more so than would be consistent with a desert rationale. On the other hand, their incapacitative effects are uncertain, because the offender score measures prior record and has not been tested for its predictive ability.

The chairman's and staff director's comments about the guidelines' aims are set forth in Kramer and Scirica, "Pennsylvania Sentencing Guidelines."

19. 18 *USC* 994(i) and (j).

20. See von Hirsch, *Past or Future Crimes,* chaps. 7 and 11.

21. See Dershowitz, "Indeterminate Confinement."

22. Desert and deterrence conceptions do not give much weight to the prior record, if any; incapacitation strategies—using forecasts of offender risk—give it preeminent weight. See chapter 5 and von Hirsch, *Past or Future Crimes,* 11–12, 132–36.

23. Martin, "Interests and Politics in Sentencing Reform," 74–75.

24. Minnesota Sentencing Commission Act, sec. 9(5); New York Sentencing Commission Act, sec. 2(4); 18 *USC* 994(g).

25. Minnesota Sentencing Guidelines Commission, *Report to the Legislature,* 13–14.

26. See Association of the Bar of the City of New York, "Testimony Regarding Proposed Sentencing Guidelines."

27. Washington Sentencing Reform Act, sec. 4(6).

28. Pennsylvania's initially proposed guidelines did provide an exclusive list of aggravating and mitigating factors, but this feature was subsequently dropped; see Martin, "Interests and Politics in Sentencing Reform," 82–83, 95–97. Minnesota's list of factors is summarized in the appendix and discussed in chapter 5 of this volume. Washington's list is also summarized in the appendix to this volume.

29. State v. Evans, 311 N.W.2d 481 (Minn. 1981).

30. *Minnesota Sentencing Guidelines,* sec. II.D.

31. Washington Sentencing Reform Act, sec. 7; New York Sentencing Commission Act, sec. 3.

32. Minnesota Sentencing Commission Act, sec. 9(12).

33. Under recent U.S. Supreme Court decisions, these restrictions apply to the legislative veto in federal rule making (see Immigration and Naturalization Service v. Chadha, 103 S. Ct. 2764 [1983]); whether they apply to a state depends on the provisions of the particular state constitution.

34. See chapter 2; see also Martin, "Interests and Politics in Sentencing Reform," 89–97.

35. Minnesota Sentencing Commission Act, sec. 12(2).

36. Washington Sentencing Reform Act, sec. 21(4).

37. 18 *Pennsylvania Consolidated Statutes,* sec. 1386(c)(1).

38. The Washington statute explicitly bars appeal of sentences that are within the standard ranges (Washington Sentencing Reform Act, sec. 21[1]); the Minnesota guidelines provide that the sentencing court *may* depart for aggravating or mitigating circumstances (*Minnesota Sentencing Guidelines,* sec. II.D); the state supreme court has interpreted "may" as meaning that the judge usually has discretion to deny departure even when plausible aggravating or mitigating circumstances appear to be present (State v. Kindem, 313 N.W.2d 6 [Minn. 1981]).

39. 18 *Pennsylvania Consolidated Statutes,* sec. 1386(c)(2). For further discussion of possible standards for appellate review, see Ozanne, "Bringing the Rule of Law to Criminal Sentencing," 744–53.

40. Minnesota Sentencing Commission Act, sec. 11.

41. Washington Sentencing Reform Act, sec. 21(2).

42. Parole supervision remains only for defendants sentenced before the guidelines took effect.

43. Minnesota Sentencing Commission Act, secs. 4, 5.

44. *Pennsylvania Sentencing Guidelines,* sec. 303.9(a).

45. von Hirsch and Hanrahan, *The Question of Parole.*

46. Ibid., chap. 7.

47. New York Sentencing Commission Act, adopted in 1983. The proposed guidelines are set forth in New York State, *Determinate Sentencing.* For further information on development of the proposed guidelines, see chapter 2 of this volume; Association of the Bar of the City of

New York, "Testimony Regarding Proposed Sentencing Guide
Goldstein, "Sentencing Guidelines"; and Keeler, "Debate over Sentei
The descriptions of the New York developments are drawn also fro
own observations and conversations with commission members, co
sion staff, and other interested persons.

48. The grid places too much emphasis on prior convictions to i
a desert rationale yet does not use a validated prediction score as a
capacitative rationale would require. See note 18, above, and chapi
For the problems involved in the commission's reliance on existing
served averages, see Association of the Bar of the City of New Y
"Testimony Regarding Proposed Sentencing Guidelines."

49. Martin, "Interests and Politics in Sentencing Reform."

50. For developments leading up to enactment of Pennsylvania's
abling statute, see ibid., 61–66.

51. Ibid., 58–59.

52. New York Penal Law, sec. 70.06; People v. Ferrar, 52 N.Y.2d
(1981).

53. Letter from Kenneth Gribetz, president of New York State Disti
Attorneys Association to Joseph Bellacosa, chairman of New York Sti
Committee on Sentencing Guidelines (Oct. 19, 1984).

54. New York State, *Determinate Sentencing,* 62–64.

55. When the guidelines took effect, the Minnesota parole boarc
discretionary release power was terminated; see also Martin, "Interests ar
Politics in Sentencing Reform," 59.

56. Maine Statutes, Title 17A, chaps. 47–53. For discussion of th
Maine developments, see chapter 2 of this volume.

57. von Hirsch, *Past or Future Crimes,* chap. 15.

58. Martin, "Interests and Politics in Sentencing Reform," 45–46, 49–
50, 58–60.

59. Jacobs, "The Politics of Prison Expansion."

60. Association of the Bar of the City of New York, "Testimony Regarding Proposed Sentencing Guidelines."

61. New York State, *Determinate Sentencing,* 62–64.

62. These opponents included the state attorney general and the mayor
of New York City.

63. The bill creating the commission had been proposed by the governor; he voiced no support, however, after the commission's guidelines
were made public.

64. Cohen and Blumstein, "Sentencing of Convicted Offenders."

65. Elazar, *American Federalism,* chap. 5.

66. Ibid.

Chapter 5

1. The commission's explanation of its guidelines' rationale is set forth
in its 1981 report to the legislature, Minnesota Sentencing Guidelines

Commission, *Report to the Legislature.* References throughout this chapter to the commission's views are based on this report (hereinafter cited as *1981 Report,*) except where otherwise indicated.

2. *1981 Report,* 4–5.

3. *Minn. Statutes,* secs. 609.11, 401.01–4.05.16; *1981 Report,* 9.

4. *1981 Report,* 8–10.

5. My views on the role of the previous criminal record are set forth in von Hirsch, *Past or Future Crimes,* chap. 7. Fletcher's and Singer's views are summarized ibid., and set forth in Fletcher, *Rethinking Criminal Law,* 460–66, and Singer, *Just Deserts,* chap. 5.

6. There have been two general incapacitation strategies discussed in the literature. The first is the so-called collective incapacitation research conducted in the United States in the late 1970s. One estimates an average rate of felony offending. Then one develops scenarios for alternative sentencing policies having different criteria for invoking imprisonment and different durations of confinement. On the basis of the assumed felony rate, the number of crimes prevented under the different scenarios is then estimated. It has proven difficult, however, to develop reliable estimates of the average rate of offending, the average length of criminal careers, and replacement effects (von Hirsch, *Past or Future Crimes,* 115–16).

A more modest and perhaps more workable approach is "categorial" incapacitation, pioneered by Jacqueline Cohen, in her "Incapacitation as a Strategy of Crime Control." She has examined the rates of recidivism associated with conviction for particular categories of crime. She found in one U.S. jurisdiction that conviction for robbery was, on average, associated with more frequent and more serious subsequent crimes than conviction for burglary. If true, this means that incarcerating robbers would have a higher categorial-incapacitation effect than confining the burglars. Since risk is defined here in terms of the conviction offense, the strategy (unlike selective restraint) would not involve punishing differently those convicted of similar criminal acts. Elsewhere, I address whether such a strategy could be consistent with desert requirements—and conclude that, under certain conditions, it could (von Hirsch, *Past or Future Crimes,* chap. 13).

7. I am speaking of traditional prediction methods, which try simply to forecast whether the offender would recidivate without attempting to identify the rate or seriousness of the forecasted offenses (ibid., 105–7). There has recently been much discussion of so-called selective incapacitation techniques, which attempt to target the high-rate, serious offenders—those likely to commit frequent robberies or violent crimes. These more ambitious techniques, however, still suffer from serious methodological problems and cannot be reliably applied to sentencing contexts using the data available to sentencing courts at present (ibid., 107–27). For a summary of the major findings on prediction, see Cohen, "Incapacitation as

a Strategy for Crime Control." For discussion of prediction and prior convictions, see von Hirsch, *Past or Future Crimes,* 132–38.

8. Ibid., chap. 13.

9. Ibid., chap. 4.

10. Ibid., chaps. 3, 5, 11.

11. Ibid., 111, 126–27.

12. See Sparks et al., "Stumbling toward Justice," 423, table 9.2.

13. *1981 Report,* 9–10.

14. See, e.g., von Hirsch and Hanrahan, *The Question of Parole,* 18–19; von Hirsch, *Past or Future Crimes,* 162–65.

15. *Minn. Statutes,* sec. 609.52(3).

16. von Hirsch, *Past or Future Crimes,* chaps. 7, 11, 14.

17. *Minnesota Sentencing Guidelines,* sec. II.B. The scoring system is summarized in the appendix to this volume.

18. *1981 Report,* 13–14.

19. In 1978, Minnesota had the fourth-lowest per capita rate of confinement in state prisons among American states. However, this may in part be due to Minnesota's decentralized criminal justice system, in which a substantial portion of incarcerated offenders was confined in county jails.

20. von Hirsch, *Past or Future Crimes,* 40–43.

21. Ibid., 43–45.

22. Ibid., 44.

23. For fuller analysis of this issue, see ibid., chap. 8.

24. Sparks et al., "Stumbling toward Justice," 427–38. Under these researchers' formula, cell values were "predicted" by multiplying the median duration for the whole matrix by a "row" effect signifying the weight given to seriousness, and a "column" effect signifying the weight given to the record.

25. *Minnesota Sentencing Guidelines,* sec. II.A.

26. See von Hirsch and Mueller, "California's Determinate Sentencing Law," 274–77.

27. Oregon's parole guidelines took this approach: the broader statutory offense categories are subcategorized by the guidelines and assigned separate seriousness ratings. See Taylor, "In Search of Equity," 58–59.

28. The procedure for sentencing hearings is set forth in *Minnesota Statutes, Rules of Criminal Procedure,* sec. 27.03.

29. The commission thus has stated that "serious legal and ethical questions would be raised if punishment were to be determined on the basis of alleged, but unproven, behavior." *Minnesota Sentencing Guidelines,* sec. II.A.01. See also chapter 9 of this volume and Tonry, "Real Offense Sentencing."

30. Minnesota Sentencing Commission Act, sec. 9(6).

31. *Minnesota Statutes,* sec. 609.582.

32. *Minnesota Sentencing Guidelines,* sec. V. Burglary of an occupied dwelling now has a seriousness rating of 6 on the grid's ten-point scale;

burglary of an unoccupied dwelling a rating of 5; and nonresidential burglary a rating of 4.

33. von Hirsch, *Doing Justice*, 133.

34. See Zimring, "Making the Punishment Fit the Crime."

35. Premeditated homicide is excluded from the guidelines.

36. For a full description of the technique used, see *1981 Report*, 6–7.

37. Indiana's sentencing standards, for example, rely on the preexisting statutory offense classifications. See von Hirsch, "The New Indiana Sentencing Code."

38. This method is proposed in Wolfgang, "Seriousness of Crime and a Policy of Juvenile Justice."

39. von Hirsch, *Past or Future Crimes*, 65–66.

40. Ibid., 66–71; using this conception, I categorize harms according to whether they infringe "welfare interests" (the most important), "security interests" (intermediate), or "accumulative interests" (less important). This taxonomy is derived from Feinberg, *Harm to Others*. See also von Hirsch, "Injury and Exasperation," 702–6.

41. *Washington Sentencing Guidelines*, table 1; see also the appendix to the present volume.

42. *Minnesota Sentencing Guidelines*, sec. V.

43. These factors are expressly ruled out by *Minnesota Sentencing Guidelines*, sec. II.D.I. For the rationale for excluding them, see *1981 Report*, 5.

44. Letter from Dale G. Parent to Andrew von Hirsch (Sept. 24, 1979).

45. Letter from Andrew von Hirsch to Dale G. Parent (Oct. 8, 1979).

46. Ibid.

47. *Minnesota Sentencing Guidelines*, sec. II.D.2; for a fuller description of these factors, see the appendix to this volume.

48. California's list of aggravating and mitigating factors, for example, includes explicitly predictive criteria. See von Hirsch and Mueller, "California's Determinate Sentencing Law," 279.

49. For a summary of Minnesota Supreme Court cases holding that "dangerousness" is *not* grounds for departure above the guidelines and that amenability or nonamenability to probation is a mitigating or aggravating factor, see Knapp, *Minnesota Sentencing Guidelines and Commentary Annotated*, 48–49.

50. Minnesota Sentencing Guidelines Act, sec. 9(5).

51. Minnesota House of Representatives, Committee on Criminal Justice, *Resolution* (March 17, 1982); Minnesota Sentencing Guidelines Commission, *The Impact of the Minnesota Sentencing Guidelines*, 129–30.

52. Minnesota Sentencing Guidelines Act, sec. 9(5)(1).

53. See Meehl, *Clinical versus Statistical Prediction;* Gottfredson, "Assessment and Prediction Methods in Crime and Delinquency."

54. *Minnesota Sentencing Guidelines*, sec. II.D.

Chapter 6

1. The suggestions made in this chapter are based on the author's own experience as research director and later executive director of the Minnesota Sentencing Commission, and on conversations with members and staffs of other state sentencing commissions.

2. The failure to develop prison-impact projections, for example, created difficulty for the Pennsylvania and New York sentencing commissions; see chapters 2 and 4.

3. For a description and analysis of these efforts, see Blumstein et al., *Research on Sentencing.*

4. Even for such descriptive guidelines, however, there has been skepticism expressed about the need for complex modeling techniques; see ibid.

5. Pennsylvania's guidelines provide a range of several years' width for the more serious offenses; New York provides a range of more than three years' width for a first offense of the common crime of armed robbery; see chapters 2 and 4.

6. von Hirsch, "Commensurability and Crime Prevention."

Chapter 7

1. Staff from the New York, Washington, Pennsylvania, South Carolina, and Florida sentencing commissions as well as staff from the Canadian sentencing study commission kindly provided information on the organization and staffing of their commissions and also shared insights.

2. Tonry, "The Sentencing Commission in Sentencing Reform," 333–42.

3. Gottfredson, "Sentencing Guidelines."

4. See Minnesota Sentencing Guidelines Commission, *The Impact of the Minnesota Sentencing Guidelines,* 15; see also chapter 8 of this volume.

Chapter 8

1. Minnesota Sentencing Guidelines Commission, *Preliminary Report on the Development and Impact of the Minnesota Sentencing Guidelines.*

2. Sarason, *The Creation of Settings and the Future of Societies,* 140.

3. Ellickson and Petersilia, *Implementing New Ideas in Criminal Justice,* 43–44.

4. Minnesota Sentencing Guidelines Commission, *The Impact of the Minnesota Sentencing Guidelines.*

5. This and the other recent shifts in sentencing patterns discussed herein are described more fully ibid.

6. State v. Randolph, 316 N.W.2d 208 (Minn. 1982). See also Knapp, *Minnesota Sentencing Guidelines and Commentary Annotated,* 89–90.

7. 311 N.W.2d 41 (Minn. 1981). See Knapp, *Minnesota Sentencing Guidelines and Commentary Annotated,* 41, 44–45.

8. Sarason, *The Creation of Settings and the Future of Societies,* 5–6.

9. The commission has the authority to develop such guidelines for nonprison sanctions but as a practical matter would probably need a further legislative mandate to implement them successfully.

10. A reporter who had covered the commission for some time observed in a private conversation with the author that it appeared commission members felt durational reductions were more feasible politically than changing the dispositional line, which would be more visually dramatic.

11. Minnesota Sentencing Guidelines Commission, "Discussion Paper on Possible Modifications to the Sentencing Guidelines."

12. The language in the 1981 intrafamilial sexual abuse statute that appears to have encouraged mitigated dispositions reads as follows: "[T]he court may stay imposition or execution of sentence if it finds that a stay is in the best interest of the complainant or the family unit." *Minn. Statutes,* sec. 609.3641(2).

13. *Minn. Statutes,* secs. 609.342–609.345.

14. *Minn. Statutes,* sec. 609.15(1).

15. Minnesota Sentencing Commission Act, sec. 9(2).

16. For a discussion of these different role conceptions, see Tonry, "The Sentencing Commission in Sentencing Reform."

17. Ellickson and Petersilia, *Implementing New Ideas in Criminal Justice,* 60–70.

Chapter 9

1. For "discount," see Gottfredson, Wilkins, and Hoffman, *Guidelines for Parole and Sentencing;* for "charge reduction guidelines," see Schulhofer, "Due Process of Sentencing."

2. Eisenstein and Jacob, *Felony Justice.* For an overview, see Nardulli, *The Study of Criminal Courts,* 101–30.

3. For California's experience, see Blumstein et al., *Research on Sentencing;* for the experience with voluntary guidelines, see Rich et al., *Sentencing Guidelines;* Carrow et al., *Guidelines without Force.*

4. See chapters 2 and 8. See also Minnesota Sentencing Guidelines Commission, *The Impact of the Minnesota Sentencing Guidelines;* Washington Sentencing Commission, *Report to the Legislature.*

5. Alschuler, "Sentencing Reform and Prosecutorial Power." See also Schulhofer, "Due Process of Sentencing."

6. For example, see Polinsky and Shavell, "Contribution and Claim Reduction among Anti-Trust Defendants."

7. Blumstein, Cohen, and Nagin, *Deterrence and Incapacitation.*

8. Knapp, "Impact of the Minnesota Sentencing Guidelines on Sentencing Practices."

9. A third, somewhat more romantic possibility—blind sentencing, in which the sentencing judge is unaware whether the defendant was convicted after trial or plea—is discussed in Coffee and Tonry, "Hard Choices."

10. See Arthur D. Little, *An Evaluation of Parole Guidelines in Four Jurisdictions,* concerning Washington and Oregon; National Conference of Commissioners on Uniform State Laws, *Model Sentencing and Corrections Act;* for local sentencing guidelines, see, for example, Wilkins et al., *Sentencing Guidelines.*

11. Coffee and Tonry, "Hard Choices."

12. The matter is addressed in sec. 2.19 of the commission's regulations (28 C.F.R. 2.19).

13. Coffee and Tonry, "Hard Choices."

14. American Bar Association, *Sentencing Alternatives and Procedures,* sec. 18–6.4; National Conference of Commissioners on Uniform State Laws, *Model Sentencing and Corrections Act,* secs. 3–206, 3–207.

15. Schulhofer, "Due Process of Sentencing."

16. Schwartz, "Options in Constructing a Sentencing System."

17. See chapter 8. See also Minnesota Sentencing Guidelines Commission, *The Impact of the Minnesota Sentencing Guidelines.*

18. Zeisel, "The Offer That Cannot Be Refused."

19. Rubinstein, Clarke, and White, *Alaska Bans Plea Bargaining,* 213–17.

20. Gottfredson, Wilkins, and Hoffman, *Guidelines for Parole and Sentencing.*

21. Schulhofer, "Due Process of Sentencing."

22. Ibid.

23. Ibid.

24. Schulhofer, "Is Plea Bargaining Inevitable?"

25. Rich et al., *Sentencing Guidelines;* and Carrow et al., *Guidelines without Force.*

26. Zeisel and Diamond, "Search for Sentencing Equity."

Bibliography

Allen, Francis A. *The Decline of the Rehabilitative Ideal: Penal Policy and Social Purpose.* New Haven: Yale University Press, 1981.

Alschuler, Albert W. "Sentencing Reform and Prosecutorial Power." *University of Pennsylvania Law Review* 126 (1978): 550–77.

American Bar Association, Task Force on Sentencing Alternatives and Procedures. *Sentencing Alternatives and Procedures.* 2d ed. Washington, D.C.: American Bar Association, 1979.

Arthur D. Little, Inc. *An Evaluation of Parole Guidelines in Four Jurisdictions.* Washington, D.C.: National Institute of Corrections, 1981.

Ashworth, Andrew. "Techniques of Guidance on Sentencing." *Criminal Law Review* (1984): 519–30.

Association of the Bar of the City of New York, Council on Criminal Justice. "Testimony Regarding Proposed Sentencing Guidelines." *Record of the Association of the Bar of the City of New York* 40 (1985): 257–75.

Blumstein, Alfred, Jacqueline Cohen, Susan E. Martin, and Michael H. Tonry, eds. *Research on Sentencing: The Search for Reform.* Washington, D.C.: National Academy Press, 1983.

Blumstein, Alfred, Jacqueline Cohen, and Daniel Nagin, eds. *Deterrence and Incapacitation: Estimating the Effects of Criminal Sanctions on Crime Rates.* Washington, D.C.: National Academy of Sciences, 1978.

Boerner, David. *Sentencing in Washington: A Legal Analysis of the Sentencing Reform Act of 1981.* Seattle: Butterworth, 1985.

Bruns, Hans-Jurgen. *Das Recht der Strafzumessung* (The Law of Sentencing). 2d ed. Cologne: Carl Heymanns, 1985.

Carrow, Deborah M., Judith Feins, Beverly N. W. Lee, and Lois Olinger. *Guidelines without Force: An Evaluation of the Multi-jurisdictional Sentencing Guidelines Field Test.* Cambridge, Mass.: Abt Associates, 1985.

Casper, Jonathan D., David Brereton, and David Neal. "The California Determinate Sentence Law." *Criminal Law Bulletin* 19 (1983): 405–33.

Bibliography

Coffee, John C., Jr., and Michael Tonry. "Hard Choices: Critical Trade-offs in the Implementation of Sentencing Reform through Guidelines." In *Reform and Punishment*, edited by Michael Tonry and Franklin E. Zimring, 155–203. Chicago: University of Chicago Press, 1983.

Cohen, Jacqueline. "Incapacitation as a Strategy for Crime Control: Possibilities and Pitfalls." In *Crime and Justice: An Annual Review of Research*, edited by Michael H. Tonry and Norval Morris, 5:1–84. Chicago: University of Chicago Press, 1983.

Cohen, Jacqueline, and Alfred Blumstein. "Sentencing of Convicted Offenders: An Analysis of the Public's View." *Law and Society Review* 14 (1980): 223–61.

Cullen, Francis T., and Karen E. Gilbert. *Reaffirming Rehabilitation*. Cincinnati: Anderson Publishing, 1982.

Dershowitz, Alan M. "Indeterminate Confinement: Letting the Therapy Fit the Harm." *University of Pennsylvania Law Review* 123 (1974): 297–339.

Eisenstein, James, and Herbert Jacob. *Felony Justice*. Boston: Little, Brown, 1977.

Elazar, Daniel J. *American Federalism: A View from the States*. 3d ed. New York: Harper and Row, 1984.

Ellickson, Phyllis, and Joan Petersilia. *Implementing New Ideas in Criminal Justice*. Santa Monica, Calif.: RAND Corporation, 1983.

Feinberg, Joel. *Harm to Others*. New York: Oxford University Press, 1984.

Fletcher, George. *Rethinking Criminal Law*. Boston: Little, Brown, 1978.

Frankel, Marvin E. *Criminal Sentences: Law Without Order*. New York: Hill and Wang, 1972.

Frankel, Marvin E., and Leonard Orland. "Sentencing Commissions and Guidelines." *Georgetown Law Journal* 73 (1984): 225–47.

Goldstein, Tom. "Sentencing Guidelines: The Search for Fairness: A Report on the Fourth Annual Retreat of the Council on Criminal Justice." *Record of the Association of the Bar of the City of New York* 40 (1985): 1–36.

Gottfredson, Don M. "Assessment and Prediction Methods in Crime and Delinquency." In *Task Force Report: Juvenile Delinquency and Youth Crime*, President's Commission for Law Enforcement and Administration of Justice, 171–87. Washington, D.C.: U.S. Government Printing Office, 1967.

———. "Sentencing Guidelines." In *Sentencing*, edited by Hyman Gross and Andrew von Hirsch, 310–14. New York: Oxford University Press, 1981.

Gottfredson, Don M., Leslie T. Wilkins, and Peter B. Hoffman. *Guidelines for Parole and Sentencing*. Lexington, Mass.: D. C. Heath, 1978.

Greenwood, Peter W. *Selective Incapacitation*. Santa Monica, Calif.: RAND Corporation, 1982.

Gross, Hyman, and Andrew von Hirsch, eds. *Sentencing*. New York: Oxford University Press, 1981.

Jacobs, James B. "The Politics of Prison Expansion." *New York University Review of Law and Social Change* 12 (1983–84): 209–41.

Jareborg, Nils, and Andrew von Hirsch. " 'Neoklassizismus' in der skandinavischen Kriminalpolitik: Sein Einfluss, seine Grundprinzipien und Kriterien" (" 'Neoclassicism' in Scandinavian Sanctioning Policy: Its Influence, Rationale, and Criteria"). In *Neuere Tendenzen der Kriminalpolitik: Beiträge zu einem Deutsch-Skandinavischen Strafrechts-Kolloquium,* edited by Albin Eser and Kavin Cornils. Freiburg: Max-Planck Institut für Ausländisches und Internationales Strafrecht, 1987.

Keeler, Bob. "The Debate over Sentencing: Albany Considers Revising Laws that Put Convicts Behind Bars. *Newsday,* June 16 and 17, 1985.

Kleinig, John. *Punishment and Desert.* The Hague: Martinus Nijhoff, 1973.

Knapp, Kay A. "Impact of the Minnesota Sentencing Guidelines on Sentencing Practices." *Hamline Law Review* 5 (1982): 237–70.

———. *Minnesota Sentencing Guidelines and Commentary Annotated.* St. Paul: Minnesota Continuing Legal Education Press, 1985.

Kramer, John H., and Robin L. Lubitz. "Pennsylvania's Sentencing Reform: The Impact of Commission-Established Guidelines." State College: Pennsylvania Commission on Sentencing, 1984.

Kramer, John H., Robin L. Lubitz, and Cynthia A. Kempinen. "Sentencing Guidelines: A Quantitative Comparison of Sentencing Policy in Minnesota, Pennsylvania and Washington." State College: Pennsylvania Commission on Sentencing, 1985.

Kramer, John H., and Anthony J. Scirica. "Complex Policy Choices: The Pennsylvania Commission on Sentencing." State College: Pennsylvania Commission on Sentencing, 1985.

———. "Pennsylvania Sentencing Guidelines: Just Deserts vs. Individualized Sentences." State College: Pennsylvania Commission on Sentencing, 1983.

Martin, Susan E. "Interests and Politics in Sentencing Reform: The Development of Sentencing Guidelines in Minnesota and Pennsylvania." *Villanova Law Review* 29 (1984): 21–113.

McCloskey, John P. "The Effectiveness of Independent Sentencing Commission Guidelines: An Analysis of Appellate Court Decisions in Two Jurisdictions." State College: Pennsylvania Commission on Sentencing, 1985.

Meehl, Paul. *Clinical versus Statistical Prediction: A Theoretical Analysis and a Review of the Evidence.* Minneapolis: University of Minnesota Press, 1954.

Miethe, Terance D., and Charles A. Moore. "Socioeconomic Disparities under Determinate Sentencing Systems: A Comparison of Preguideline and Postguideline Practices in Minnesota." *Criminology* 23 (1985): 337–63.

Minnesota Sentencing Commission Act. 1978 Minn. Laws, chap. 723.

Minnesota Sentencing Guidelines and Commentary. Revised August 1, 1986. St. Paul: Minnesota Sentencing Guidelines Commission.

Minnesota Sentencing Guidelines Commission. "Discussion Paper on Possible Modifications to the Sentencing Guidelines." St. Paul: Minnesota Sentencing Guidelines Commission, April 1986.

———. *The Impact of the Minnesota Sentencing Guidelines: Three-Year Evaluation.* St. Paul: Minnesota Sentencing Guidelines Commission, 1984.

———. *Preliminary Report on the Development and Impact of the Minnesota Sentencing Guidelines.* St. Paul: Minnesota Sentencing Guidelines Commission, 1982.

———. *Report to the Legislature* (Jan. 1, 1981).

Morris, Norval. *Madness and the Criminal Law.* Chicago: University of Chicago Press, 1982.

Nardulli, Peter F. *The Study of Criminal Courts.* Cambridge, Mass.: Ballinger Publishing, 1979.

National Conference of Commissioners on Uniform State Laws. *Model Sentencing and Corrections Act,* 1978.

New York Sentencing Commission Act. 1983 N.Y. Laws, chap. 711.

New York State, Committee on Sentencing Guidelines. *Determinate Sentencing: Report and Recommendations.* New York, 1985.

Note. "Appellate Review of Primary Sentencing Decisions: A Connecticut Case Study." *Yale Law Journal* 69 (1960): 1451–78.

O'Donnell, P. D. Curtis, and M. Churgin. *Toward a Just and Effective Sentencing System.* New York: Praeger, 1977.

Ozanne, Peter A. "Bringing the Rule of Law to Criminal Sentencing: Judicial Review, Sentencing Guidelines, and a Policy of Just Deserts." *Loyola University of Chicago Law Journal* 13 (1982): 721–89.

Pennsylvania Commission on Sentencing. *1983 Report: Sentencing in Pennsylvania.* State College: Pennsylvania Commission on Sentencing, 1984.

———. *1984 Report: Sentencing in Pennsylvania.* State College: Pennsylvania Commission on Sentencing, 1985.

———. *Proposed Sentencing Guidelines. Pennsylvania Bulletin,* Jan. 24, 1981, 463–76.

Pennsylvania Sentencing Commission Act. 1978 Penn. Laws, chap. 319.

Pennsylvania Sentencing Guidelines. In *Pennsylvania Administrative Code,* tit. 204, sec. 303.1 through sec. 303.9.

Phillips, H. J. "Final Report of the Maine Sentencing Commission." A report submitted to the 111th Maine Legislature. Augusta, 1984.

Polinsky, A. Mitchell, and Steven Shavell. "Contribution and Claim Reduction among Anti-Trust Defendants: An Economic Analysis." *Stanford Law Review* 33 (1981): 447–71.

Posner, Richard A. *Economic Analysis of Law.* 2d ed. Boston: Little, Brown, 1977.

Rathke, Stephen C. "Plea Negotiating under the Sentencing Guidelines." *Hamline Law Review* 5 (1982): 271–91.

Rich, William, Paul Sutton, Todd Clear, and Michael Saks. *Sentencing Guidelines: Their Operation and Impact on the Courts*. Williamsburg, Va.: National Center for State Courts, 1982.

Rubinstein, Michael L., Stevens H. Clarke, and Teresa J. White. *Alaska Bans Plea Bargaining*. Washington, D.C.: U.S. Government Printing Office, 1980.

Sarason, Seymour B. *The Creation of Settings and the Future of Societies*. San Francisco: Jossey-Bass, 1972.

Schulhofer, Stephen. "Due Process of Sentencing." *University of Pennsylvania Law Review* 128 (1980): 733–828.

———. "Is Plea Bargaining Inevitable?" *Harvard Law Review* 97 (1984): 1037–107.

Schwartz, Louis. "Options in Constructing a Sentencing System: Sentencing Guidelines under Legislative or Judicial Hegemony." In *Reform and Punishment*, edited by Michael Tonry and Franklin E. Zimring. Chicago: University of Chicago Press, 1983.

Sechrest, Lee, Susan O. White, and Elizabeth D. Brown, eds. *The Rehabilitation of Criminal Offenders: Problems and Prospects*. Washington, D.C.: National Academy of Sciences, 1979.

Shane-DuBow, Sandra, Alice P. Brown, and Erik Olsen. *Sentencing Reform in the United States: History, Content, and Effect*. Washington, D.C.: U.S. Government Printing Office, 1985.

Singer, Richard G. *Just Deserts: Sentencing Based on Equality and Desert*. Cambridge, Mass.: Ballinger Publishing, 1979.

Sparks, Richard F., Bridget Stecher, Jay Albanese, Peggy Shelly, and Donald Barry. "Stumbling Toward Justice: Some Overlooked Research and Policy Questions about Statewide Sentencing Guidelines." Newark, N.J.: Rutgers University, School of Criminal Justice, 1982.

Stone-Meierhoefer, Barbara, and Peter B. Hoffman. "Presumptive Parole Dates: The Federal Approach." *Federal Probation* 46, no. 2 (1982): 41–57.

Swedish Ministry of Justice. *Påföljd för Brott* (Sanctions for Crime). Stockholm: Stadens offentliga utredningar, 1986: 13–15.

Taylor, Elizabeth. "In Search of Equity: The Oregon Parole Matrix." *Federal Probation* 43, no. 1 (1979): 52–59.

Thomas, D. A. *Principles of Sentencing*. London: Heinemann, 1979.

———. "Sentencing Guidance: The Court of Appeal and the Crown Court." Cambridge: Institute of Criminology, Cambridge University, 1985.

Tonry, Michael H. "Real Offense Sentencing: The Model Sentencing and Corrections Act." *Journal of Criminal Law and Criminology* 72 (1981): 1550–96.

———. "The Sentencing Commission in Sentencing Reform." *Hofstra Law Review* 7 (1979): 315–53.

Twentieth-Century Fund. Task Force on Criminal Sentencing. *Fair and

Certain Punishment. New York: McGraw-Hill, 1976.

United States Sentencing Commission. *Sentencing Guidelines: Preliminary Draft*. Washington, D.C., 1986.

von Hirsch, Andrew. "Commensurability and Crime Prevention: Evaluating Formal Sentencing Structures and Their Rationale." *Journal of Criminal Law and Criminology* 74 (1983): 209–48.

―――. "Constructing Guidelines for Sentencing: The Critical Choices for the Minnesota Sentencing Guidelines Commission." *Hamline Law Review* 5 (1982): 164–215.

―――. "Dangerousness and Deservedness in Sentencing Policy." *Criminal Law Review* (1986): 79–91.

―――. "Desert and Previous Convictions in Sentencing." *Minnesota Law Review* 65 (1981): 591–634.

―――. *Doing Justice: The Choice of Punishments*. New York: Hill and Wang, 1976. Reprint, Boston: Northeastern University Press, 1986.

―――. "Guidance by Numbers or Word?—Numerical vs. Narrative Guidelines for Sentencing." In *Sentencing Reform: Guidance or Guidelines?*, edited by Ken Pease and Martin Wasik. 46–69. Manchester: Manchester University Press, 1987.

―――. "Injury and Exasperation: An Examination of *Harm to Others* and *Offense to Others*." *Michigan Law Review* 84 (1986): 700–714.

―――. "The New Indiana Sentencing Code: Is It Indeterminate Sentencing?" In *An Anatomy of Criminal Justice: A Systems Overview*, edited by Cleon Foust and D. R. Webster. 143–56. Lexington, Mass.: D. C. Heath, 1980.

―――. *Past or Future Crimes: Deservedness and Dangerousness in the Sentencing of Criminals*. New Brunswick, N.J.: Rutgers University Press, 1985. U.K. ed., Manchester: Manchester University Press, 1986.

―――. "Principles for Choosing Sanctions: Sweden's Proposed Sentencing Statute." *New England Journal on Criminal and Civil Confinement* 13, no. 2 (1987).

von Hirsch, Andrew, and Kathleen J. Hanrahan. "Determinate Penalty Systems in America: An Overview." *Crime and Delinquency* 27 (1981): 289–316.

―――. *The Question of Parole: Retention, Reform or Abolition?* Cambridge, Mass.: Ballinger Publishing, 1979.

von Hirsch, Andrew, and Nils Jareborg. "Provocation and Culpability." In *Responsibility, Character and the Emotions: New Essays in Moral Psychology*, edited by Ferdinand Schoeman. New York: Cambridge University Press, 1987.

von Hirsch, Andrew, and Julia M. Mueller. "California's Determinate Sentencing Law: An Analysis of Its Structure." *New England Journal on Criminal and Civil Confinement* 10 (1984): 253–300.

Washington Sentencing Commission. *Report to the Legislature: January 1, 1986*. Olympia: Washington Sentencing Commission, 1986.

————. *Sentencing Practices under the Sentencing Reform Act: A Preliminary Report*. Olympia: Washington Sentencing Commission, 1985.

Washington Sentencing Guidelines. In *Revised Code of Washington*, secs. 9.94A.340 through 9.94A.420 and tables 1, 2, and 3.

Washington Sentencing Reform Act of 1981. 1981 Wash. Laws, chap. 137, as amended by 1983 Wash. Laws., chap. 163.

Wasik, Martin. "Excuses at the Sentencing Stage." *Criminal Law Review* (1983): 450–65.

————. "Guidance and Guidelines in Sentencing." Manchester: Manchester University, Faculty of Law, April 1985.

Wilkins, Leslie T., Jack Kress, Don M. Gottfredson, J. Calpin, and Arthur Gelman. *Sentencing Guidelines: Structuring Judicial Discretion*. Washington, D.C.: National Institute of Law Enforcement and Criminal Justice, 1978.

Wilson, James Q. *Thinking About Crime*. Rev. ed. New York: Basic Books, 1983.

Wolfgang, Marvin E. "Seriousness of Crime and a Policy of Juvenile Justice." In *Delinquency, Crime, and Society,* edited by James Short, Jr., 267–86. Chicago: University of Chicago Press, 1976.

Zeisel, Hans. "The Offer That Cannot Be Refused." In *The Criminal Justice System,* edited by Franklin E. Zimring and Richard Frase. Boston: Little, Brown, 1980.

Zeisel, Hans, and Shari S. Diamond. "Search for Sentencing Equity: Sentence Review in Massachusetts and Connecticut." *American Bar Foundation Research Journal* (1977): 881–940.

Zimring, Franklin E. "Making the Punishment Fit the Crime: A Consumer's Guide to Sentencing Reform." *Hastings Center Report* 6, no. 6 (1976): 13–17. Reprinted in *Sentencing,* edited by Hyman Gross and Andrew von Hirsch. 327–35. New York: Oxford University Press, 1981.

Index

Italicized page numbers indicate tables

Acquittal, 149, 150; real-offense sentencing following, 155
Advisory body for technical assistance to courts, 58–59
Aggravated dispositional departures, 129
Aggravating and mitigating factors, 54, 55; advisory guidelines for, 59; appellate sentence review and, 74; in drug sentences, 135–36; lists of, 9, 102–5, 195n13, 198n28; in state sentencing guidelines, 5, 6, 21, 23, 24, 25, 58, 71–72
Aggravating durational departures, 131
Alaska, 5, 163
Amendments to sentencing guidelines, 116, 141
Appellate courts: sentencing principles, development of, 50–52, 57–58; tariff development, assistance for, 58–59
Appellate sentence review, 9, 16, 17–18, 198n38; appeal rate, 42; appeals by other participants, 171–72; prosecutorial appeals, 168–71; as provision of statutes, 73–74; in Sweden, 55
Armed robbery, 102, 159, 203n5
Attorneys: attitude re sentencing guidelines, 143, 144; as counsel to probation department, 162; guilty-plea discounts and, 165, 167; plea bar-

gaining and, 160; as sentencing commission members, 118, 119, 121–22, 136

Bench trials, 166
Blind sentencing, 205n9
Burglary, 94, 97–98, 102n32

California sentencing guidelines, 5; aggravating and mitigating factors, 202n48; offense classifications, 97; sentence reconsideration requests, 172; sentencing ranges, 155
Cardinal proportionality of punishment, 95
Case law: real-offense sentencing and, 156–58; sentencing principles established by, 50–52
Case processing, evaluation of, 115
Categorial incapacitation, 200n6
Charge bargaining, 31, 114–15, 143, 146; illusory plea bargaining and, 158, 159, 170; increase in, 39–40, 41
Child abuse, sentences for, 134–35, 204n12
Collective incapacitation, 200n6
Colorado, 5
Commensurate-deserts principle, 53
Community Corrections Act (Minnesota), 85
Computer use by sentencing commissions, 124
Connecticut sentencing commission, 16, 21, 42–43

219

Index

Consecutive sentences, 23, 24
Constituent representation by commissioners, 136–37
Constitutionality concerns: appellate sentencing appeal and, 169; guilty-plea discount and, 165–66
Consultants to sentencing commissions, 118
Consumer reform efforts, 161
Convictions, multiple, 48, 49, 50, 102
Corbitt v. New Jersey, 165–66
Corrections officials as sentencing commission members, 118, 119
Courts, cooperation of, 59–60
Crime rates, sentencing policy and, 88–89
Crimes, rating of, 96; "enhancements" and, 101–2; offense classifications, 97–99; offense score, 108–9; seriousness ratings, 99–101
Criminal codes, 122
Criminal history score, 40; method of computing, 48, 96, 102; multiple charges and, 48, 129, 133–34; negotiation of, 140; in preguideline practice study, 108–9; rationale and, 90, 92, 93
Criminal record, 13, 66, 78; advisory guidelines for, 59; and duration of imprisonment, 96; rationale and, 11, 12, 54, 68–69, 86, 87, 197n18, 197n22, 199n48

Defendants: personal factors of, 19; preferences for prison vs. nonprison sentences, 129–30; sentencing risks weighed by, 147–48; social history of, 87, 103
Defendants' rights: to appeal, 168–69, 171; to fair treatment, 6, 79; in plea bargaining, 143, 151; real-offense sentencing and, 153–54, 158, 162
Descriptive sentencing guidelines, 19, 21, 108, 110
Desert rationale, 4, 11, 19; aggravating and mitigating factors, 103–4; criminal history and, 102, 197n18, 197n22, 199n48; debate re, 88; and disparity reduction, 10, 114; and

dispositional line, 85–86, 90, 91; enabling legislation and, 65, 66, 67, 68–69; limits on sentencing and, 194n10; prison population and, 13–14, 94–95; purpose of, 89; in statutory statements of purpose, 53, 54. *See also* Modified desert rationale
Determinate sentencing law (Indiana), 5, 6
Determinate sentencing system, 21
Deterrence rationale, 51, 66, 68–69, 148, 197n22
Deviation from sentencing guidelines, 59–60, 64–65, 106, 140–41; statutory provision for, 71–72
Discounts. *See* Guilty-plea discounts
Discrimination against defendants, 19
Disparity in sentences: evaluation of, 114; reduction of, 9–10, 19
Dispositional departures, 27–29, 30, 127, 129, 130
Dispositional line, 8–9, 48, 49, 57, 204n10; elevation of, 93–95; slope of, 11–12, 84–85, 89–90, 91, 92–93, 134
Dispositions, mandated, as provision of statutes, 67–69
District size representation in research sample, 109
Double jeopardy clause, 155, 169
Drug dealers, sentences for, 135–36
Durational departures, 28–30, 131

Economic crimes, 101
Elazar, Daniel, 82–83
Elite model of sentencing commission membership, 118
Emergency release, 12
Enabling legislation, provisions of: appellate sentence review, 73–74; deviating sentences, 71–72; legislative review of the guidelines, 72–73; mandated dispositions, 67–69; parole release and supervision, 74–75; policy-making role of the commission, 62–63; prison and jail sentence guidelines, 63–64; prison capacity considerations, 69–70; rationale selection, 65–67, 69; sentencing com-

mission composition, 117; sentencing guidelines, binding effect of, 64; sentencing guidelines, structure and definiteness of, 65

England, sentencing principles in, 51–52, 56

"Enhancements" of crime seriousness ratings, 101–2

Evaluation research, design of, 113–15

Federal court system, 135, 155

Federal sentencing commission, 8, 16, 67, 153

Federal sentencing law, 67, 68, 69

Felony convictions: compliance rate for, 29, 30–31; criminal history and, 84, 102; dispositional line and, 90, 92; guidelines for, 25, 37; mandated dispositions for, 67, 68, 78

Females in research sample, 109–10

Fines for low penal value crimes, 55

Finland, statutory statements of purpose in, 53–54, 195n13

Firearms offenses, 32–33, 34, 85, 131

Firearms sentencing laws, 157

First offenders, 35, 40, 67, 68, 84–85, 196n5

Fletcher, George, 86, 90

Florida sentencing commission: funding for, 123–24; membership of, 118

Frankel, Marvin E., 7–8, 18

Funding for sentencing commissions, 21, 123–24

General incapacitation, 86, 87

Germany, statutory statements of purpose in, 53, 194n10

Good-behavior allowance, 5, 131, 191n19

Governors: sentencing guidelines, support of, 79; "toughness" of campaigns, 81

Guilty-plea discounts, 143, 144; effects of, 163–64; methods of, 164, 166–67; problems with, 164–65, 167

Guilty pleas: incentive for, 42, 163–64, 165; sentencing guidelines and, 146, 147, 148, 149, 150, 151, 152

Harms, grading of, 101, 202n40

"Horizontal" charging and bargaining practices, 40, 170, 171

Hybrid rationale, 66–67

Incapacitative rationale, 4, 10, 11; criminal record and, 197n18, 197n22, 199n48; and dispositional line, 85; mandated dispositions and, 68–69; types of, 86–87, 200n6

Indiana determinate sentencing law, 5, 6, 202n37

Individualistic style of politics, 82, 83

In-out line. *See* Dispositional line

Institutionalization of programs, 127–28, 140–41

Interest-group representative role of commissioners, 136–37, 138

Jacobs, James, 80

Jail sentences, 201n19; disparity in, 38; guidelines for, 25, 35, 36, 63–64, 105

Judges: adverse publicity and, 174–75; appellate sentencing appeal and, 168, 169; departure reports, 140–41; interpretation and application of sentencing guidelines, 7, 8; real-offense sentencing and, 162; as sentencing commission members, 117–18, 119, 120, 136; sentencing guidelines, opposition to, 21, 24–25, 26, 42, 78–79, 144

Judicial discretion, 3–5, 21, 47, 145, 146; limits on, 105–6

Judicial model of sentencing commission membership, 117–18

Jury determination of offense severity, 158

Jury trials, costs of, 166

Jury-trial waiver discounts, 166

Kennedy, Edward, 18

Larceny, 154–55

Law enforcement officers as sentencing commission members, 118, 136

Legislative approval of sentencing guidelines, 7, 8, 21, 22, 24, 25, 49, 192*n*21; as provision of statutes, 72

Legislative judgments of crime seriousness ratings, 100

Legislative prescriptions re sentencing guidelines, 67–69

Legislative standards, unsuitability of, 5–6

Legislative veto of sentencing guidelines, 72–73, 192*n*21

Legislators as sentencing commission members, 119

Maine sentencing commission, 16, 20–21, 43

Maine sentencing guidelines, judicial opposition to, 79

McMillan v. Pennsylvania, 156–57

Meetings of sentencing commissions, frequency of, 120–21

Membership of sentencing commissions, 117–19, 136; part- or full-time, 120

Minnesota, sentencing reform in, 16

Minnesota sentencing commission, 8; commissioners' role definitions, 136–38; funding for, 123; "political style" of, 82–83; preguideline practice, study of, 108–9; presentence report review, 173; resources for, 138–40; role of, 63, 132–33, 172; staffing for, 124; success of, 18–20, 43, 124

Minnesota sentencing guidelines: aggravating and mitigating factors, 57–58, 102–5; appellate sentence review, 42, 73, 74, 198*n*38; binding effect of, 64, 196*n*8; compliance rates, 28–29; correctional resources, projection of impact on, 112–13; crimes, rating of, 96–102, 201*n*32; deviating sentences, 71–72; disparity and, 37–38, 114; dispositional line, elevation of, 93–95; dispositional line, slope of, 84–85, 89–90, 91, 92–93; effects of, 20; evaluation of, 127–28, 151; goals of, 133–36;

guilty-plea discounts, 164–65; implementation of, 113, 128–32; institutionalization of, 127–28, 140–41; jail sentences and, 63, 201*n*19; judicial discretion, limit on, 105–6; legislative review of, 72, 192*n*21; mandated dispositions, 67; parole release and supervision, 74–75, 191*n*19, 199*n*55; plea bargaining and, 38–40; prison population and, 12–13, 69; prosecutorial and judicial opposition to, 77–78; prosecutorial discretion, 146–47, 152; punishment issues in, 80; ranges of sentences, 65, 196*n*11; rationale, choice of, 11, 65, 96, 100–101; real-offense sentencing and, 162–63; sentencing grid, duration of imprisonment in, 96; sentencing pattern changes, 35–36; and sentencing severity, 36–37; shortcomings of, 48–49

Minnesota sentencing practice, 1982–1984: prison populations, 131–32; proportionality in sentencing, 128–30; uniformity in sentencing, 130–31

Misdemeanors, 31, 102

Mitigated dispositional departures, 134–35

Mitigating factors. *See* Aggravating and mitigating factors

Modified desert rationale, 50; and dispositional line, 48, 90, 92, 93, 96

Monitoring system for sentencing guidelines, 115–16

Moralistic style of politics, 82, 83

Morgenthau, Robert, 22

Multiple charges and convictions, 48, 49, 50, 102, 129, 133

Murder convictions, 196*n*11

New Jersey, 165–66

New Mexico, 5

Newsday, 22–23

New York City, sentence bargaining in, 163

New York sentencing commission, 16, 21–23; failure of, 8, 42, 76, 124; funding for, 123; "political style" of, 82–83; research problems, 122; staffing for, 124

New York sentencing guidelines: legislative review of, 72; prison expenses and, 80; prison population and, 69, 70; projections, difficulties of, 113; punishment issues in, 80–81; ranges of sentences, 65, 203n5; rationale, 66

Nonprison sentences. *See* Jail sentences; Probation

North Carolina, 5

Opinion survey research, 100

Ordinal proportionality of punishment, 95

Oregon, 201n27

Parent, Dale, 40

Parole, accelerated, 12

Parole administrators as sentencing commission members, 118

Parole board: discretion of, 3, 4, 145, 172; as rule-making body, 6–7

Parole release and supervision, 21, 23, 25, 191n15, 191n19, 199n55; as provision of statutes, 74–75

Penal philosophies. *See* Rationale

Penalty scale, 95

Penal value, determination of, 55, 56, 58–59

Pennsylvania sentencing commission, 8, 16, 23, 24, 43; funding for, 123, 124; staffing for, 124

Pennsylvania sentencing guidelines, 23–24; aggravating and mitigating factors, 198n28; appellate sentence review, 74; binding effect of, 64, 196n7; compliance rates, 29–33; deviating sentences, 71; disparity, extent of, 38; for jail sentences, 64; legislative review of, 72, 73; mandatory sentencing law, 157; parole release and supervision, 75, 191n19; plea bargaining and, 40–41; prison population and, 69; projections, difficulties of, 113; ranges of sentences, 65, 196n11, 203n5; rationale, 67; sentencing severity and, 36–37

Perjury cases, 51, 56

Philadelphia, trial choices in, 166–67

Plea bargaining, 38–42, 144; and compliance rates, 31–33; illusory, 143, 158–61, 170; prosecutorial practice, 78, 114–15; types of, 170–71

Policy-making role of sentencing commissions, 19, 136, 137, 138, 141; as provision of statutes, 62–63

Political issues in sentencing commissions, 19–20, 133

Political issues in sentencing guidelines, 48, 49, 50, 60, 68, 76–77; legislative and gubernatorial support, 79–82; "political styles" of jurisdictions, 82–83; prosecutorial and judicial support, 77–79

"Political styles" of jurisdictions, 82–83

Predicate felony law, 78

Predictive sentencing, 53, 66, 86–87, 88, 92–93, 200n7; as crime-prevention technique, 89

Presentence reports, 161, 162, 173

Prison construction, 12, 14

Prison expenses, 79–80, 81, 137–38

Prison population, 12–14, 19, 48, 60, 94; desert rationale and, 13–14, 94–95; evaluation of, 115; increases in, 80, 81; as provision of statutes, 25, 69–70, 75; sentencing guidelines and, 110–13, 127, 131–32, 134

Prison sentences, 37–38, 41; dispositional line and, 93–95; durations of imprisonment, 96; for property offenders, 35–36, 40, 48, 92, 102, 105, 128–29, 131; reconfinements, 75, 132; sentencing principles for, 54, 55; for violent offenders, 19, 25, 35–36, 48, 85, 127

Probation, 36, 38, 55, 105; "amenability" to, 58, 104–5, 202n49; for first offenders, 84; for violent offenders, 78

Probation department, real-offense sentencing and, 161–63

Probation officers: role of, 115–16, 140; sentencing recommendations of, 123, 173–74

Projections of sentencing guidelines' impact on correctional resources, 111–13

Property crime cases, aggravating factors in, 129

Property offenders: criminal history score and, 133–34; increase in imprisonment of, 35–36, 40, 48, 92, 102, 105, 128–29, 131; jail sentences for, 38; reduction in imprisonment of, 19, 25, 40, 68, 127, 132

Proportionality principle, 5, 53, 55, 95, 113, 128–30

Prosecutorial discretion, 145, 146–47, 152

Prosecutorial practice, 129; evaluation of, 114–15

Prosecutorial sentencing appeal, 168–71

Prosecutors: plea bargaining and, 159–60, 161, 162; power of, 25, 32, 38, 40, 102; preguideline behavior, 150; as sentencing commission members, 118, 119, 120; sentencing guidelines, attitude re, 77–78, 143–44, 145

Public as members of sentencing commissions, 118, 120

Public concern re crime, 79, 81–82

Publicity and sentencing guideline enforcement, 174–75

Public rating of crime seriousness, 100

Punishment, nature of, 88

Punishment issues, politicization of, 80–81

Punishments, comparative, 95

Rape cases, 194n4

Rationale: choice of, 10–12, 22, 48, 49–50, 65–67, 69, 100–101; comparisons of, 87–89; and disparity reduction, 114; hybrid, 66–67; and tariff development, 51–52. See also Desert rationale, Incapacitative rationale

Real-offense sentencing, 114, 152–53; illusory plea-bargaining problem, 158–61; practicality of, 161–63; trial stage, effect on, 153–58

Recidivism, 4, 11, 48, 54, 68, 92, 200n6, 200n7

Regional representation in research sample, 109

Rehabilitationism, 3–4, 53

Representative model of sentencing commission membership, 118–19

Risk aversion, 147, 148–49, 150–51, 168

Risk neutrality, 147, 151

Risk preferral, 147–48, 149–50, 151

Robbery, 94, 97, 102, 159

Rule-making body for drafting of sentencing principles, 56–57

Rural sentencing patterns, 38

Sanction scores, 9

Santobello v. New York, 160

Sarason, Seymour, 127–28, 133

Schulhofer, Stephen, 164, 166, 167

Schwartz, Louis, 159

Selective restraint, 86–87, 200n7. See also Incapacitative rationale

Sentence bargaining, 39, 40, 146, 158, 159, 170–71

Sentencing, time required for, 115

Sentencing commission model, 17–18; future of, 42–43

Sentencing commissions, 16, 17; appeal rights of, 172; commissioners' role definitions, 136–38; composition of, 117–20; funding of, 123–24; meetings, frequency of, 120–21; membership of, 7, 139–40; mission of, 7–8, 22, 24, 132–33; policy-making role, 62–63, 100; political problems, 19–20, 22, 26; question-answering service of, 139; resources for, 138–40; staffing of, 121–22, 139. See also specific state sentencing commissions

Sentencing commissions, empirical research of, 107; correctional resources, study of guidelines' impact on, 110–13; evaluation research, design of, 113–15; monitoring system and, 115–16; preguideline practice, study of, 108–10; staffing for, 122

Sentencing discretion, 111; 1900–
1960, 3; 1970–present, 3–5
Sentencing facts, 154, 155–56
Sentencing grid, 8–9, 14, 21, 90, *91*,
195*n*24; criminal record, scoring of,
96, 102; guilty-plea discount in,
164. *See also* Dispositional line
Sentencing grid ranges, 13, 19, 22, 23,
24, 25, 59–60, 65, 105–6, 196*n*11
Sentencing guidelines, 17–18, 47;
amendments to, 116, 141; binding
effect, 64–65; crimes, rating of, 96–
102; disparity and, 9–10; evaluation
of, 127–28; format of, 8–9; goals
of, 133–36; legislative review of,
72–73; limitations of numerical
guidelines, 48–49; numbers or guild-
ing principles, 49–50; for prison and
jail sentences, 63–64; resistance to,
143–45; structure and definiteness,
as provision of statutes, 65; types of,
108; voluntary, 17, 144, 168
Sentencing guidelines, effects óf, 26–
27; compliance rates, 27–33, 35;
disparities, extent of, 37–38; plea
bargaining, 38–42; sentencing patterns, 35–36; sentencing severity,
36–37; trial and appeal rates, 42
Sentencing guidelines, enforcement of,
142; adaptive responses and, 143–
45; adverse publicity and, 174–75;
internal controls for, 172–74; judicial and prosecutorial discretion and,
145, 146–47, 152; plea bargaining
and, 143, 146–52. *See also* Appellate sentence review; Guilty-plea discounts; Real-offense sentencing
Sentencing guidelines, implementation
of. *See* Minnesota sentencing
practice, 1982–1984
Sentencing patterns, changes in, 35–36
Sentencing policy: evaluation of, 7–8;
implementation of, 113
Sentencing principles, 50, 66; appellate
court involvement in development
of, 50–52, 57–58, 194*n*5; environment for, 60, 61; fuller statement of
principles (Sweden), 54–56, 57,
195*n*21, 195*n*22; prerequisites for,

56–60; statutory statements of pur-
pose (Finland), 52–54, 195*n*13;
tariff development and, 61
Sentencing Reform Act of 1984, 16, 18
Seriousness ratings of crimes, 99–101,
201*n*32
Sexual abuse of children, sentences for,
134–35, 204*n*12
Singer, Richard, 86, 90
Size of sentencing commissions,
119–20
Social history of defendants, 87, 103
South Carolina sentencing commission,
8, 16, 24–25, 43; funding for, 123,
124; research problems, 122; staff-
ing for, 124
Sparks, Richard, 96
Special prevention, 53
Staffing of sentencing commissions,
121–23
State v. Evans, 131
Statistical prediction methods, 86–87
Stratification of research sample,
109–10
Supreme court, appeals to, 74
Sweden, sentencing principles in,
54–56, 57, 195*n*21, 195*n*22

Tariff development, 14–15; court in-
volvement in, 55–56, 57, 58–59; ra-
tionale and, 49, 51–52; and sentenc-
ing-principle success, 61
Thefts, 92
Thomas, David, 51
Treatment-oriented sentences, 35
Trial facts, 154, 155–56
Trial rate, changes in, 42, 115, 151
Trials: choice of, 166–67; cost
comparisons, 166; real-offense
sentencing and, 153–58

U.S. Parole Commission, 7, 155
U.S. Sentencing Commission, 8, 16,
67, 153
Uniform Determinate Sentencing Law
(California), 5
Uniformity in sentencing, 130–31
*United States ex rel Goldberg v.
Warden, Allenwood*, 160

Index

United States v. Cook, 160
United States v. DiFrancesco, 169
United States v. Fatico, 162
Urban sentencing patterns, 38

"Vertical" plea bargaining, 39–40,
  170–71
Victim's right to appeal, 171–72
Violence, effect of, 101
Violent offenders, imprisonment of,
  19, 25, 35–36, 48, 85, 127
Voluntary sentencing guidelines, 17,
  144, 168

Washington sentencing commission, 8;
  funding for, 123; staffing for, 124;
  success of, 16, 25–26, 43, 124, 144

Washington sentencing guidelines,
  197n12; appellate sentence review,
  73–74; 198n38; compliance rates,
  35; deviating sentences, 71; disparity, extent of, 38; for jail sentences,
  63; legislative approval of, 192n21;
  parole release and supervision, 74;
  plea bargaining and, 40–42; prison
  population and, 70; rationale, 65,
  66; sentencing patterns, changes in,
  35, 36; sentencing ranges, 155
Wasik, Martin, 51
Weapons charges, 101–2, 132, 155–56
Weston v. United States, 162
"Work group" for sentencing
  decisions, 144–45

Zeisel, Hans, 163